WHY TRAVEL?

Understanding Our Need to Move
and How It Shapes Our Lives

Edited by
Matthew Niblett and Kris Beuret

With a Foreword by
Tony Wheeler

D1610483

BRISTOL
UNIVERSITY
PRESS

First published in Great Britain in 2021 by

Bristol University Press
University of Bristol
1-9 Old Park Hill
Bristol
BS2 8BB
UK
t: +44 (0)117 954 5940
e: bup-info@bristol.ac.uk

Details of international sales and distribution partners are available at
bristoluniversitypress.co.uk

British Library Cataloguing in Publication Data
A catalogue record for this book is available from the British Library

ISBN 978-1-5292-1636-3 hardcover
ISBN 978-1-5292-1637-0 paperback
ISBN 978-1-5292-1638-7 ePub
ISBN 978-1-5292-1639-4 ePdf

Cover design: by Clifford Hayes
Front cover image: iStock/SensorSpot
Bristol University Press uses environmentally responsible print partners.
Printed and bound in Great Britain by CMP, Poole

Contents

List of Figures

Image Credits

7.1   ID 19878336 © Jaimaa/Dreamstime.com
7.2a   Ababsolutum/istockphoto.com
7.2b   afby71/istockphoto.com
7.3   Wellcome Collection. Attribution 4.0 International (CC BY 4.0)
7.4   Friedrich Stark/Alamy Stock Photo
8.1   Winslow Homer 1899 The Gulf Stream, The Metropolitan Museum of Art, Catharine Lorillard Wolfe Collection, Wolfe Fund, 1906. Licensed under CC01.0 Universal (CC0 1.0) Public Domain Dedication https://creativecommons.org/publicdomain/zero/1.0/
8.2   Courtesy National Gallery of Art, Washington, Gift of Mrs. Barbara Hutton
8.3   Ansel Adams, The Tetons and the Snake River (1942), Grand Teton National Park, Wyoming. National Archives and Records Administration, Records of the National Park Service. (79-AAG-1). National Archives Identifier (NAID) 519904
8.4   Album/Alamy Stock (original artwork held by Brooklyn Museum, Museum Collection Fund, 20.640)
8.5   Artepics/Alamy Stock Photo
9.1   Westend61 GmbH/Alamy Stock Photo
9.2   Maria Yfanti/Shutterstock.com
9.3   Stefano Ember/Shutterstock.com
9.4   frantic00/istockphoto.com
10.1   Image by Gianni Crestani from Pixabay
10.2   Image by Ed Judkins from Pixabay
10.3   Image by Free- Photos from Pixabay
10.4   Image by Thomas Staub from Pixabay
11.1   L. Prang & Co, Boston (1893)
11.2   Ortelius (1570). BPL Call Number: G1006.T54 1570 View at the Norman B. Leventhal Map Center (CC BY 2.0)
11.3   Sir Francis Bacon (1620)
11.4   Henry Bowers
11.5   Saulius Damulevicius/Shutterstock.com
11.6a   John Seller (1700)
11.6b   Astronaut David R. Scott, Apollo 15 commander
12.1a   Image by Herbert Bieser from Pixabay
12.1b   narvikk/istockphoto.com
12.2   monkeybusinessimages/istockphoto.com
12.3   Volodimir Zozulinskyi/Shutterstock.com
13.1   © DSDHA

Notes on Contributors

Hazel Andrews is Reader in Tourism, Culture and Society at Liverpool John Moores University. As a social anthropologist Hazel is interested in issues of identity, selfhood and the body, principally in relation to tourism and travel. Hazel's PhD thesis was the first full-length ethnographic study of British charter tourists. The research involved periods of participant observation in the resorts of Palmanova and Magaluf, Mallorca and was published as *The British on Holiday: Charter Tourism, Identity and Consumption* (Channel View, 2011). She is also the editor of the books *Tourism and Violence* (Routledge, 2014), and *Tourism and Brexit: Travel, Borders and Identity* (Channel View, 2021).

Kris Beuret OBE is the Director of Social Research Associates (SRA). She is a sociologist, previously an academic, and a member of the Independent Transport Commission and Highways England's Research and Innovation Advisory Board. Kris has advised the House of Commons Transport Committee, Transport for London, the Department for Transport and overseas governments on disability and diversity issues. Kris's publications include *Marketing in Local Government* (Beuret and Hall, 2003), alongside many reports, conference papers and TV/radio content-writing.

Matthew Dillon is an Associate Director in Arup's City Economics and Planning team. He holds a Bachelor's degree in Mathematics and a Master's in Transport, and his subsequent career path has taken him from consultancy, to a civil service role for the Department for Transport, and back again. He is co-author, with Alexander Jan, of the chapter 'Rolling stock companies (Roscos): experience from Great Britain' in *Rail Economics, Policy and Regulation in Europe* (Finger and Messulam, 2015). He lives in London, and enjoys travelling with his young family.

Tom Greenall is an Associate Director of DSDHA. In 2019 he was a guest editor of *Architectural Design* (AD). 'Sharing The Beautiful Everyday

Journey', a toolkit to aid designers and policy makers in integrating cyclist and pedestrian journeys in our street spaces, was the result of a Fellowship in the Built Environment by the Royal Commission for the Exhibition of 1851. Tom leads an architectural design studio at the Royal College of Art and is a visiting tutor at the Sandberg Institute in Amsterdam. He has been a chair of the Wandsworth Design Review Panel since 2016.

Roger Hall has an MA in Politics and is an independent researcher specializing in business policy. He previously taught at Essex, Oregon and De Montfort universities.

Terry Hill CBE is an expert on the economics and engineering of transport and travel and is Chair of the Independent Transport Commission. He is former ISO President, UK, former Chairman of Arup Group and was a non-executive member of the Crossrail Ltd Board. He is a fellow or member of many professional associations including the UK Royal Academy of Engineering, the Institution of Civil Engineers and the World Economic Forum.

Tony Hiss is the author of fifteen books, including the award-winning *The Experience of Place* (Vintage Books, 1991). He was a staff writer at *The New Yorker* for more than thirty years, a visiting scholar at New York University for twenty-five years, and has lectured around the world. His latest book, *Rescuing the Planet: Protecting Half the Land to Heal the Earth* (Knopf, 2021), is about staving off the biodiversity crisis, safeguarding rapidly shrinking wilderness areas, and preventing the mass extinction of a million species.

Alexander Jan is Arup's former chief economist. He holds a Bachelor's degree in Economics from the London School of Economics. He is a member of the Mayor of London's infrastructure advisory group, non-executive chair of the Midtown business improvement district in central London and a fellow of the Chartered Institute for Transport and Logistics. He is co-author, with Matthew Dillon, of the chapter 'Rolling stock companies (Roscos): experience from Great Britain' in *Rail Economics, Policy and Regulation in Europe* (Finger and Messulam, 2015).

Alison Kuznets is an independent researcher, editor and writer with expertise in the fields of travel, sustainability and the relations between science and society. She holds an MA (Cantab), an MSc in History of Science and Medicine, and has taught at Cheonnam National University in South Korea. Alison has travelled extensively throughout Latin America and Asia and now enjoys the pleasures of lower impact 'slow travels'.

Glenn Lyons is Mott MacDonald Professor of Future Mobility at the University of the West of England Bristol and founding Director of the Centre for Transport and Society. Professor Lyons takes a socio-technical perspective in addressing how the digital age has collided and merged with the motor age and the implications for mobility and shaping its future in an uncertain world. He is an experienced writer and has (co)authored over 200 articles.

Matthew Niblett is Director of the Independent Transport Commission and a Fellow of the Royal Society of Arts. He oversees the ITC's research portfolio and has presented findings from this research to Ministers and Parliamentary Select Committee enquiries. Matthew holds a doctorate from the University of Oxford and was a senior research associate at Oxford's Transport Studies Unit.

Charles Pasternak is a Professor of Biochemistry (retired) and President of Oxford International Biomedical Centre. Well-known internationally as a promoter of science, Charles is also the author of a number of popular science books including *Quest: The Essence of Humanity* (Wiley, 2004), *Blinkers: Scientific Ignorance and Evasion* (Smith-Gordon & Co Ltd, 2012) and *Africa South of the Sahara: Continued Failure or Delayed Success?* (Words By Design, 2018).

Deborah Saunt is a Director of architecture, urban design and research studio DSDHA and currently the Eero Saarinen Visiting Professor of Architectural Design at Yale University. She obtained her PhD into practice-based research from RMIT and a Research Fellowship in the Built Environment from the Royal Commission for the Exhibition of 1851. She is active in democratizing architecture and the built environment, establishing the Jane Drew Prize in Architecture and co-founding the London School of Architecture.

Tom Selwyn is Professorial Research Associate and Leverhulme Emeritus Fellow in the Department of Anthropology at SOAS, University of London. He founded the SOAS Master's degree in the Anthropology of Travel, Tourism, and Pilgrimage (ATTP) and is co-convenor of the SOAS ATTP summer school. He is widely published in the field and has directed/co-directed several large research and development projects for the European Commission in the Balkan and Mediterranean regions.

Emily Thomas is Associate Professor in Philosophy at Durham University. Prior to this she obtained a PhD from the University of Cambridge, and held a NWO grant at the University of Groningen. She has published widely on the history of metaphysics, especially space and time. She is the author of the scholarly monograph *Absolute Time: Rifts in Early Modern British Metaphysics* (Oxford University Press, 2018) and the popular book *The Meaning of Travel: Philosophers Abroad* (Oxford University Press, 2020).

The Independent Transport Commission (ITC)

The Independent Transport Commission (ITC) is Britain's foremost independent transport and land use think tank. It was established in 1999 as a research charity committed to providing insight and analysis of the most pressing long-term strategic issues in the fields of transport and land use. Over the past two decades it has supported a wide range of influential research projects and events that have helped to reshape and improve policy-making in the UK. The ITC has presented extensively on the findings from its work to ministers and civil servants, and is regularly invited to contribute to parliamentary select committee enquiries.

The ITC has a particular interest in understanding better the connections between and across policy areas, thereby ensuring that transport and travel challenges are considered in a broader context than is normally the case. The 'Why Travel?' project has been an excellent example of this mission, bringing together insights from a wide range of disciplines and fields of study in order to provide a richer and more comprehensive understanding of the reasons why humans travel. Details can be found on the project website www.whytravel.org.uk.

The ITC wishes to acknowledge the generous support of our corporate members, whose help enables the charity's work to continue, and which has been essential for enabling projects such as the 'Why Travel?' study to reach completion. For more information on the ITC please visit our website at www.theitc.org.uk.

Acknowledgements

The journey to completion of this book has been a long one, and in reaching our destination the editors would like to thank all those whose work, help and advice have made it possible. First, we are indebted to all the talented chapter authors for their efforts and patience during the editing process, and whose expertise has resulted in a publication that should be of lasting interest and value.

We are especially grateful to Alison Kuznets who, throughout the book's production, has provided an immense resource of assistance and organization, and whose efforts have enabled us to meet the challenge of completing this complex project. Our thanks are also due to the excellent team at Bristol University Press, including Emily Watts, Caroline Astley, Kathryn King and Ruth Wallace, whose advice and guidance have made the process much less stressful than it would otherwise have been. We would also like to record our gratitude to those who have reviewed chapters and provided valuable advice and comment: the book is much better for their input. Others whose practical assistance has been warmly appreciated include Bright Pryde-Saha, Tiffany Lam, Sue Crockford and Neha Bajaj.

The genesis of this project is found in a number of discussions and debates that the ITC held about the nature of travel and the need to understand the motivations that lie behind it. For their insights and inspiration, we would like to acknowledge the input of many ITC members past and present, including Terry Hill, Peter Jones, Deborah Saunt, Roger Madelin, Alan Baxter, Sir Patrick Brown, Lord Andrew Adonis, Simon Linnett, Elizabeth Gilliard, Dominique Laousse and Sir Peter Hendy. The support of the ITC trustees for the project has made the volume possible and we are grateful for their longstanding and generous backing. An early concept of the project was trialled at an ITC event at which we were grateful for the insights of Lord Harries, Quentin Willson, Lord Adonis, Sir Peter Hall, Simon Calder and Lord McLoughlin.

Finally, we would like to thank all those, including friends and family, who have generously supported us throughout this process, and whose patience and understanding were invaluable.

Matthew Niblett and Kris Beuret

Foreword

Tony Wheeler, co-founder, Lonely Planet

Travel? Oh I remember that. I visited 14 countries in 2019, if we count Transnistria as a country, and 20 the year before. Even in 2020, before it all went wrong, I'd been to five countries – at home in Australia, in Japan (for a university conference on 'Overtourism', remember overtourism?), then the UK, Egypt and Yemen before I had to rush home as the gates slammed shut. And slam shut they most definitely did. Indeed, in this very book Chapter 4 on Philosophy notes that the USSR didn't like Article 13 of the UN Declaration of Human Rights, which insists that entering and leaving your own country is a basic human right, but today it's Australia which has totally tossed out that right. You're trapped in Australia, unless you're a movie or sports star or billionaire friend of the government of course.

So every chapter of *Why Travel* underlines just how important travel has been and will continue – one day – to be in my life. Since writing Lonely Planet's first guidebook – almost 50 years ago – travel has been my work and my life, but just as football is much more important than mere life and death, so travel has been much more for me. Fortunately, like many of us suffering an enforced travel-free diet, it's been surprising how much travel I still enjoyed, certainly I've rediscovered and extended the boundaries of my own back yard. The pandemic has emphasized how much nature and how many birds pop up right outside my kitchen window, I've rediscovered so many travel memories, partly through finally getting around to sorting out my much too extensive pre-digital (i.e. colour slide) photo collection.

Perhaps most important, I've had plenty of time to ponder just why travel is so important. Certainly the pandemic has been an enforced opportunity to look at the problems travel brings – from overtourism to environmental and climate damage – and examine how we can do things differently post-pandemic. But there has also been plenty of opportunity to think about the good stuff that travel does and worry about people, far from our sheltered first world, who have been doing it really hard over the past year. 'Come back, we miss you', has been a message from an awful lot of tourist destinations and most emphatically from those developing world locations where tourist income was a huge part of the local economy.

Why Travel? points out comprehensively that travel is such a fundamental – even hard-wired – part of human existence that it's inevitable that it will come back. Economic shocks, terrorist attacks, natural disasters and previous pandemics have all taken their toll, but on every occasion travel has bounced back. Even Spanish Flu and the Black Death were just temporary potholes. Inevitably there will be differences, some of them big ones, between travel pre- and post-pandemic. It's easy to contemplate possible changes – big ticket travel bounces back, people who can afford chartered boats and private jets are going to feel insulated and safe and they can afford it, but what about the budget travellers, the backpackers? I've always felt that the gap year trip, that first big experience of independent travel, was almost an essential part of growing up, a more valuable spell of education than years of school. Why travel? Well that's a very good reason why.

Why Travel? An Introduction

Matthew Niblett and Kris Beuret

Why travel? We have all done it and, for most of us, travel fills our lives. Whether strolling to the shops, joining the commuter conveyer belt to work, or jetting off to foreign climes, we move and we travel. The importance of travel is seen in the way it shapes our society. Hence our strongest form of civil punishment is to imprison, to stop transgressors travelling and moving freely. Some of the most difficult aspects of the COVID-19 pandemic have stemmed from the ways in which it has resulted in restrictions on movement, and forced us to confront the extent to which we miss the freedoms associated with travel.

The place of travel at the core of our lives is hinted in our language and everyday interactions. We love to talk about travel, to moan about obstacles to travel and to dream about where it can take us; it is as good an ice-breaker as the weather and with far more conversation 'mileage'. Indeed, there is no more frequent idiom than travel to describe our 'life's journey'.

While we often view travel as a chore, the popularity of luxury liners and heritage trains (in which the journey is as important as the destination), and the undying appeal of a good walk to clear the head, suggest that we do not just do it because we have to but because we love to; because, on some fundamental level, we need to. Travel seems to have utility itself, and this appears no more clearly than at the current time, when the COVID-19 pandemic has dramatically reduced travel globally as a result of social distancing restrictions. Confined and limited in where we can move, people across the world have developed a fresh appreciation of the importance of travel to our existence.

When asked to identify the most basic elements of human existence, the immediate responses usually include breathing, eating, drinking or, perhaps, even reproduction. Movement, in spite of being as fundamental a part of human life as these other principles, is a less common response. But what drives human movement, and particularly our propensity to travel? On the surface such a question can appear facile, but on deeper reflection it unfolds as an issue of great complexity and, as such, has exercised human minds for millennia. The Greek philosopher Aristotle, when thinking two and a half thousand years ago about the motion of animals, classified movement into categories including non-voluntary, such as sleeping and breathing, and voluntary, such as when we choose to take a walk. To explain voluntary movements Aristotle turned to the principle of desire: the rabbit flees from the fox because it desires to survive; just as the human travels to the theatre because he/she desires to be entertained.[1] This faculty of desire, he suggested, was allied with our capacity for practical reason, which focuses upon an object and makes it desirable. Having determined the object or objective we desire, we then move to pursue it.

This book asks why? Why travel? What are the fundamental motivations that underpin the journeys we make? And how can we create places and policies that better satisfy these motivations and improve the quality of our travel and, thereby, our lives, without wreaking environmental harm on our planet? In other words, can we travel better?

Understanding travel behaviour: the value of movement

Traditionally, in academic circles, travel has been viewed as a derivative of other human activities. Transport economists have frequently described travel as a 'derived demand': it is not undertaken for its own sake but is derived from our desire to access activities in different locations. The result of this view is that travel becomes a cost to be minimized or something that has to be reduced in order that it uses as little time as possible. We see the results of this way of thinking evident in much transport planning and economic policy, whereby the monetary value of travel is related to time savings. If travel is merely a demand derived from other activities, it is reduced to something we do only when we need to: a behaviour we have outgrown, a hangover from our days roaming the savannah or steppes searching for food.

There is growing evidence, however, that travel behaviour is rooted in the desire to move as a purpose in itself: an issue determined by social, physical, psychological and cultural factors. The economic importance of travel, which contributes at least ten per cent of global GDP and underpins the globalized economy, is well-recognized, all the more so at a time when this has been jeopardized by the COVID-19 pandemic travel restrictions. But this view tends to overshadow a more holistic and realistic picture of travel; it overlooks the diverse and complex reasons for travel and the impacts of travel on people's lives, the environment and society. This has two crucial implications. Firstly, these important factors are often missed in travel demand analysis and forecasting, meaning that policy decisions on travel and transport can lose the full picture and risk impaired travel experiences and costly mistakes. Secondly, it suggests that the quality of our journeys is much more important than has previously been realized, and we need to see travel and transport as a central aspect of human wellbeing.

We perhaps ought here to consider the recognized distinction between 'mobility' and 'accessibility'. Getting to the things we need (and want) – access – is related to the derived demand for travel and can be achieved with all kinds of travel and transport provision. If you need a loaf of bread it might be acceptable to take a ten-minute walk to a local corner shop (or even bakery). In other circumstances, the nearest loaf might mean a 30-minute drive to a superstore. The access to meet the need is key, while on the other hand mobility involves improving our ability to and our experience of travel. By paying attention to the latter we can better understand the full utility of these trips. Is the long drive as satisfying for our exploratory and curious instincts as the long walk? What is the comparative 'benefit' for our well-being (in all senses) of a two-hour budget airline flight with lengthy connections to the airports at each end and all the hassle that involves, or of a two-hour walk through a park or along a beach with the waves lapping at our feet, or even through a well laid out and pedestrian-friendly urban landscape? Perhaps providing a range of 'travel opportunities' to any individual is a better policy goal. Should not everyone have the mobility to take a stroll in a stimulating environment near their home, or to hop on a bus 'to somewhere different', or have access to (not necessarily through ownership) a car or bike?

If there does exist a fundamental human need for mobility, this also points us in the direction of achieving a much improved understanding of travel demand: one that takes account not only of derived, but also intrinsic, motivations and satisfactions. This in turn can help us better plan and design our travel and transport systems – not only through thinking about the connectivity we require, but also the *conditions* in which we undertake the journey.

At the same time, we need to recognize that unlimited travel can generate external problems that can undermine and ultimately inhibit the quest for better journeys. The most obvious problem is the huge carbon footprint arising from modern travel, which contributes to climate change. But other externalities include environmental degradation and overtourism, both of which can blight particular destinations and communities. There are many thinkers who would argue that this means we should reduce and restrict human travel. But rather than focus on travelling less, this book considers these challenges in the context of how we can travel better. If travel is a human need, then we also need to explore how we can fulfil this in ways that are sustainable and positive both for the traveller and those around them.

From a policy perspective, it has been clear that we still understand too little about the motivations that underpin travel, in spite of its critical importance for our whole way of life and our future. In this book, we aim to start filling that gap by exploring these motivations from a wide range of perspectives to offer an original and holistic picture of why we travel. The authors, expert across a wide range of fields not normally considered in travel and transport thinking, have brought together a fascinating array of insights into human travel, ranging across cultures and eras, and from the inner psyche to outer space. Consolidating perspectives from across the humanities, social and natural sciences, the book provides a broader understanding of travel than is normally possible within transport studies, in order to develop a deeper understanding of the journeys we all make.

Our starting point

The ITC is the UK's only dedicated pan-transport and land use think tank. Our combined role is to research key issues in travel, transport policy and related subjects. We also hold discussion groups, lectures and seminars to encourage the free-flow of ideas related to human movement. It has always been apparent to the ITC that we need to develop a much more holistic understanding of the motivations driving travel if we are to develop better policy. Happily, the need for a fresh investigation into why we travel has also become apparent to policy makers at the highest levels of government.

As a result, the subject of this book is not the 'how' of travel, or the mechanics of conventional transport, but rather the 'why' of travel, and the human motivations that drive it. Many questions arise from this quest: from whether there is an inherent need to travel, to how does travel moderate our lives; where does this need come from and, critically, what might this mean for how we can travel better in the future?

We have decided to explore this subject by drawing on the views of those from outside the conventionally circumscribed transport world. To do so we have brought together experts in economics, sociology, evolutionary biology, anthropology, philosophy, technology, exploration, land use and other related subjects. It is important to be clear that we cannot hope to be able to cover every aspect of travel in a single book (had space permitted, we could have included at least a dozen further subject areas such as music, geography and politics). Furthermore, the subject matter reflects the fact that most of the authors are working in a British and European context, although global examples are also widely used. Yet, taken together, the insights within this study help to provide a fresh and illuminating insight on this crucial aspect of human existence.

Feedback from the project website (www.whytravel.org), which has generated interest since this project started, has revealed that the subject is of fascination to a wider audience beyond transport professionals, including those who see opportunities for new forms of travel implied by the broader perspectives depicted in the book.

Brief biographies of our distinguished authors are included to explain her/his perspective and we would like, before the readers move further, to record our appreciation to all our expert contributors who have donated their time, intellect and energies for this book.

Our path: a voyage of discovery

The chapters in this book take us on an exciting journey across a wide field of human knowledge: given the central role of travel within our lives, it makes sense to explore far and wide. Our authors therefore start by looking at the question 'why travel?' from a range of disciplinary perspectives, starting with biological and psychological foundations and moving through the social and cultural phenomena we have created – our philosophies, literature and art as well as our economic and social structures. We then examine some major types of travel that humans have engaged in across centuries and cultures – exploration, religious travel and tourism – in order to understand at a deeper level what motivates such journeys. Having surveyed the range of motives that drive human movement, the book concludes by thinking about the future of our travel; considering our natural and built environment and, in the light of technological developments, we look at the limits and new frontiers that we might face as part of the continuing story of human travel over the next century. A crucial question is whether humans can continue to indulge our travel desires while reducing the negative impacts that arise from this, whether that be emissions contributing to air pollution and climate change, or the impacts of over-tourism.

Fundamental motivations: the pleasure of travel

The human need for travel is often instinctive and can be a pleasure in itself. Early railways extolled in their advertising the positive joys of travel (often in luxury). As the market for transporting passengers by ship across the Atlantic (and other sea routes) declined in the 20th century, the ocean-going passenger companies developed cruises as a replacement through which the act of travel was an intimate part of the excitement and experience. In the same way, great railway journeys have developed as an end in themselves, to be enjoyed as an experience without a particular need to reach a certain destination.

At other times we do not have to venture far to discover the inherent desire to travel; experts in animal behaviour have demonstrated that dogs go for a walk and break into impromptu runs in the park, not to get to the other side, or even because they have seen a squirrel, but because of the sheer exhilaration of movement and the drive to know what is around them. At a different end of the spectrum, many humans find the act of walking a positive therapy as they pace the office or take a short walk in the lunch hour. We may not know we are doing it but we do it all the time, in many different ways.

The book opens with an evolutionary biologist's perspective on travel by Charles Pasternak, who provides evidence on the origins of human movement and its link to the evolution of our brains and bipedal posture. This is followed by an investigation of travel and the mind by Tony Hiss, in which the psychology of travel is explored as well as the impacts of travel on our mental wellbeing. In the next chapter, Matthew Niblett explores some of the philosophy of travel, and how the question of travel motivations has occupied thinkers down the centuries. He explains how thinkers have identified both good and bad reasons behind our desire to travel. To conclude this section, Matthew Dillon and Alexander Jan examine the economics of travel, challenging the traditional view of travel as merely a derived demand, and showing how the intrinsic utility and pleasures of travel should lead to a new understanding of how we value this essential human activity.

Travel as exploration and to discover ourselves

Travel has also become an important expression of identity for individuals and societies. Do we go on protest marches to communicate our displeasure to those in power or to express it to ourselves? Are religious pilgrimages more than simply a means of getting the pilgrim to where the festival or icons are located; and, if not, what are the acts of ritual involved in the journey? Why otherwise would the climbers on the 1921–24 expeditions to Everest have discovered Tibetans making pilgrimages to the mountain?

These issues are explored in the second part of the book, with Kris Beuret and Roger Hall looking at sociological perspectives on travel and investigating how travel affects social structures and identities. In the following chapter, Alison Kuznets explores religion and travel and uncovers why travel is at the core of so many world religions and their spiritual practices. To understand the relationship between travel and self-expression and cultural identity, the next chapter, by Alison Kuznets and Matthew Niblett, investigates the links between travel, art and literature. Through an exploration of the ways in which travel has affected language and human creativity, the chapter reveals the centrality of movement in culture.

Today the world may seem to have grown much smaller but still the act of travel is seen as an important statement of intent: of freedom; of generosity, of courtesy. The event of travelling has its own rituals: state visits, business deals and home-stays all involve us in exchanges of culture and rituals of hospitality, including giving and receiving well.

To explore these themes, the book continues with Tom Selwyn's investigation of anthropological insights on travel. He shows how travel features at the core of many myths of origin in ancient cultures, and explains how travel enables individuals and societies to discover their own identities. In the chapter by Hazel Andrews, the phenomenon of travel as tourism is explored. She uncovers the wide range of motivations that lie behind tourist travel, and reveals how this has become such a central part of the global economy. Travel for discovery is examined in Emily Thomas's chapter on exploration. The human need to search beyond the horizon dates back to the pre-modern age, but she shows how such travel became a defining part of the early-modern world and, inspired by thinkers such as Francis Bacon, led to the development of travel for scientific exploration.

The future of human travel: limits and new horizons

We conclude by reviewing what we have learned about the motivations driving human travel, and use this to look towards the future and how this better understanding of travel might be used to improve our lives. Our authors examine how our travel behaviours interact with the world around us — our natural and built environment and the technological world we have created — and they try to unpick how we might travel better in the future, considering the constraints and opportunities we face.

This final part opens with a chapter by Glenn Lyons examining the way in which technology is reshaping travel. He explains how travel is both enabled and transformed through technological innovation, which also holds the potential to address some of the environmental challenges generated by mass travel. In the penultimate chapter by Deborah Saunt and Tom Greenall on travel and placemaking, the role of travel in the built environment is explored. The authors demonstrate how travel and movement have been at the core of where and how our settlements have developed. Looking ahead, they explain how cities and the built environment should be designed with movement in mind. Finally, Terry Hill explores the critical question of travel and the environment. The negative impacts of mass travel on the environment are well-known, but does this have to mean that we must restrict travel or can we find ways of travelling better? The chapter provides an optimistic view that environmentally sustainable travel is achievable, and encourages policy makers to make this a priority.

Our destination

Our goal is to stimulate people to think about and discuss more deeply the reasons behind our travel and the often hidden impacts movement has on our lives. This book is written in the belief that a better comprehension of the nature of travel and its relation to human behaviour will be crucial if we are to make good decisions as individuals and as a society. We expect it to be useful at a number of levels.

First, for policy makers, this investigation offers an opportunity to rethink how we plan and design for our travel needs. Several aspects for policy makers emerge. At a local and national level, it is important that we plan our travel infrastructure and built environment in a way that is environmentally sustainable and improves our quality of life. In order to do this, we need to understand how far people can really change their travel choices. The implications of there existing some underlying psychological and physiological foundations beneath our desire to move around – or achieve variety in our experience of our surroundings – are significant for policy making.

The insights in this book also suggest that we might need to rethink the characterization of travel time as a disutility, and begin to consider mobility more along the lines of a basic component of human wellbeing. There are potentially important social and economic considerations that arise from travel having an intrinsic utility. It indicates that the opportunity to travel well should be considered an essential aspect of social equity. It is well known that those on low incomes have more limited access to various travel modes, which tends to mean that they travel less far or suffer worse conditions when travelling. Limited mobility due to poverty might well be a problem not only from the access that is lost to goods and opportunities, but also as a result of the negative effects on the mental and physical health of those who face such restrictions. At a time when governments are restricting travel it would be wise to bear in mind the importance of maintaining travel opportunities for those with restricted mobility. Such considerations are not only relevant to policy makers in the transport field, but also in the arenas of health, social services and land use/planning. The way in which we design our cities and places, for instance, could be improved by reflecting on the importance of promoting mobility (particularly of the human-powered kind) across the settlements that we build, as well as incorporating features into our built landscapes that encourage the use of our innate sense of curiosity.

Better insights such as those offered in this book will also allow us to address some of the key conundrums that travel generates. Travel is essential to the functioning of the global economy, and yet is a major generator of carbon emissions. Can we satisfy our desire to travel without making so many journeys? Travel is also fundamental to the working of our communities and cities, yet when planned badly can be a blight on our lives. How can we improve the quality of the journeys we make while ensuring they enhance our surroundings? Travel is a rich source of happiness and fulfilment, and yet is also the cause of more than a million road deaths and serious injuries worldwide. Can we still experience the thrill of travel while reducing the risks?

We believe that the thought-provoking and practical new perspectives in this book will be vital for those working within and studying transport and travel, and fascinating for all those who journey near and far and have ever wondered why we travel and how it could be improved. This book should also provide a 'voyage of discovery' (one cannot escape the travel metaphor for long) for the reader, a tour through a wide range of perspectives on travel, and we would like to acknowledge our gratitude to all those who have contributed their intellect and time in shaping this guide.

Note

1   Aristotle, *De Anima* iii 10, 433 a31–b1.

PART I

Fundamental Motivations

2

Biological Perspectives on Travel

Charles Pasternak[1]

As a species, humans are the world's great travellers. We have travelled to every continent on the planet, and even to the moon. On an individual level, over a billion people travel outside their own country every year.[2] Every day most of us will make a journey of some sort, usually spending about an hour per day travelling, regardless of our country or culture of origin (Marchetti, 1994). It seems common sense that such a ubiquitous behaviour must have some sort of biological basis: that travel is in some way 'hard-wired' into us. Yet travel is so rarely considered this way: it is thought of as a waste of time, a 'derived demand', in economist-speak, to be minimized and insulated against. Such a view ignores the biological basis of our travel behaviour, and risks our wellbeing as well as that of the planet's other biological systems.

To explore this idea of 'hard-wiring', we must look beyond just the more obvious biological motivations for travel – those shared with all mobile organisms – like access to food, shelter or a mate. We must step outside our narrow view of the modern world and look back deep into our evolutionary past, and inside our brains and bodies. This chapter therefore begins its story six million years ago, to understand how 'coming down from the trees' changed our basic mode of travel and, with it, expanded our physical and mental horizons. The second part of the chapter turns our gaze inwards to try to understand the effects travel has on our bodies and brains. Bringing together research in diverse fields of biology, we will see how travel is implicated in physical, mental and cognitive health; how travel is processed in our brains; and even how travel might play a role in human social groups.

In doing so we can better understand human travel – why we have travelled in the past and why we will continue to do so.

'The travelling ape' – travel and human evolution

When Tony Hiss, author of the next chapter ('Travel and The Mind'), terms *Homo sapiens* the 'travelling ape', is this fanciful or do we really show a propensity to travel not exhibited by other primates? If we take a look back at our prehistory (rather than at the age of modern travel, when the odds seem so stacked in our favour), were humans such great travellers? The answer is yes. Our ancestors, *Homo erectus*, travelled out of Africa to Asia and Europe some 1.8 million years ago and our own species has travelled even further and spread more quickly. Modern humans, *Homo sapiens*, evolved in Africa around 300,000 years ago. Gradually they spread throughout Africa and, apart from a few small groups who settled in Arabia, they mostly stayed within Africa for the first 200,000 years of their existence. While expanding across such a large continent is no mean feat, it was the following 80,000 years that really mark humanity out as a great traveller. Between 60,000 and 80,000 years ago bands had migrated to the Middle East. 15,000 years on, *Homo sapiens* had reached south east Asia, from where they managed to reach Australia. Because ice still locked up large amounts of water, sea levels were considerably lower than today. Many of the Indonesian islands were a single land mass ('Sunda Land'), as were New Guinea, Australia and Tasmania ('Sahul'). But to get from Sunda Land to Sahul still meant crossing a considerable amount of open water, a remarkable achievement. Around 40,000 years ago, humans also entered Europe (which was then dominated by the cold of the last ice age). Here they met Neanderthals, whom they gradually supplanted. Neanderthals are thought to have become extinct some 25,000 years ago.

By 20,000 years ago, groups who had reached the cold tundra of north east Asia continued their easterly trek. They arrived in north western America, crossing the isthmus that became the Bering Straits some 5,000 years later when the ice melted. From here they spread out, some walking gradually southwards. Within a thousand years, they had infiltrated North, Central and South America as far as Patagonia. So by this time humans had travelled to every continent (except Antarctica). In the lands they inhabited, our ancestors led nomadic lifestyles, their movements probably driven by basic biological

Figure 2.1: Map showing prehistoric migrations of *Homo sapiens*

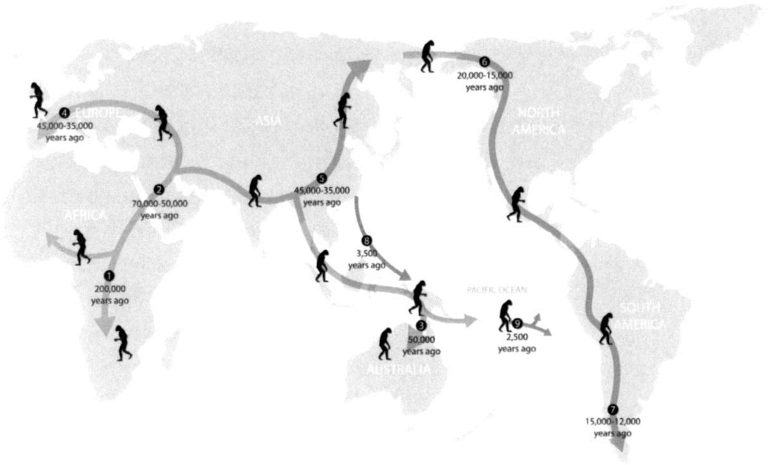

Early *Homo sapiens* migrated across all continents, except Antarctica, relatively quickly, showing a propensity to travel not exhibited by other primates.

needs for food, water, favourable climate and to escape from hostile groups of their own species. Even when humans began to form settled societies and develop agriculture some 10,000 years ago (a development called 'sedentism', which will be covered in more detail in the following chapter), humans did not stop travelling. Indeed, with the invention of the wheel and the domestication of horses and camels, travel became quicker and easier, and trade became an important motivator for travel, exchanging goods between different settled communities. Migrations also continued and, in general, historical migrations (ie those we have written records of) seem to have been for reasons of escape from persecution, poverty or natural disaster (Collier, 2013; Fisher, 2014). This pattern has continued to this day – according to the UN the number of people forced to migrate due to conflicts and violence had reached over 70 million in 2019.

We may never know what motivated the early prehistoric migrations of our ancestors (although I believe that curiosity was a strong motivating factor) but we can say that without four crucial characteristics, it would not have been possible. It is to those that we now turn: bipedalism, a large brain, dextrous hands and speech. These four characteristics – often considered to be defining aspects of humanity – have much to tell us about why we travel and how travel is woven into our physical and mental make-up.

Evolution of bipedalism

The genetic similarity between humans and our closest living relative – the chimpanzee – is very high, but in the small genetic variations there lie hints at some of our defining differences. One of the most striking is that we walk upright on two legs and chimpanzees do not. Walking upright is our original mode of travel. Understanding the origins and consequences of human bipedalism gives us a deep-time perspective on human travel. If travel is in some way 'hard-wired' into our physical and mental development, appreciating how that came about may help us better understand our own travel behaviours today. In this section we will go back to the evolutionary origins of ancient humans (our ancestors, including other species in the genus *Homo)* to trace the development of bipedalism and to look at what this tells us about human travel. While the story could start hundreds of millions of years ago, with the origin of the first mobile life-forms, I will start around six million years ago in Africa, with the common ancestor of chimpanzees (*Pan*) and humans (*Homo*). Since that time the lineage leading to *Homo* changed much more than that leading to *Pan*, and one of the key modifications was bipedalism.

From fossilized tracks along the East African Rift valley that stretches from Ethiopia to Lake Malawi, scientists have been able to deduce that 3–4 million years ago *Australopithecus,* an ancestor of *Homo,* was walking upright. Why this change came about is still debated. It seems likely that habitat changes, from dense jungle to savannah, favoured an upright stance. As the habitat changed, the increasingly long distance between trees and other shelters now had to be traversed quickly and safely and with a view of approaching danger or prey. There is evidence that such habitat changes did occur in Africa at this time, between three and six million years ago, due to massive tectonic and climatic changes that changed the geography of Africa, forcing up a high plateau of land and volcanoes and changing the habitat from tree-dominated to grass-dominated.[3] More recent research has suggested that the habitat change behind bipedalism may have been not just increased grassland but increased variability of terrain, including rocky outcrops and mountains being pushed up by these tectonic changes. Bipedalism, it is argued, offered flexibility in ways of travelling across such rugged terrain, including walking, running, climbing and scrambling ability (Winder et al, 2013). These habitat changes did not happen overnight – rather habitats changed slowly with trees becoming more spread out, grasslands more expansive and rocky outcrops and uneven terrain more common, over a few million years. This fits with the equally gradual

Figure 2.2: Chimpanzee and human skeletons

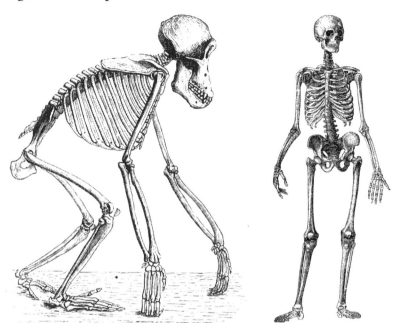

Many anatomical differences between humans and chimpanzees, our closest living relatives, are due to the different requirements of quadrupedal and bipedal locomotion (NB: illustrations here are not to the same scale).

change in the way that hominin species evolved: bipedalism was not 'all or nothing' – rather a mode of travel that may at first have conveyed benefits in certain circumstances. Indeed there is some debate as to whether the development of bipedalism was 'linear' (moving from 'occasional' to 'habitual' to 'obligate' in a straight trajectory) or whether it was more complex than this, with bipedalism perhaps evolving a few times in independent lineages (Harcourt-Smith and Aiello, 2004). Whatever the exact pattern, the earliest species we know of that could walk on two legs (around six million years ago) were 'occasional bipeds', covering only short distances bipedally. *Australepithecus,* ancestors of early humans, were 'habitual bipeds', walking when it suited but not yet constrained to do so as their only mode of travel. The first 'obligate biped', *Homo erectus,* seems to have emerged around two million years ago, with longer legs and more slender in build than earlier hominins, able to walk quickly and run over long distances as modern humans can, with feet adapted for walking and running, not for climbing or gripping trees. It may be that, as well as walking, long-distance running ability, played a key role in the evolution of the human body form. Humans tend to out-perform all other animals at this challenge, particularly in hot conditions, suggesting we may have evolved as 'persistence hunters' (Bramble and Lieberman, 2004). With the development of obligate bipedalism came the first expansion of early humans out of Africa, across south and south east Asia. Perhaps not coincidentally, *Homo erectus* was also possibly the first species to develop technology to extend this ability to travel: there is evidence that suggests that *Homo erectus* may have fashioned simple boats to travel across the sea.

Human curiosity and the consequences of bipedalism: brains, hands and speech

When we travel, we do so not only to reach a safe haven for the night, or to seek food. As humans, we travel not only from necessity but also from desire; from – I would argue – curiosity. As Aristotle (Ross, 1924) said: 'All men by nature desire to know.' Sir Alister Hardy (Professor of Zoology at Oxford during the 1950s) put this into a modern, biologically-framed context:

> out of this process of evolution, from *somewhere* has come the urge, or love of adventure, in Man that can drive him to risk his life in climbing Everest or in reaching the South Pole or the Moon. Is it altogether too naive to believe that this exploratory drive, this *curiosity* [my italics], has had its beginnings in some deep-seated part of animal behaviour which is fundamental to the stream of life? (Pasternak, 2003: 11)

Following Hardy's suggestion, are there evolutionary developments in the deep past of humanity that might shed some light on human curiosity? Indeed, may bipedalism itself have something to do with our curiosity? All animals are curious (and some individual humans more so than others), but as a species, *Homo sapiens* developed three characteristics that make them able to exercise their curiosity more intensely than any other creature. You might think this has to do with eyesight, sense of smell, or hearing, but you would be wrong. A dragonfly has more sophisticated vision, a bear's ability to smell is 2,000 times more acute, and a tiger's hearing is three times finer than that of a human being. It is the human hand, speech, and larger brain that are crucial. These characteristics enabled ancient humans to travel so far and wide, and to so effectively pursue our curiosity. Without the abilities to solve complex problems, plan for the future, make and use complex tools and communicate such ideas with their social groups, ancient humans would not have been able to adapt so quickly to the many different habitats they encountered in their rapid migration across the world. As I have argued in my book *Quest* (2003), I believe that our innate curiosity is a major motivating factor of human travel. It is little surprise then that travel and curiosity should share such biological bases. How these characteristics evolved, and their close ties to bipedalism and travel, we will now see.

The human brain

The human brain is about three times as large as that of the chimpanzee, and we have just to look at the name we have chosen for our species – *Homo sapiens*: 'wise man' – to see in what high regard we hold this characteristic. There is much to be explored about the brain and human travel, and this will be covered in this book's next chapter by Tony Hiss. For now, let us look at how our brains evolved and how, if at all, this was related to walking upright. How do the evolutionary histories of our brains and human travel intertwine?

The brain of *Australopithecus* was barely larger than that of the common ancestor of chimpanzees and humans six million years ago, or indeed of today's chimpanzees. But since then, mutations in a region of DNA that specifies the number of neurons (nerve cells) in a brain began to lead to ever more neurons, with a concomitant increase in brain size. Modern humans have three times as many neurons (around 86 billion) as a chimpanzee, and our brain is accordingly three times as large. Around 20 per cent of the brain's neurons are found in the cortex (outer layer) of the brain, which, because of extensive folding, actually makes up most of the brain of primates (Herculano-Houzel, 2009). It is in the cortex (especially its frontal part) where thinking, short-term memory, language, and some sensations are processed. So, a three-fold increase in the number of nerve cells (each of which makes thousands of connections with other nerve cells) provides the additional complexity in humans that allows us to work out problems as complicated as how to travel to the moon. Such a large brain enables humans to realize their curiosity better than any other animal, and to travel far and wide in an attempt to satisfy their curious nature. For good reason was the robotic rover on NASA's Mars mission in 2011 called 'Curiosity'.

Casting back 80,000 years, to when *Homo sapiens* embarked on its great migrations out of Africa, we can see the brain leading the way. It has been suggested that this time was a 'dynamic period of innovation' for humanity in which tools seem to have increased in complexity.

There is also evidence that around this time humans first began to exploit the sea for food, gaining a highly nutritious source of fatty acids for the energy-hungry human brain. Complex tools and brain food (and windows of favourable climate) seem to have helped prompt the rapid spread of humans across the globe.[4]

Being curious not only drives us to seek new information, it also has an effect on the brain that makes it easier to remember information: curiosity enhances learning (Gruber, 2014). So when we take a new track to travel along out of curiosity, our brain simultaneously remembers the details of that route better than if we had taken it out of necessity or by command. Such reinforcement is of obvious benefit if we wish to repeat the journey. Thus, curiosity conveys advantages in spatial learning, and may in part be responsible for much of humanity's success in colonizing and exploiting the world.

The hand

The hand is a key feature of humans, enabling complex tool use and manufacture. It has long been debated whether this in itself was a driving pressure behind the development of bipedalism. The discovery of the 3.7 million-year-old Laetoli Tracks seemed to settle this, placing habitual bipedalism a full million years before confirmed tool use. It seems likely that the human hand was a consequence of bipedalism: that bipedalism 'freed' the hands from the task of locomotion, enabling them to become better adapted to other tasks, from tool use to communicative gestures.

Mutations in the genes leading to the development of the thumb and other parts of the hand meant that early humans (*Homo habilis*, around two million years ago) were able to grasp and manipulate objects with a more powerful and better controlled 'precision grip' (thumb apposed to first finger) than our ancestors. Our primate relatives have both the 'precision' and 'power grip' (fingers clenched, thumb outside) that humans do, but human anatomical features and greater neural control evolved in early humans alongside tool use (Key and Lycett, 2011). Some researchers have explored the evolutionary links between the human hand and bipedalism by looking at our ability to throw objects: an ability that links an upright stance, free hands, a mobile upper body and the power grip. Accurate throwing is a crucial skill in hunting and in fighting off predators and rivals, and something that humans excel at in relation to other animals (Young, 2003).

Figure 2.3: Nordic Bronze Age petroglyphs of ships and men

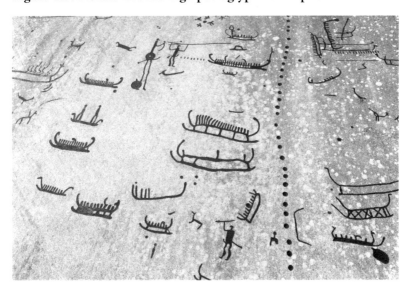

The ability (and desire) to build boats, and to represent those boats in artwork, are a result of humanity's large brains, language abilities and dextrous hands. These petroglyphs from Sweden date from 1700–500 years BCE, but the earliest boats may have been made by *Homo erectus* 900,000 years ago.

And what did this increased dexterity mean for human travel and curiosity? The impacts were profound. *Homo habilis* and their descendants were better able to fashion tools used for hunting and for scraping meat from a carcass. This in itself could be linked to increased brain size since meat – particularly if cooked – is a high-energy food that can help meet the nutritional demands of a large brain (Milton, 1999). The ability to make tools and scrape furs for clothing and shelter would have helped early humans adapt to the new environments they encountered as they moved around and out of Africa – no other animal was or is able to manipulate its environment in quite the same way. As for 'travel technologies', at some point, perhaps as early as 900,000 years ago, early humans learnt to shape a fallen tree trunk into a boat: for a long time this was the only form of travel apart from walking and running (Rose, 1998). And, of course, making things with our hands has enabled us to fulfil our innate curiosity: telescopes to see stars, microscopes to discover microbes, X-ray crystallography to probe the structures of proteins and DNA. It is clear that we would not be able to travel so far and wide today without the technological developments our dextrous hands have enabled us to create.

Speech

None of the technological advances and social changes I have mentioned would have been possible had humans not learned to communicate complex ideas with each other. Discussion in a project even as simple as making and launching a log-boat facilitates the process – not to mention deciding where to travel as a group, or telling others about your travels on your return. Crucial to such communication was the development of speech. This involved the evolution of a number of complex and interrelated features in the brain, nerves and anatomy, including the lowering of the larynx (voice box) and related changes to the tongue, improved control of breathing, and the ability to vocally imitate sounds. This vocal imitation is something that humans, parrots and dolphins can do, but that it seems our primate relatives cannot (though they do, through particular sounds, communicate specific dangers like 'snake' or 'eagle'). We do not know when these changes occurred, as vocal cords and imitative abilities do not leave a fossil record (Fitch, 2010). We think that *Homo sapiens*, modern humans, may be the only species of *Homo* to have acquired the facility of speech, but that *Homo neanderthalensis*, Neanderthal man, who emerged around 500,000 years ago (but is not a direct ancestor of *Homo sapiens*), may have communicated through some type of singing discourse (Mithen, 2006).

These changes are likely to have been related to bipedalism in a few ways. Humans have better control over breathing than our ape relatives, and this breath control is an important requirement for human speech. It involves the ability to control the muscles between the ribs, which first requires that the thorax (upper body) be independent of locomotion – as it is when walking on two legs rather than four. It has also been suggested that the 'freeing up' of hands as a result of bipedalism enabled not only improved tool use, but also the use of hands in communication through gestures. The origins of language are much debated but many believe that language first evolved in early humans with hand gestures, followed later by vocal speech (Fay et al, 2014). There is also some evidence to suggest that speech evolved as part of a vocal recognition system, enabling human ancestors to better recognize individuals and to discriminate between individuals of their own group and of competing groups; such an ability would be of clear use to groups who travelled a lot. It seems that speech and human travel may have been linked from early on.

★ ★ ★ ★ ★

The biology of travel

We have seen how travel played a key role in human evolution, shaping and being shaped by the development of our anatomy and cognitive abilities. We turn now to look at how travel affects our bodies and minds and what this might teach us about our continuing desire to travel.

Active travel and health: body and mind

The physical activity involved in more active forms of travel, particularly human-powered travel such as walking, running and cycling, and even horse riding, rowing or sailing, has a wide range of benefits for physical health. According to the World Health Organization (WHO):

> Sedentary lifestyles increase all causes of mortality, double the risk of cardiovascular diseases, diabetes, and obesity, and increase the risks of colon cancer, high blood pressure, osteoporosis, lipid disorders, depression and anxiety. … 60 to 85% of people in the world – from both developed and developing countries – lead sedentary lifestyles, making it one of the more serious yet insufficiently addressed public health problems of our time. It is estimated that nearly two-thirds of children are also insufficiently active, with serious implications for their future health.[5]

And the WHO also says that one of the major causes in our decline in physical activity is a reduction in active travel such as walking and cycling.[6]

Benefits of active travel are not limited to our bodies; it has long been known that physical exercise has a strongly beneficial effect on the brain. In the short term, as many exercise enthusiasts will tell you, exercise has been associated with a feeling of exhilaration and happiness. The molecular details of this – the so-called 'runner's high' – have been established. We have in our brain certain proteins to which substances like morphine and other opiates (or opioids) attach. When they do so, they engender within us a feeling of euphoria (as well as analgesic – pain reduction – and other effects). But you do not have to ingest opiates, because these molecules occur naturally within us. Various activities increase the amount of endogenous opiates, which leads to euphoria. A group of German scientists studied ten athletes at rest, or immediately after two hours of endurance running for about 20 kilometres. They found that 'the level of euphoria was significantly increased after running' as expected, 'and was inversely correlated with opioid binding' in various regions of the brain (Boecker et al, 2008). In other words the 'runner's high' is due to an increased production of opioids in the body.

Short term it gives you a sense of euphoria but, more importantly, continued exercise has several benefits, including a reduction in the development of cognitive disorders like Alzheimer's, reduced anxiety and depression, and increased self-esteem (Morgan, 1985; Norton et al, 2014). There is even evidence that walking can assist with recovery from brain injury. According to neuroscientist Sean O'Mara (who is so passionate about walking and its positive impacts on our brain that he has written a book entitled *In Praise of Walking*):

> '[I]t is reasonable to surmise that supervised walking may help with acquired brain injury, depending on the nature, type and extent of injury – perhaps by promoting blood flow, and perhaps also through the effect of entraining various electrical rhythms in the brain. And perhaps by engaging in systematic dual tasking, such as talking and walking.' (quoted in Fleming, 2019)

Active travel may therefore have a very important role to play in both preventative and therapeutic forms.

Travel of course may also have negative impacts on our health. Although major air accidents grab the headlines, it is automobiles that are the serious killers. Road traffic accidents are a major cause of death and injury throughout the world, especially among the young, and particularly in developing countries. In 2018 alone, an estimated 1.35 million people lost their lives on the roads, a third of whom were travelling on foot or bicycle (WHO, 2019). Somewhat ironically, the inactivity caused on long journeys by air, road or rail can actually damage health too, not least in the form of increased risk of deep vein thrombosis. Despite these risks, there is no doubt that travel (at least if it is active) can be enormously beneficial for your physical, mental and cognitive health; and it makes sense that doing the activities we evolved to do provide such benefits.

Processing travel within our brains

The *experience* of travel, like other knowledge, is retained by structures in the brain such as the hippocampus, where long-term memory is encoded. The hippocampus is also where spatial navigation, imagination and future thinking take place in the brain, underpinned by a common set of neurological processes that researchers have described as 'scene construction' (Maguire et al, 2010). So navigation (an essential thought process within travel) and imagination and future thinking (which are both key parts of curiosity) all seem to be linked at a fundamental neurological level. As O'Mara explains, "the brain systems that support learning, memory and cognition are the same ones that are very badly affected by stress and depression ... And by a quirk of evolution, these brain systems also support functions such as cognitive mapping" (quoted in Fleming, 2019).

There is some evidence that even the idea of travel may impact the way we think by increasing our capacity for creativity. Researchers have found that participants asked to solve a problem that they are told originates from a place far away (eg students in the US asked to solve a problem reportedly set by Greek university professors) give more creative solutions to the problem than those participants who believe the problem is local in origin. Researchers concluded that a sense of 'psychological distance', in which the self is separated from an event or problem by spatial, social or temporal distance, promotes more creative thinking (Jia et al, 2009). This suggests that the benefits of travel asserted by many cultures past and present – travel as an experience that broadens the mind – may have a neurological basis, lying within the 'scene construction' process of the hippocampus.

Indeed some scientists, Sean O'Mara included, take a 'motor-centric' view of the evolution of animal brains, ie that the brain evolved to support movement, illustrating this view with examples of marine animals who have mobile larval forms, which do have a brain, and sessile adult forms, which have lost their brain. Similarly, influential 20th-century psychologist, James Gibson, argued that visual perception is deeply linked to motion: 'We must perceive in order to move, but we must also move in order to perceive' (1979: 223). This of course does not mean that we cannot perceive things if we are sitting still in a room but that if all we get is a snapshot view, our perception will not be 'adequate'. Also that perception contains integrally a 'perception of how to approach and what to do about it' (1979: 226). As Gibson puts it:

> Looking around and getting around do not fit into the standard idea of what visual perception is. But note that if an animal has eyes at all it swivels its head around and goes from place to place. The single frozen field of view provides only impoverished information about the world. The visual system did not evolve for this. (1979: 2)

Sharing the travel experience: humans as social animals

Our personal memories, experiences and imaginings of travel do not remain locked in our own brains (specifically the hippocampus, where long-term memory is encoded). The information is then retrieved and recounted. Sharing our experiences and plans for the future is an important part of social bonding and organization for us as social animals. Humans share information in a number of ways, including verbally, from chats with friends to the epic spoken poems of ancient times, and visually (think of how the fashion for travel in the 18th-century Grand Tour era changed European visual culture, or the great travel photography competitions and thousands of travel-themed Instagram accounts). Travel writing, from writers like Joseph Conrad, Ernest Hemingway and Wilfred Thesiger, to the countless travel blogs online today, testify to the process by which one person's evocation of travel is conveyed to thousands through speech, art and literature. This will all be covered in much more depth in later chapters (specifically, see 'Travel in Art and Literature') but the biological basis of this desire to share experiences – both to tell our own experiences and hear about those of others – is worth looking at here. Sharing experiences bonds groups and increases the knowledge base of the group as a whole, allowing us to create social 'productive networks' for solving problems and achieving the groups' aims. But 'sharing' can also involve 'showing off': ie sharing our experiences can be used to gain higher social status. The promotion of group cohesion, and the competitive process of vying for a place in a hierarchy, are both important social processes found across all social primates, humans included. The traveller has, throughout history, had an ambiguous social status (the 'outsider') but, at least in more recent times, long distance travel has often conveyed higher social status upon the traveller when returning to their home community (although of course travellers from other communities are often treated with distrust).

The importance of actually *travelling: unconscious environmental cues*

If you are curious to see the Taj Mahal or Red Square, no need to queue for a visa. If you want to see a crocodile devouring a young hippo, no need to invest in a safari suit or take out expensive travel insurance. All is available to you from your armchair at the flick of a switch. If you are the CEO of a multinational conglomerate and wish to discuss progress with your team on another continent, just turn on Skype. Yet people continue to travel, and CEOs spend long hours on aeroplanes (first class) in order to meet subordinates or competitors. Why? Because there is something special about seeing a monument in a certain light or touching it with your finger and because it can be hard to judge a social situation unless you are really there. For many, their curiosity is satisfied only by actually being there. The reason for this may lie in part in the importance of environmental and communicative cues that cannot be effectively transmitted 'virtually'. In communication, non-verbal cues like gestures and facial expressions convey a lot of information, even if unconsciously, to both parties (Benedetti, 2011: 138–48) and although these visual cues could be conveyed by high-quality video links, there may be other factors that cannot, including touch and smell. Researchers in fields like neuropharmacology and biometeorology are studying the relatively new field of environmental influences on our bodies and brains and finding that everything from the smells, ions in air and inaudible noises to electromagnetic fields in our surroundings can have huge impacts on our mood and health. Thus environmental factors, like the quality of the light on the monument, or the smell of a local market, can greatly – and often unconsciously – shape a person's experience of travel, both of their journey and the destination (Hiss, 1991).

Curiosity, travel and scientific discovery

I could give many examples of curious travellers over the ages, from Marco Polo to Ibn Battuta, but perhaps the two who most appositely exemplify the curious traveller, especially in a chapter focussed on biology, are Charles Darwin and Alfred Russell Wallace. Each man – quite independently of the other – integrated the observations made over years of travelling into the most innovative theory ever proposed concerning living creatures: the origin of species through natural selection. In the words of historian Eric J. Leed (1991: 70), Darwin's five years aboard *The Beagle* (and by implication, Wallace's travels in South America and the Malay Archipelago), enabled him to see both the 'enormous variety of species but also ... the role played by context in the change of species character'. Leed describes travel as a 'generalising activity' that, by taking the traveller out of their familiar environment, enables them to see more general patterns and relations – what some have described as the 'objectivity' of the traveller. This certainly seems true of these two curious travellers, Darwin and Wallace, whose insight has proved to be the greatest advance in biology ever made. Their revolutionary theory, which came about as a result of curiosity-driven travel, enables us to study our own evolutionary origins[7] including, rather aptly, the questions we are asking here about why we travel.

Figure 2.4: *HMS Beagle,* by Conrad Martens (1831–36)

The famous voyage of HMS Beagle played a key role in the development of Darwin's theory of evolution by natural selection. Thus one of the greatest scientific advances emerged from curiosity-driven travel.

Conclusions: Why do we travel – and how might we make travel better?

All of this brings us back to the core question: why do we travel? What can we conclude from all we have covered about the biological basis, origins and consequences of human travel? We can now access virtually so many of the needs and desires that previously only travel could provide. But even with all of our modern abilities to obviate travel, we still travel, and in increasing numbers and increasing distances. Even at the more local scale, home-working technologies have not rid us of the daily commute and, despite online shopping, local markets are gaining popularity. For some reasons, actually making the journey, and actually being in the destination yourself, still matters. As we have seen, we can start to understand these reasons by looking at our basis as biological beings – and if we understand this biological basis we can then start to imagine ways in which we might shape our travel to better suit our biological needs, through our personal behaviours and on a larger scale in our travel infrastructure and planning.

It is clear that active, 'human-powered' travel conveys all the health benefits of exercise, improving both physical and mental health.

Individuals, governments and organizations are recognizing this (indeed, have long recognized this) and efforts are being made to promote walking and cycling – for example the Welsh Sennedd's 2014 Active Travel Bill, the popular 'Boris Bikes' of London, and the WHO's Global Action Plan on Physical Activity 2018–30. If travel is necessary for our physical and mental wellbeing, we need to take account of such needs in making travel accessible to all members of society, whatever their physical capabilities. Bringing biological health into the core of transport planning and other policies is of vital importance in tackling a public health crisis as well as environmental and social problems (for more on this see the 'Placemaking and Travel' chapter).

Evidence of how environmental and communicative factors affect our experience of places and people gives an insight into why, despite the advances of a digital age, we still travel to have the experience ourselves. It is interesting to consider whether improved virtual reality technology, which could simulate at least some of these environmental factors, might in future more effectively replace actual travel.

Travel also seems to fulfil some social functions, which humans, as social primates, need in order to be members of a functioning group. While it is the cultural interpretation of travel that provides meaning (for example that travel is a good thing, which raises the social status of the traveller), some of the functions that travel is being used to fulfil are the social functions of group cohesion and of social hierarchy that are common among other social primates. These social aspects of our travel motivations must of course be understood in much more depth if we are to plan better travel and transport policies (see, for example, the chapters 'Why Travel? The Sociological Perspective' and 'Why People Travel: An Anthropological View', for more on social and cultural perspectives).

The evolutionary links between bipedalism – our original mode of travel – and other key human characteristics, such as the hand, large brain and speech, suggest that how we travel is linked to other very fundamental parts of human life. Appreciating this core place of travel within our pre-history, our very origins, helps place human travel within a deeper and more profound context than we usually might consider it. Travel is not just a walk to the shops or even a round-the-world tour; it has played a fundamental part in creating us and in helping us to create the world we see today. From the first steps of our bipedal ancestors and the earliest migrations of *Homo sapiens* out of Africa, to the invention of trains, planes and automobiles, travel has and continues to shape our lives. It is now time we placed travel back at the heart of our understanding of humanity.

Notes

[1] I thank the editors of this volume for skilfully expanding my original contribution. I am grateful to Kasia Lewis, Director of the Oxford International Biomedical Centre, for office facilities, and to the staff of the London Library for their efficient handling of my many demands.

[2] According to the United Nations World Tourism Organization (UNWTO) this reached 1.4 billion in 2018.

[3] www.geotimes.org/jan08/article.html?id=feature_evolution.html

[4] www.smithsonianmag.com/history/the-great-human-migration-13561/#50PbxVfW74emySF6.99

[5] www.who.int/mediacentre/news/releases/release23/en/

[6] www.who.int/ncds/prevention/physical-activity/inactivity-global-health-problem/en/

[7] Darwin (1871) even proposed that changes in habitat from forest to savannah may have driven evolution of arboreal ancestors to terrestrial bipedalism.

References

Aristotle and Ross, W. D. (1924). *Aristotle's Metaphysics : A Revised Text With Introduction and Commentary*, Oxford: The Clarendon Press.

Benedetti, F. (2011) *The Patient's Brain*. New York: Oxford University Press, pp 138–48.

Boecker, H. et al (2008) 'The runner's high: opioidergic mechanisms in the human brain', *Cerebral Cortex,* 18: 2523–2531.

Bramble, D. M. and Lieberman, D. E. (2004) 'Endurance Running and the Evolution of Homo', *Nature,* 432(7015): 345–52. doi.org/10.1038/nature03052.

Collier, P. (2013) *Exodus: Immigration and Multiculturalism in the 21st Century,* London: Allen Lane.

Darwin, C. R. (1871): *The Descent of Man, and Selection in Relation to Sex*, John Murray.

Fay, N., Lister, C. J., Ellison, T. M. and Goldin-Meadow, S. (2014) 'Creating a communication system from scratch: gesture beats vocalization hands down', *Frontiers in Psychology*, 29 April 2014. doi: 10.3389/fpsyg.2014.00354.

Fisher, M. H. (2014) *Migration: A World History,* New York: Oxford University Press.

Fitch, W. T. (2010) *The Evolution of Language,* Cambridge: Cambridge University Press.

Fleming, A. (2019) "It's a superpower': how walking makes us healthier, happier and brainier', *The Guardian*, 28 July 2019. https://www.theguardian.com/lifeandstyle/2019/jul/28/its-a-superpower-how-walking-makes-us-healthier-happier-and-brainier

Gibson, J. (1979) *The Ecological Approach to Visual Perception*, Boston, MA: Houghton Mifflin.

Gruber, M. J., Gelman, B. D. and Ranganath, C. (2014) 'States of curiosity Modulate hippocampus-dependent learning via the dopaminergic circuit', *Neuron*, 84: 486–96

Harcourt-Smith, W. E. H. and Aiello, L. C. (2004) 'Fossils, feet and the evolution of human bipedal locomotion', *Journal of Anatomy*, 204(5): 403–16.

Herculano-Houzel, S. (2009) 'The human brain in numbers: a linearly scaled-up primate brain', *Frontiers in Human Neuroscience*, 9 November 2009. doi: 10.3389/neuro.09.031.2009.

Hiss, T. (1991) *The Experience of Place*, New York: Alfred A. Knopf.

Jia, L., Hirt, E.R. and Karpen, S.C. (2009) 'Lessons from a faraway land: the effect of spatial distance on creative cognition', *Journal of Experimental Social Psychology*, 45(5): 1127–31.

Key, A. J. M. and Lycett, S. J. (2011) 'Technology based evolution? A biometric test of the effects of handsize versus tool form on efficiency in an experimental cutting task', *Journal of Archaeological Science*, 38: 1663–70. doi:10.1016/j.jas.2011.02.032.

Leed, E. J. (1991) *The Mind of the Traveler,* Basic Books (p 70).

Maguire, E. A, Vargha-Khadem, F. and Hassabis, D. (2010) 'Imagining fictitious and future experiences: Evidence from developmental amnesia', *Neuropsychologia*, 48(11–2): 3187–92. doi: 10.1016/j.neuropsychologia.2010.06.037.

Marchetti, C. (1994) 'Anthropological invariants in travel behavior', *Technological Forecasting and Social Change*, 47: 75–88.

Milton, K. (1999) 'A hypothesis to explain the role of meat-eating in human evolution', *Evolutionary Anthropology*, 8: 11–21. doi:10.1002/(SICI)1520-6505(1999)8:1<11::AID-EVAN6>3.0.CO;2-M

Mithen, S. J. (2006) *The Singing Neanderthals: The Origins of Music, Language, Mind and Body,* Cambridge, MA: Harvard University Press.

Morgan, W. P. (1985) 'Affective beneficence of vigorous physical activity', *Med. Set. Sports Exerc.* 17: 94–100.

Norton S., Matthews F. E., Barnes D. E., Yaffe K., and Brayne C. (2014) 'Potential for primary prevention of Alzheimer's disease: an analysis of population-based data', *Lancet Neurology*, 13(8):788–94. doi:10.1016/S1474-4422(14)70136-X.

Pasternak, C. (2003) *Quest. The Essence of Humanity,* Chichester: Wiley.

Rose, M. (1998) 'First Mariners', *Archaeology*, 5 (May/June 1998).

WHO (2019) *Global Status Report on Road Safety 2019,* WHO. https://archive.archaeology.org/9805/newsbriefs/mariners.html.

Winder, I. C., King, G. C. P., Devès, M. and Bailey, G. N. (2013) 'Complex topography and human evolution: the missing link', *Antiquity*, 87(336): 333–49.

Young, R.W. (2003) 'Evolution of the human hand: the role of throwing and clubbing', *Journal of Anatomy*, 202(1): 165–74. doi: 10.1046/j.1469-7580.2003.00144.x.

3

Travel and the Mind

Tony Hiss

Introduction

The title of this book – *Why Travel?* – is one of those questions that dates us, because modern human beings have been asking it in a succession of languages for about the last 11,500 years. Before that, back when travel was a given, not a choice, asking 'Why travel?' would have made no more sense than asking 'Why sleep?'

Simplifying the back-story somewhat, modern humans left Africa about 60,000 years ago. But for fully four-fifths of that long time span, as they dispersed across the continents throughout almost 50,000 years, they were wanderers, people who hunted, fished and foraged, settling down at night, but moving on again and again, as the animals and plants they relied on were depleted or shifted seasonally or with changing climates.

Then as a species we came to a halt. Not everywhere, not all at once, but at some point over the past 400 generations of people, staying put became the norm, along with permanently growing a community's plants and animals on site. The technical term for this great shift is 'sedentism' – from the Latin word for 'to sit', which also led to sedentary, sediment, settlement.

Why travel? Set aside the profound and transformative economic, social and environmental changes sedentism has created, and look instead to the (in evolutionary terms) still only lately formed, inwardly focused, stay-at-home mindset that sedentism has brought with it.

Figure 3.1: Women walking in the savannah, eastern Kenya

Travel can open up our minds to a wider sense of awareness, a bigger 'here', a longer 'now'. There is evidence that the evolution of bipedalism within an open savannah landscape – with long vistas to the horizon – may have encouraged the development of human imagination and curiosity.

Innocently posed by the book's editors, the simple, two-word question is simmering with attitudes and expectations that immediately and usefully open up for close examination the psychology of travel and the effect it has on our minds.

'Why travel?' is actually a tightly knit collection of questions, and down at their heart lurks an entrenched sedentist scepticism, ambiguity and ambivalence about what travel can accomplish. There is a grudging quality here: is travel really necessary? If it has to happen, is it not likely to be more trouble than it is worth, and unpleasant and dangerous?

Such questions linger and smolder in 21st-century societies – where most people commute, where younger people who can afford to travel so far and so frequently they are called the 'first globals', and where involuntary dislocations of large groups of people from countryside to city and from country to country are increasingly commonplace. For all our restlessness, the underlying assumption remains that homes and communities are somehow unmoving and unshakeable. Why venture forth when we are already right where we belong? The 'here' we know is more real and more reliable than the 'over theres' and the 'elsewheres'.

How, then, can we explain the persistence of the travel urge over the past 11,500 years, a force that remains vigorous even after being degraded and frowned upon? Perhaps it is simply because travel, even when no longer a constant state, continues to serve as a unique mental stimulus with its own unsurpassed and still much-prized ability to lead our minds in new directions. In this chapter, using themes adapted from my book *In Motion*, I will explore how this legacy of travel came about, how it still shapes our minds today, and how we might use this understanding to improve and expand – rather than minimize – our daily travel experiences and thus reclaim and augment that part of our lives we otherwise risk losing.

Deep Travel: a human mentality of travel

To begin this exploration of travel and the mind, I would like to introduce the concept of 'Deep Travel' – a way of using the mind that opens us up on all channels to new experiences. Deep Travel is key, I believe, to understanding why, despite millennia of sedentist habits, a desire to travel persists in our minds. It is something of a built-in Cinderella ability, because in our schooling we hear only about two ways in which the waking mind can organize its thinking – daydreaming and closely focused attention (schools warn us about the first and try to train us to get better at the second). Both these mental capacities operate by sealing us off from the world, while Deep Travel is alert to everything around us.

A young British paleoanthropologist, William E. H. Harcourt-Smith, at the American Museum of Natural History in New York, helped me understand that in pre-sedentist days Deep Travel may have been a default setting of the human mind, since it is doubly important for our brains to be alert to new opportunities and new dangers in new places, and that is what life constantly exposed our ancestors to. It still appears spontaneously whenever we travel to new places – and it can appear whenever we remind ourselves that any trip we take is new.

We have all experienced that exhilarating quality of feeling a place for the first time. Deep Travel is like waking up while already awake; everything seems fresh, vivid and memorable. Even when it is not at the forefront of our minds, we use this capacity to evaluate the trips we take, both daily commutes and long-distance business trips and vacations to faraway places. Here is the policy implication: if roads and train lines and ships and airlines are not built in a way that offers nourishment and stimulation to the Deep Travel part of our minds, trips will fall short of offering the fulfillment the mind craves; they will have a bitter residue and be perceived as drudgery.

The origins of human movement and the development of the human mind

Travel, navigation and the animal mind

Animals, in general, are travellers (motion is at the heart of a number of the root words for 'animal', such as the Greek *anemos*, or 'wind') and, over hundreds of millions of years, animals have devised a series of movement strategies that automatically guide and shape their many travels. Since animals' independent, self-propelled motion has been connected almost from the start with staying alive, and since animals began to move around long before they became sociable, these inward and self-protective 'guidance traits' are probably one of the most fundamental underpinnings of an animal's essential capacities.

University-led 'spatial cognition' and 'way-finding' studies have picked apart the workings of these animal travel strategies – and have shown that many of them appear in human beings as well. Two-year-old children being observed by Elizabeth Spelke, a cognitive psychologist at Harvard, rely solely on 'contour navigation' when moving through a room and looking for an object that has been hidden from them, meaning that they use only the shape of the walls to tell them where they are and how to go, and ignore any other feature that might catch the eye of a grown-up, such as colours or the placement of objects around the room. This is the very same technique that rodents rely on when seeking food rewards placed inside a box. Our heritage as animals, as movers, has profoundly shaped our brain and how we navigate space.

The travelling ape

As we saw in Chapter 2 by Professor Pasternak, approximately two million years ago, with the appearance of *Homo ergaster* ('the working human') and *Homo erectus* ('the upright human'), smooth and fluid walking almost identical to that of modern humans became for the first time an everyday part of the life of human ancestors. Once they

Figure 3.2: Migrating birds fly in the night sky

Animals are travellers: only a few groups have evolved to be completely sessile. Like these birds, many animals migrate thousands of miles a year, using navigating senses humans do not possess.

became obligate bipeds they acted as if a restraint had been lifted; they developed bigger brains and more sophisticated tools.

This was the moment when long-distance travel began for hominins: they diffused throughout Africa and, within about 100,000 years, groups of them had left the home continent and spread out across Asia as far as China and Java (over 5,000 miles away). Roaming and ranging was the norm for the next two million years – first for them and later for the species (including ours) that followed them. Sedentism became a viable alternative to almost continuous movement perhaps 11,500 years ago – or during the last one-half of one per cent of this period.

In the decades since World War II, humanity has given itself a series of unprecedentedly humble nicknames that, instead of just asserting our uniqueness, present us as an unusual and sometimes highly idiosyncratic member of a larger clan, the primate or hominoid family. The most famous of these redefining terms is 'the naked ape', from Desmond Morris's 1967 best-seller. Morris proposed several additional terms, including 'the hunting ape' and 'the killer ape', and since then other writers, partly in admiration and partly in rebuttal, have countered with 'the moral ape' and 'the empathetic ape'. At the same time, another part of our own substance has not yet been caught and distilled in any catchphrase, a quality whose distinctiveness deserves its own recognition as a hominoid achievement. So let us give it a name – and say that two million years ago, we emerged as the only 'wandering ape', a transformation that also let us become, uniquely, 'the travelling ape'.

New horizons: the development of heightened awareness

Astonishing changes in human capacities followed from becoming bipedal. As anthropologist Robin Fox (1997) expresses it: 'Concentration and persistence are there in the apes, but they had to be applied systematically and across a wide range of behaviors' for humanity to emerge. 'The attention span, as we now like to call it, had to be lengthened and focused on something other than food and sex.' To what extent was the process assisted or even accelerated by having access to the 'bipedal perceptual platform', the new arrangement of feelings and perceptions that standing up had made possible?

In an extended conversation on the subject, Will Harcourt-Smith told me that the idea makes best sense to him "if you think of this larger awareness as something that really kicked in at the time of obligate bipedalism." His conclusions (slightly abbreviated):

> 'We know that obligate bipedalism coincides with the grasslands opening up, with the emergence of tools, with brain enlargement, and with having to travel farther on a daily basis for food, while avoiding different predators. So this was a really critical period. It required us – well, hominins, because up to a point these creatures were still not human – to pay attention to a wider range of stimuli just to get what was needed in terms of the search for nourishment and safety. And it was the moment when we finally had no other strategy available. It wasn't possible any longer to shinny up a tree, since our feet didn't work that way anymore.
>
> So we had to use whatever intelligence we had. In these circumstances there could be a very strong selection pressure for the ability to use this larger and more intensive awareness of our surroundings, to sustain it throughout the day, and to retain it from one generation to the next. When you're an obligate biped and seeing vistas to the horizon 80 to 90 per cent of the day – vistas that give

you an overview of the entire landscape – maybe that's when a threshold of inquisitiveness is crossed, and *curiosity* takes over.

A new physical capacity to be more exploratory, thanks to our longer legs, overlapped with a new mental capacity to be more exploratory, that desire to range a little further which heightened excitedness and sharper perceptions bring. So maybe what we're really saying is that becoming bipedal helps you get smart. Your legs bring you into the savannah, but your new perceptual platform brings you into an even more expanded realm, and it's the stimulation and new information that is the precursor of smartness, the backbone of cognitive development.'

These suggestions are also supported by the work of Jonathan Kingdon (2003: 249-52), an Oxford zoologist, who discusses what he calls the gradually widening and concentric 'circles of alertness' that organized the hominin approach to the world. In an early pre-walking era, much of a hominin's attention stayed focused within the tightest of these circles, concentrating on collecting and processing food 'within a perceptual field narrowed to the reach of their arms'. Surrounding this was a broader 'zone of immediate action' within the woods that was roughly 25 to 30 feet across. Habitual and obligate walking in a more open landscape added something new, a third and greatly expanded circle of alertness – the 'distant ambit', which extended 'beyond the range of immediate action to the horizon'. From Kingdon's book *Lowly Origin*:

> The act of scanning would have mainly concerned perceiving the movements of distant con-specifics, enemies, prey, or patterns made by attractive vegetation types, fires, rain clouds, and the sun's cycle. Judgments would have centered on assessments of direction, relative distance, and an awareness of events such as the comings or goings of rain, smoke, dust, or dusk. Because the act of long-distance scanning was relatively slow, passive, and did not involve the need for immediate action, there would have been a potential for reflection and planning. (2003: 251)

With its emphasis on 'long-distance scanning', on the combined noticing of sights, sounds and scents, and on an ability to detect hitherto hidden patterns in the land and the sky, this immediately sounds like a description of Deep Travel's moment of arrival – and seems just as clearly to have emerged as a consequence of moving around in a new way, a revelation summoned into being by standing upright. Making it a case of the feet (and legs) directly influencing and rearranging the mind.

Walking brought with it access to an enriched, inner impression-gathering device: our previously undeveloped, multi-sensory, wide-angle awareness. And this suddenly wider awareness helped hominins find reliable paths through the almost immeasurably wider world they then began to inhabit. Thus was inaugurated humanity's twin travel inheritance, an inseparable mind/body continuum that is still with us, one that is both a complex physical matter of bodies in motion, a matter of acceleration and deceleration and comfort and safety and, at the same time, exists as a constantly updated internal process whose unending concern is assessing, appreciating, absorbing and responding to the information and impressions that motion brings to us.

And what of curiosity, which as Professor Pasternak argued in the previous chapter, has been developed in humans to a peculiar degree, and which forms a central part of the heightened awareness of Deep Travel: the noticing and the desire to know more? It has been nearly half a century since Desmond Morris first suggested that 'neo-philia' – meaning a love for the novel and for innovation, and a passionate curiosity – is a trait that developed among primates and has been inherited by humanity. Once neo-philia puts us in touch more and more often with novel situations, a new kind of curiosity arises, and we find ourselves 'wanting to get better at knowing more', just to keep pace with ourselves. Maybe standing upright simultaneously heightened two different awarenesses – of the possibilities in the world and of its perils. The 'fight' and 'flight' impulses were suddenly balanced. And as a result something else became possible, almost a 'sit tight' kind of response: a wish to know more in safety before deciding what to do. Which may not quite sound like 'wanderlust', but which does sound a good deal like 'curiosity'.

Sedentism and our diminishing capacity for awareness

In another conversation with Harcourt-Smith, he had a question of his own. If an expanded awareness – or a 'travel chip', as he called it – was useful enough to have been offered permanent residence in our minds something like two million years ago, why is it that people today who have inherited it often feel estranged from it, or have a

Figure 3.3: 17th-century city walls of Khiva, Uzbekistan

Sedentism arose some 11,500 years ago, helping to relax the need for constant awareness, isolating us from a higher sense of awareness of the wider world, and generating a mistrust of travel. This image shows the city walls of Khiva, built (as in so many settlements) to protect inhabitants from external dangers.

hard time even acknowledging its presence? That was a question I had frequently found myself thinking about – it seems so odd to be cut off from something that offers so much enjoyment and insight. I told him I had come up with several theories. Sedentism and its effects seemed to be at the bottom of things.

We have said that our larger awareness is a unique amalgam of heightened feelings, characterized by a curiosity blended from vigilance and anticipation. But one of the first accomplishments of sedentism was to set up a perimeter that excludes dangerous wild animals, thus creating a permanent zone where some parts of alertness could be relaxed. These altered circumstances reset the fear–opportunity balance, and so made our larger awareness less 'necessary' as a constant state of mind, while offering new scope for other forms of awareness, such as focused attention and daydreaming, where any consciousness of our surroundings (not to mention the sense of time passing) virtually disappears. Noting that the human brain has become smaller over the past 35,000 years, biologist and anthropologist John Allman (1999) suggests: 'Perhaps humans, through the invention of agriculture and other cultural means for reducing the hazards of existence, have domesticated themselves.'

The arrival of settlements also set up the distinction we still make between 'here-ness', as it could be called, meaning places where we expect to find a relaxed state of affairs, and 'there-ness', or everywhere else. At first, 'here-ness' did not occupy very much ground, since people, once settled, did not move around much. Gradually, however, as humanity grew and spread, 'there-ness' shrank in size and, along the way, the 'wildness quotient' of the remaining 'theres' was repeatedly reduced, tamed. To which can be added the fact that we have been able to turn 'here-ness' into a portable commodity we often carry around with us, and can alter the focus of travel by imposing either a 'never left' sense in which we find ourselves preoccupied by the thoughts that had dominated our thinking before departure or, by contrast, an 'almost there' overlay based on anticipating our arrival and what it is we will be doing when we get to our destination.

Our brains on (Deep) Travel: lessons from neuroscience and psychology

Humans as 'infovores': the pleasure of novelty

Work by two neuroscientists, Irving Biederman and Edward A. Vessel, about how the brain processes visual information, does not address the question of when or how our larger awareness arose but does show us another aspect of its staying power, once it had become a part of us. Namely, that, like any of the great human drives – say, for food or reproduction – it is intrinsically pleasurable. As they describe us, humans are 'infovores', meaning we crave information. According to Biederman and Vessel (2006), 'the neural pathways through which we learn about the world tap into the same pleasure networks in the brain as are activated by drugs like heroin.' They say that, 'for humans, only the basic urges of hunger, harm avoidance and the need to find a mate can distract us from this info-craving.'[1]

There is more than one surprise here. It has been known for some time that the brain rewards itself (after exercise, for instance: see Chapter 1 of this book) by generating its own 'opioids' (endorphins and endomorphins) but it is new to think that visual areas of the brain are also equipped with 'opioid receptors' of their own. Even more startling is Biederman and Vessel's (2006) discovery that these receptors are most densely clustered in an area of the brain 'where visual information engages our memories.' 'So', they sum up, 'our hypothesis proposes that the rate of endomorphin release ... determines at least partially, the human preference for experiences that are both novel ... and richly interpretable.' Under the terms of this analysis, any awareness state would have its rewards, since an open eye is always processing some measure of visual information. But only the widest awareness – such as is brought about during Deep Travel – would bring the greatest pleasure, since its specific function is to be alert for new meanings that may reveal themselves through intricate and unexpected sights of the sort that Biederman and Vessel call 'novel ... and richly interpretable'.

How Deep Travel upsets our 'field of promoted action'

Beginning in 1950, a new way of explaining how people perceive the world began to emerge from visual studies being made by eminent American psychologist, J. J. Gibson. At the heart of traditional Western psychology was the idea that the mind is something acted upon, a recipient and a processor – responding to, and trying to make sense of, the many stimuli that reach it from the world outside. In the Gibsonian view, also known as ecological psychology, the emphasis is reversed, and the mind itself is the active force, reaching out for information that the world readily provides. Awareness, and not some external agent or force, is the central factor guiding human and animal behaviour.

Because awareness resides within, another consequence of this point of view is to give new standing to the mind and the role it plays in human life. Edward S. Reed, a philosopher of science and expert on Gibson's work, explained it thus:

> Mind has had no home in the universe for the past few hundred years. Since Descartes' day, mind has been relegated to whatever area of the cranium is least well understood ... retreating from one shelter to another or taking refuge in a nonphysical existence. Finally, with ecological psychology, the mind has found a home, not alongside the complex physical relations of the brain, but amidst us, the mental being conceived as our ability to experience the environment ... and act appropriately in it. (cited in Hiss, 2010: 89–90)

Gibson is probably best remembered for putting forward the idea of 'affordances', the basic insight behind which is that the world is intelligible because it has a structure the mind can take in. What the mind notices, in a nutshell, is not abstractions like space or time but the fact that there are some things in the environment that are persistent and others that undergo more frequent changes. Using this interplay between persistence and change as a background, the mind can then pick out things meaningful for its purposes – things to approach because they can be used, and that offer information about how to go about using them; and things, on the other hand, to avoid.

For a Gibsonian, a principal benefit that children pick up from the adults around them is the ability to recognize the affordances that will be of continuing importance to them in their lives. This is the basic human need that led over countless generations to the creation and constant elaboration of each culture's 'field of promoted action'. And it also explains why these fields are universally present within human communities.

Deep Travel, as travel writer Pico Iyer (2000) has said, 'spins us round in two ways at once' – changing both our inward view, as it shows us part of ourselves we do not know well, and our view out into the world, putting in front of us 'sights and values and issues that we might ordinarily ignore'. When we see people in a new place doing something we do not know how to do, we are seeing a 'sight' and a 'value' at the same time – an affordance that was not part of our own training. So noticing actions we do not understand is a way of noticing a hole in our own field of promoted action, and we have a chance to move beyond limitations we have just identified.

Although Deep Travel lets us see the gaps and incompleteness of our field of promoted action, that field is often not lightly abandoned: any number of travel accounts show that it is very common that people encountering strange affordances – customs or creatures or unexpected capacities – at first almost reflexively try to keep their preconceived notions intact. When the known no longer seems to offer guidance, the ache and sense of loss that wells up are feelings of having been cast adrift, cut off from the source; and of being becalmed and rudderless – when all that is really happening is people have moved beyond the orbit of the field they grew up in and have been carrying with them ever since.

The two-day rule: Deep Travel fading

The one drawback to Deep Travel that some people have pointed to is its impermanence: an observation poignantly presented by Thomas Mann, in *The Magic Mountain* (1924):

> The first few days in a new place have a youthful swing to them, a kind of sturdy, long stride – that lasts for about six

to eight days. Then, to the extent that we 'settle in,' the gradual shortening becomes noticeable… The first few days at home after a change of scene are likewise experienced in a new, broad, more youthful fashion – but only a few, for we are quicker to grow accustomed to the old rules than to their abrogation. And … within twenty-four hours it is as if we were never gone and our journey were merely last night's dream.

For medical anthropologist Dana Raphael the 'youthful swing', described by Mann as lasting six to eight days, lasts only a couple of days, leading her to warn her students: "The first 48 hours in a place are so critical they're almost the only time you really have there."

Raphael said that the "two-day rule" was something she had herself gradually figured out and started to live by during many years of travel. She looks forward to the first 48 hours in a place because this is the only period when she is almost compelled to notice things she has never seen before and in many cases finds herself totally unprepared for: "It's more than just a 'learning moment'", she said, "because it's practically inescapable. All you have to do is leave your hotel room and you get the full impact of whatever's there."

Echoing Pico Iyer (and his sense of the need to 'scribble and scribble and scribble' to 'catch all the experiences and impressions and feelings that are flooding through me' as soon as he arrives somewhere),[2] Raphael says that "to capture it, you really want to write and write and write throughout the first 48 hours." Raphael continues:

> 'Inevitably, after a couple of days, or even sooner, someone is going to, as they think, throw you a lifeline. Maybe by showing you how to do something the way it's done by people in that community … Or you will see people assuming roles that are familiar to you from any other group and then they take form as recognizable individuals, and once they're not so mysterious, you're more comfortable.'

During the first two days, one part of you is reaching out for the wholly unknown, but another part of you is already eagerly searching for the familiar, even if that means pieces of the unknown that begin to reappear or repeat themselves and thereby become more predictable – "and the result of that", she says, "is that once you get used to certain things, you start taking them for granted. And you no longer notice them."

She thinks some of this return to a more normal condition of avoiding available information is probably good for you and keeps you from being overwhelmed:

> 'It's possible that this very withdrawal of interest is part of a long-term survival mechanism – we've moved around as a species so often since we left Africa, many of us may need this kind of protection or cloak so that we can keep moving on when necessary. And at that point it's up to you to take the process into your own hands, so to speak, and to start to think carefully about what it is that's going on around you that you want to try to keep alive to, and what on the other hand that you may want to dissociate from.'

Travel and our cognitive and emotional mental health

The benefits of alert travel

A great deal could be written – and I think is about to be written – about the long-term health benefits of travel, and Deep Travel in particular, once the overlap with established health data is more clearly recognized. For instance, Marian C. Diamond (2001), a neuroanatomist at the University of California, Berkeley, who decades ago discovered that even aged rats grew new brain cells when placed in an 'enriched' environment (that gave them more to do and to explore), more recently looked at 'successful aging' among people, identifying five factors she considered 'essential for keeping our brains healthy and active throughout our life span'. Two of the five factors (diet and human love) are not particularly connected to deep travel, but one (exercise) certainly could be, and the other two are directly relevant:

We must CHALLENGE the brain. It gets bored; we know that well. We need NEWNESS, new pursuits, new ideas, new activities in our life.

Travel brings both novelty and the challenge of the unexpected; it is a dissolver of boredom, even during an otherwise repetitive activity, like a trip to the supermarket.

Figure 3.4: Senior couple waiting for a train in Amsterdam

Travel, by providing challenge and novelty, helps keep the brain healthy as we get older.

There is also evidence that travel can impact our ability to think flexibly and creatively. One experiment indicated that 'people who had spent time living outside their own countries' were 'less fixed' in their thinking and 'more able to accept and recombine novel ideas', as evidenced by the fact that they were 'more likely ... to solve the "Duncker candle problem": given only a box of thumbtacks and a candle and told to fix the candle to a wall, you need to divine that the tack box can be used as a shelf' (Maddux and Galinsky, 2009).

Dangers of a sedentary lifestyle, confinement and the great move indoors

Some of the benefits of travel – some of the answers to that central question 'why travel?' – are most starkly illuminated when we consider the impacts of *not* travelling. The physical health problems associated with a sedentary lifestyle are well documented, as are the impacts on our emotional and cognitive wellbeing (see previous chapter). But the benefits to the mind go beyond just the act of physical exercise; a fact demonstrated clearly, and sometimes disturbingly, by the effects of confinement. According to a report by the American Association for the Advancement of Science (AAAS), solitary confinement of prisoners has been linked to 'extreme paranoia, self-mutilation, hypersensitivity to sound, light and touch, and severe cognition dysfunction'. While much of this may be linked to a lack of social interaction rather than physical confinement per se, there is other evidence for the very negative psychological consequences of confinement. Speaking at the AAAS symposium on solitary confinement, 'Robert King, a former prisoner held in solitary confinement for 29 years ... described how his experience permanently distorted his eyesight and physical orientation.'[3] Psychologists have also raised concerns about the impacts of confinement and the lack of novel environmental stimulation on future deep space missions. According to one article about the mental health risks for colonists on the much publicized Mars One mission: 'Animal studies show that captivity can stunt the normal development of young primates, leading to abnormally high fear and reduced exploration behaviours.'[4] In addition to the lack of environmental stimulation that confinement entails, we might wonder: what are the long-term psychological effects on a creature that evolved to scan the horizon and roam free?

Fortunately, the majority of us are not confined by force and in such constricted circumstances; but across much of the industrialized world we are increasingly confining ourselves *indoors*. In all the millennia since human ancestors learned to walk upright across the savannah, we have never before made changes capable of impairing those of our internal systems that rely on light or scent or other aspects of the environment. Now, all of a sudden, it has happened: in America today, for instance, almost all of us spend almost all of our time inside, breathing recycled air and absorbing artificial light. And as our internal systems begin to react – badly, more often than not – to this new environment, we become aware of their existence. In the words of Dr Richard Wurtman, emeritus professor of neuropharmacology at the Massachusetts Institute of Technology, "We are all unwitting subjects of a long-term experiment on the effects of artificial lighting on our health."[5]

Since Deep Travel is an internal mechanism that can combine the responses of all our senses, any change in our surroundings which our senses can register – in the light, in colours, in sounds, in smells – alters the information that this mechanism receives. But what kind of changes, large or small, or what combinations of changes, will actually alter its workings? This we do not yet know, but our great 'indoor experiment' risks reducing our access to Deep Travel experiences and the benefits to our mental health that its form of heightened and broadened awareness can bring.

Modern travel: jet lag and hypermobility

One form of Deep Travel time is an entirely modern invention – jet lag. Before jet airliners began flying across the Atlantic Ocean in 1958 (which also happened to be the same year that for the first time more people crossed the Atlantic in planes than on ocean liners), it was impossible for travellers moving east and west to 'outrun the sun' – or at any rate to cross more than two time zones while still awake. (So this was also the moment, as has become even clearer in retrospect, when 19th-century railroad time, which gave rise to the idea of time zones, was superseded by 20th-century airline time, which is no longer bound by them.) As we have since discovered, this disrupts people's internally recording biological clocks, and often leads to headaches, to eating or digestion or sleep problems, and to changes in the way people feel that have been characterized in one online chart as 'disorientation, grogginess, irritability, mild depression'.

Many travel writers of our time leave jet lag out of their stories, treating it either as an occupational hazard, like malaria, or, as Pico Iyer suggests in a travel blog (2007), as a distraction they can with practice learn to ignore or silence. 'Jet lag', Iyer writes, 'remains one of the great unmentionables of long-distance travel, as if not to speak of it is to help it go away.' Iyer, on the other hand, not only acknowledges jet lag, he celebrates it – not surprisingly, perhaps, for a writer for whom the 'first point' of travel is always to 'slip through the curtain of the ordinary', as he says in one of his books (2004). For Iyer, time in jet lag is a trip to 'a deeply foreign country'; a trip which allows him 'to see a world, a self, I would never see otherwise' (2004).

Despite the potential Deep Travel experiences that jet lag may allow, it is not without its problems. According to research gathered and analyzed by Dr Scott Cohen and Professor Stefan Gössling (2015), jet lag's 'interference with the body's rhythms reflects a widespread disruption of many biological processes, including gene expression that influences aging … Jet lag can even switch off genes that are linked to the immune system, thereby raising the risk of having a heart attack or stroke.' And 'long-term chronic jet lag among airline cabin crew is associated with cognitive deficits including memory impairment.'

In their study, Cohen and Gössling look at the modern phenomenon of 'hypermobility': an academic term for the fact that, with the invention of jet aircraft and the increased availability of cheaper flights, a small but significant proportion of the world's population are travelling far and often. Their findings suggest that, despite the often glamorized lifestyle, 'hypermobility can contribute to a significantly higher risk of developing psychological disorders.'

> In more extreme cases, mobility can engender psychological disorders and mental illness. Studies from consular psychiatry have examined how 'pathological tourism' fosters 'mad [leisure] travellers' who have severely disrupted conceptions of personal identity.... [And] a study of the medical insurance claims of 10,000 World Bank staff [found] a nearly three-fold increase in psychological claims by business travellers (4000 of those staff) as opposed to non-travellers.

While much of this chapter is devoted to the benefits of travel, such research suggests it is worth pausing to consider if there could be too much of a good thing; or, perhaps more to the point, that it needs to be done in the right way to be good for us. Travel that does not engage the heightened mental awareness of Deep Travel – that opening of the mind to novelty and challenge – may in fact cause us harm.

What this might mean for policy makers

It is clear that travel should not simply be viewed as a 'disutility' to be minimized and removed, but that on a deep level the desire to travel is built into us and forms a central part of our wellbeing. While it may sound simplistic, or vague, the importance of a true appreciation of the centrality of travel to the human condition cannot be underestimated when we are thinking about policies and practices to make transport and planning work better for us all. Such an understanding could cause a ground-shift in how we make decisions. This applies broadly: widening access to transport for the disabled, elderly or poor, for example, becomes not just a transport issue but a decision that relates, on a macro-level, to economics and healthcare costs and, at an individual level, to empowerment, wellbeing and the ability to participate more fully in the world.

On the other side of the coin, a huge number of us, by choice or necessity, spend a considerable portion of our lives on the move. The world over, people devote an average of an hour a day to travel (Marchetti, 1994); and by some estimates Americans spend a tenth of their waking lives travelling, mostly in cars.[6] What we need now is a 21st-century approach to travel and transportation that opens up the benefits of Deep Travel, so that the huge amount of time devoted to travel no longer feels wasted or lost or, worse, risks psychological harm.

We are still getting used to the fact that when it comes to being in motion we have several ways of travelling. We can be indifferent to motion: technology makes us even better at this – iPods promote reverie; mobile phones maintain narrowly focused attention. Or – unlike a parcel or an oil drum – we can be changed, even transformed by motion. Movement itself in this state can be a part of 'becoming more fully ourselves'. We need an approach that, for the first time, makes an inviolable distinction between living cargo and inanimate objects, and redefines the art of moving people around to accommodate everyone in all our dimensions. Because when blinders are placed over the workings of Deep Travel by anyone – travellers themselves, the vehicles that carry them, the roads and train tracks and other rights of way – we are starving ourselves, letting ourselves down. We need to re-examine the physical components of our journeys (vehicles, buildings, rights of way) with an eye toward updating them so that they can serve the full range of our travel needs. They must continue to be safe and comfortable, reliable and on time. But because humans are a hybrid, they have another mission as well. Each element of a trip needs to contribute to the chance that any trip at all can be a Deep Travel exploration of the unknown and the not-yet-known, that the time involved can be used profitably to help us become more fully ourselves.

This is actually not a new idea – more than 2,200 years ago the Indian emperor Ashoka beautified the roadways of his country with shade-giving Banyan trees, wells and rest-houses in order 'that the people might practice the *Dhamma*'. By the *Dhamma*, Ashoka meant kindness, restraint from cruelty, non-violence, tolerance. Modern parkways, invented by Frederick Law Olmsted, the great landscape architect and designer of New York's Central Park, carry forward his idea that roads, if 'so planted and constructed never to be noisy', can extend outward the 'tranquility and rest to the mind' that his parks induced (1997: 81–83).

When making our 'ways' appealing and conducive to Deep Travel, we can look to the insights that studies of psychology have shown us. Research psychologists Drs Stephen and Rachel Kaplan (1982), who have looked at how people respond to a diversity of environments, think that we may have an inborn preference for landcapes which provide 'mystery' and 'legibility'. Such landscapes 'give the impression that one could acquire new information if one were to travel deeper into the scene' and that 'one could explore extensively *without* getting lost: enough openness to see where one is going, as well as distinctive enough elements to serve as landmarks.'

The good news here is that changes need not be huge. The great post-war American urbanist William H. Whyte found that people's perceptions of a landscape are affected disproportionately by small changes. Albert F. Appleton Albert F. Appleton, New York City's former Environmental Protection Commissioner, even came up with a rough mathematical formula for this: "The first five percent of development in a countryside region generally does fifty percent of the damage, in terms of altering people's mental geography of an area." Whyte saw hope in such statistics (Whyte, 1968: 274, 277): 'In these disproportions lie great opportunities', he wrote. 'If relatively small elements of the scene have such a leverage effect, relatively small actions can, too. A scenic clearing to open up a meadow, a row of sycamores planted along a riverbank, a screen of signs removed at the crest of a hill: individually such projects seem trivial.' But taken together, 'these tremendous trifles can have a major impact on the environment' – and whether it's still cherished.

Then there are the vehicles we enter – our 'third skins'. To what extent can our several awarenesses 'breathe' through these skins, which are mostly made of metal, plastic and glass? To what extent are they suffocated or simply not taken into account? Nowadays most travel seems to involve packing passengers in as if they were freight; or it aims to cocoon us from the very experience of travel with in-journey entertainment and distractions. But the appeal of many of the most popular journeys has been intimately tied up with the vehicle in which the journey is made and the experience that vehicle provides. The *California Zephyr*, for example, 'immediately captured the nation's imagination' when it first ran in 1949 – despite being ten hours slower than other trains on the line – because its 'sleek, silvery, air-conditioned fluted stainless steel cars featured glass-enclosed penthouses that gave the rider a fish-eye lens's 180-degree vista' (Kisor, 1994). Such beloved vehicles are a 'third skin' that allow the traveller to feel their movement through the world and thus help the traveller to invoke the excitement and wider awareness that comes with Deep Travel.

With such insights in mind we might yet recapture the full mental benefits from our travelling nature.

Notes

[1] 'The word: infovore', *New Scientist*, July 2006, www.newscientist.com/article/mg19125612-200-the-word-infovore/

[2] https://rolfpotts.com/pico-iyer/

[3] www.aaas.org/news/solitary-confinement-fundamentally-alters-brain-scientists-say

[4] www.theguardian.com/science/head-quarters/2013/sep/09/neuroscience-psychology

[5] https://www.nytimes.com/1981/06/23/science/from-fertility-to-mood-sunlight-found-to-affect-human-biology.html

[6] *A Look Under the Hood of a Nation on Wheels* was a 2005 survey jointly commissioned by ABC News, Time Magazine, and the Washington Post.

References

Allman, J. (1999) *Evolving Brains,* New York: W. H. Freeman & Co.

Biederman, I. and Vessel, E. (2006) 'Perceptual pleasure and the brain', *American Scientist*, 94(3): 247.

Cohen, S.A. and Gössling, S. (2015) 'A darker side of hypermobility', *Environment and Planning A*, 47: 1661–79.

Diamond, M. C. (2001) 'Successful Aging of the Healthy Brain', originally presented at the Conference of the American Society on Aging and The National Council on the Aging 10 March 2001, New Orleans, LA First Joint Conference. http://silverinnings.in/wp-content/uploads/2016/10/Successful-Aging-of-the-Healthy-Brain.pdf

Fox, R. (1997) *Conjectures & Confrontations: Science, Evolution, Social Concern*, New Jersey: Transaction Publishers.

Hiss, T. (2010) *In Motion: The Experience of Travel*, New York: Alfred A. Knopf.

Iyer, P. (2000) 'Why We Travel', *Salon*, (18 March), https://www.salon.com/2000/03/18/why/

Iyer, P. (2004) *Sun After Dark: Flights Into the Foreign*, New York: Alfred A. Knopf.

Iyer, P. (2007) 'The Uninvited Guest', *Jet Lagged Blog*, (27 December 2007), New York: The New York Times.

Kaplan, S. and Kaplan, R. (1982) *Cognition and Environment: Functioning in an Uncertain World*, New York: Praeger Publishers.

Kingdon, J. (2003) *Lowly Origin: Where, When, and Why Our Ancestors First Stood Up*, Princeton: Princeton University Press.

Kisor, Henry (1994) *Zephyr: Tracking a Dream Across America*, New York: Random House.

Maddux, W. W. and Galinsky, A. D. (2009) 'Cultural borders and mental barriers: the relationship between living abroad and creativity', *Journal of Personality and Social Psychology*, 96(5): 1047–61.

Mann, T. (1924) *The Magic Mountain*, Berlin: S. Fischer Verlag.

Marchetti, C. (1994) 'Anthropological invariants in travel behaviour', *Technical Forecasting and Social Change*, 47(1): 75–8.

Morris, D. (1967) *The Naked Ape: A Zoologist's Study of the Human Animal*, London: Jonathan Cape Publishing.

Olmsted, F. L. (1997) 'Public Parks and the Enlargement of Towns, in S. B. Sutton (ed) *Civilizing American Cities: Writings on City Landscapes*, New York: Da Capo Press.

Whyte, W. H. (1968) *The Last Landscape*, New York: Doubleday.

4

Philosophy and Travel: The Meaning of Movement

Matthew Niblett

Introduction

'What is life but a form of motion and a journey through a foreign world?' That was the rhetorical question posed by the Spanish-American thinker George Santayana – an inveterate traveller and migrant himself – in his famous essay on 'The Philosophy of Travel'. Santayana believed that movement was a fundamental characteristic of human existence, closely related to thought and desire and, as such, was a worthy subject of philosophical investigation (1968: 5–17). Although it rarely attracts much attention in the transport world, many of the greatest thinkers have shared Santayana's view and enthusiastically mused on the relevance of travel to our lives. This is less surprising than it might at first appear. Philosophy, in the sense of trying to obtain a deeper understanding of our existence, values and motivations, has much to offer an investigation of why we travel. Questions about travel are often philosophical in nature, and help us to comprehend who we are. What, for instance, are we hoping to achieve from our journeys? Will travel lead to the good life, or is it a fool's errand? Can we improve ourselves through travel to new places? And, topically, is it ethical to travel if it damages the environment? Through such questions philosophers can help us understand better both the nature of travel as well as our behaviour.

In this chapter, we will take a tour through some of the insights that philosophers over the centuries have brought to our appreciation of why humans travel. A short essay can, of course, only skirt the foothills of such a rich body of writing and reflection, but it will try to offer a brief introduction to some of the giants who have explored the philosophy of travel. We will begin by examining travel in the ancient world and the insights classical philosophers in Europe and Asia have brought to these questions. Moving forward, the chapter will then track some of the key motivations behind travel identified by more modern philosophers, before considering perspectives that have been sceptical of travel and encouraged deeper thought about our journeys before we leave home. Finally, we will investigate some of the more recent controversies about why travel, and the moral questions and dilemmas philosophers have raised.

The ancients on travel

The pathway to insight

To understand thought about travel in the ancient world, it is helpful to consider both how it was similar and different to today's experience. For those thinkers working in the cradle of European philosophy – ancient Greece and Rome – their societies and cultures were fundamentally shaped by travel as part of a seafaring Mediterranean world. In building their empires and extending their influence, travel would be undertaken for trade, diplomacy and warfare, as well as for social reasons, such as pilgrimages to sacred sites, journeys to festivals or even as a form of early tourism to see cultural monuments. At the same time, travel was incalculably more hazardous and challenging than is the case today. Journeys by sea and land were slow, highly dangerous given the vagaries of storms and the potential for encountering hostile bandits or pirates and, usually, very uncomfortable. Travel over longer distances was also expensive, requiring porters, attendants, or a seafaring crew, as well as sufficient provisions. One needed resourcefulness on top of stacks of courage and resilience.

It should not be a surprise, therefore, that travel was held in high regard in these cultures. Evidence of this celebration can be found widely across the myths, epics and literature of ancient Greece and Rome. From the myth of Jason and the Argonauts to Homer's *Odyssey*, early Greek literary traditions praised the adventures and benefits that could arise from epic journeys. In the 5th century BCE, the celebrated *Histories* of Herodotus provided a cornucopia of insights gleaned from travelling around the eastern Mediterranean. And the fundamental Roman myth of origins, the *Aeneid* as told by the poet Virgil, is based upon the epic wanderings of its hero Aeneas, who survives the fall of Troy to become the ancestor of the Romans. The centrality of travel to the identities and culture of the ancient world was not limited to the Mediterranean. Travel also played a central role in ancient Asian societies: in Chinese mythology a central concept is travel between the heavens, the earth and the underworld, while the great Indian epic *Ramayana* narrates the exile, travels and homecoming of Lord Ram. As the travel historian Peter Whitfield has observed: 'When we think of travel in the remote past a number of powerful and resonant words come into our minds: Exodus and Odyssey, Epic and Saga, Quest and Pilgrimage .... An ordeal, a challenge, an experience to be endured' (2011: 2).

In this context, it is not surprising that many ancient philosophers believed that there was a connection between travelling and thought. Contrary to the popular view today of philosophers meditating quietly alone in a sedentary space such as a library or study, in the ancient world it was more common for philosophers to be actively moving around as they debated and contemplated fundamental questions about life. Travel outside one's homeland was also frequently associated with the development of wisdom. The earliest philosophers in ancient Greece, who dominated intellectual life before the age of Plato and Aristotle, were the Sophists, who spent much of their time as wandering teachers, travelling from place to place rather like itinerant lecturers to give talks and classes offering ideas and information. This wandering was believed to help the formation of wisdom through the opportunities that arose to learn from foreigners and through the development of a more detached viewpoint on problems. Although Plato was critical of the Sophists, he too found travel formative for his thinking, having spent 12 years travelling around the eastern Mediterranean after the death of his mentor Socrates, gathering experiences and wisdom that he would end up teaching in his academy. The Roman philosopher Cicero would later praise Plato, as well as other Greek philosophers such as Pythagoras and Democritus, for their willingness to travel and search widely for new knowledge which could not have been found at home (Cicero, 2001: 146). Others, such as Diogenes the Cynic, sought out a wandering life as part of his belief that one must reject the norms of society and live as a homeless nomad to find true wisdom and happiness. Famous for his claim that he was a 'citizen of the world' – a sentiment as unpopular in ancient Athens as it is in contemporary Britain – Diogenes notoriously spent much time living in a wine barrel, which can perhaps be seen as a Greek variant on the tents of modern nomads.

Figure 4.1: Detail of Plato and Aristotle from *The School of Athens*, fresco by Raphael (1509–11)

The ancients believed there were strong links between wandering and wisdom, movement and thought. Here we see a detail of Raphael's fresco *The School of Athens*, showing Plato walking and debating with his student Aristotle.

More fundamentally, there developed in the ancient world a widespread belief that active movement, particularly walking, could be the handmaiden of thought. When Plato's pupil, Aristotle, came to establish his own school in Athens, he was given a plot of land with walkways and colonnades, where his students would gather and listen to him teaching while walking to and fro. From the Greek word for these walkways, *peripatoi*, came the description of Aristotle's school of philosophy as the *Peripatetics*, which retains its original meaning of 'given to walking about' in English today. The link between walking and thinking was also evident in other philosophical schools in ancient Athens, including the Stoics, whose name derived from the *Stoa* – a painted colonnade where the adherents of the school would meet and debate philosophical tenets whilst perambulating around (see Craig and Casey, 2018: 51–67). In so doing, they may have actually been benefiting from a physiological and psychological truth about human nature, explored in our earlier chapter on 'Travel and the Mind' (Chapter 3), which pointed out the ways in which active movement, including walking, can improve our vascular and mental health.

Something of this appreciation of the links between moving and thinking is also evident in various ancient cultures in Asia. Travel is a central concept in the ancient Chinese philosophical tradition of Taoism, which itself is based upon a concept, Tao, with an original meaning of 'the way or road for travel'. The semi-legendary founder of the tradition, Lao Tze, is traditionally supposed to have made great journeys to the West, and the *Zhuangzi*, a foundational text of Taoism, contains aphorisms in which travel becomes a metaphor for life. Some scholars credit Taoism for introducing the concept of wandering: travelling for its own sake without a particular destination in mind. 'Wander where there is no path', tells the *Zhuangzi*: since the goal of life is losing one's desires and joining with the flow of the universe, which is always in flux, a state of indefinite and infinite travel is almost a utopian end in itself (Xiang, 2014). In the case of Siddhartha Gautama, better known as the Buddha, wandering was a central feature of his life after the attainment of enlightenment. These journeys were a core part of his teaching mission, and he encouraged his first disciples to wander forth and do the same. Furthermore, the freedom offered by the ascetic wandering life also appears to have been appreciated by the Buddha in terms of developing a clear mind. From this practice has developed the meditative exercise of *kinhin* in several forms of Buddhism which involves careful walking while practising meditation and mindfulness.

The challenge of travel

What though of travels to far destinations, in the sense of our motivations to visit new places and gain fresh experiences? On this, ancient philosophers were divided, and often questioned the purposes and effects of travel. For some, such as Democritus, Pythagoras and his followers, travel was a key requirement to gain knowledge, insights and wisdom on human affairs. Later scholars would speak of these philosophers as *polyplanos*, or those who wandered across many lands (Montiglio, 2005: 156–79). The 1st-century philosopher Apollonius of Tyana, whose thinking is best known through a semi-fictional biography written by Philostratus, was a wandering scholar, whose wisdom was said to be derived from his experiences travelling across much of what was then the known world, from the Caucasus to India, and Egypt to Spain. Others suggested that it was important to interrogate the purposes of travel before one set out on a journey. For the Stoics, travel should be seen in terms of why one was undertaking it. Since the physical world was an object of wonder worthy of study, travel could help expand the mind and one's understanding. At the same time, travel was often part of one's duty. The Greek Stoic Epictetus quoted approvingly the willingness of Socrates to be sent on campaign when it was required of him, and encouraged travel if it was truly part of one's responsibilities. The important aspect when travelling was to distance oneself from expectations or desires and to treat with equanimity whatever may befall the journey. For instance, Epictetus chastized those who developed anxiety and homesickness when far from home: such sentiments, he argued, leave the traveller 'more wretched than ravens or crows, which, without groaning or longing for their former home, can fly where they will, build their nests in another place, and cross the seas' (Stephens, 2007: 127–40).

The problems with much travel, Stoic philosophers suggested, lay in the flawed motivations of the traveller. For the Roman Stoic philosopher Seneca, many travellers made the mistake of embarking on journeys as a means of escaping or distracting themselves from more fundamental problems. Travel could not be an antidote for suffering, Seneca wrote in his letter *On Travel as a Cure for Discontent*, for 'though you may cross vast spaces of sea, and though, as our Virgil remarks, lands and cities are left astern, your faults will follow you withersoever you travel'. Reaching a new destination will not fundamentally cure one of unhappiness or depression, he counselled his reader, for 'one must change the mind, not the venue'. On this basis, Seneca saw too much travel as a frequent sign of discontent, particularly if pursued in an aimless way. Until one has mastered one's emotions and developed mental wisdom, travel was unlikely to bring much in terms of self-improvement. 'Believe me, there is no journey that could deposit you beyond desires, beyond outbursts of temper, beyond your fears', Seneca explained, for 'if that were so, the human race would have headed there in droves' (2015). Seneca's scepticism about the motivations that drove many travellers was shared by other ancients. Plato in his *Republic* indicated that foreign travel had no role in the education of the citizenry, and he mistrusted the phony erudition that many well-travelled contemporaries displayed, which he contrasted with the development of true understanding. The Epicurean school of philosophy also taught the value of finding wisdom and pleasure in the simple quiet life, rather than in foreign adventures and relentless travel. Epicurus was well known for teaching in the private groves of his garden outside Athens, a retreat where he could think and walk undistracted by the disturbances of the city: a perspective that resonates strongly in an age of virus-induced lockdowns.

The moderns on the benefits of travel

Although the ways and means of our travel have changed significantly since these ancient philosophers were writing and thinking, questions on why and to what purpose we travel have continued to absorb philosophers in more recent centuries. Unsurprisingly, the responses to this questioning have been varied and offer a kaleidoscope of insights on our travel motivations. Some thinkers have taken a sceptical view on what drives us to travel, while others have focused on the benefits that drive us to seek out new places and experiences. In this section, we will look at five key motivations that modern thinkers have identified behind our urge to travel.

Broadening the mind

The first idea is that travel can be undertaken for broadening the mind. From the late 16th century onwards, there was an increasing emphasis upon the benefits that travel could bring for knowledge and learning. At this time in Britain, the literate public began to develop a voracious appetite for travel writing and insights from foreign journeys. This was fed by publications from writers such as Samuel Purchas, whose collection of travellers' reports was hugely popular, and Thomas Coryat, who published an account of his grand tour of Europe, and was widely credited with introducing the table fork to England, the use of which he had witnessed in Italy. At a time when scientific enquiry was making rapid advances, and the practice of empiricism – emphasizing the role of evidence and sensory experience in the formation of knowledge – was beginning to emerge, it is not surprising that philosophers also began to give greater consideration to the educational value of travel. We will see in Chapter 11 on 'Travel as Exploration' how the English philosopher Francis Bacon played a key role in this development. Bacon devoted one of his popular *Essays* to the subject of travel, which he opened with the observation that: 'Travel, in the younger sort, is a part of education; in the elder, a part of experience.' In keeping with his scientific method, Bacon advised his younger readers to keep a diary of their travels in order to evaluate all their observations and experiences, which could then later be used to improve their understanding and discourse (Bacon, 1985). In this way, the traveller would return home with a prize – knowledge – of much greater value than mere souvenirs and fancy fashions.

The proposition that travel was a formative part of learning was strengthened during the Enlightenment. The 18th-century Genevan philosopher Jean-Jacques Rousseau was convinced that travel could be an important aspect of education, and that, if undertaken properly, a traveller should return home wiser and more learned than before. How we travel was therefore an essential question. 'It is not sufficient to stroll through countries', Rousseau explained, but one needed 'to observe', and turn our eyes 'toward the object we wish to examine'. Rousseau acknowledged that not all people could do this, and so serious travelling, he suggested, should be limited to those with 'sufficient self-control' and 'whose good nature has been well cultivated' (2003). Such people ought to 'return better and wiser than when they started out'.

Rousseau's contemporary and critic Mary Wollstonecraft was in agreement that travel was an important aspect of a liberal education, and declared in one of her frequent reviews of travel writing that 'the art of travel is only a branch of the art of thinking'. Moreover, Wollstonecraft appreciated the effects that travel could have on broadening a person's understanding through the use of comparison and observation. In her *Letters Written During a Short Residence in Sweden, Norway and Denmark*, she explained how travel stimulated curiosity, thereby 'exciting to the comparison which leads to improvement'. By 'mixing with mankind', Wollstonecraft observed that 'we are obliged to examine our prejudices,

Figure 4.2: Mary Wollstonecraft's travels in Scandinavia

Mary Wollstonecraft travelled through Scandinavia in the 1790s and wrote in her travel account about her philosophy of travel.

and often imperceptibly lose, as we analyse them' (1796: Letters III and XIII). This sense that travel, if pursued with empirical vigour, can improve our understanding has been acknowledged by more recent thinkers. The American thinker and writer Mark Twain, perhaps expressed this most eloquently in his book *The Innocents Abroad*, where he observed that 'Travel is fatal to prejudice, bigotry and narrow-mindedness.... Broad, wholesome, charitable views of men and things can not be acquired by vegetating in one little corner of the earth all one's lifetime' (2003: 490–4).

Travel for wonder

Around the time when Rousseau and Wollstonecraft were writing, there emerged growing interest in a second idea about the beneficial motivations for travel: that it could be pursued to generate a sense of wonder and to experience the sublime. The concept of the sublime was developed by the philosophers Edmund Burke and Immanuel Kant, the latter oddly being notorious for never having travelled more than 100 miles from his home city of Königsberg in Prussia. Burke distinguished the sublime from beauty by suggesting that the former was capable of provoking both fear and attraction at the same time, and could create a sense of danger and awe that touched our instinct for self-preservation. Kant developed this further by adding a transcendental quality to the sublime, observing that it forced us to reflect on our sense of place in the universe, however minute (Burke, 1757; Kant, 1790; Nivala, 2016). Objects that could invoke a feeling of the sublime could therefore range from natural features such as mountains and waterfalls, to the wonders of the built environment, such as cathedrals and monuments. In terms of travel, it was no coincidence that the idea of the sublime was taken up by the Romantic movement with its emphasis upon the exploration of nature and the benefits this could bring to the mind. For the Romantic tourist, seeking out a sense of danger and wonder in the natural world through objects such as mountains, oceans and glaciers, in order to experience the sublime, was an important aspect in choosing a travel destination. As Mary Wollstonecraft was to explain, the importance of exploring nature came through its ability to 'give birth to sentiments dear to the imagination, and inquiries to expand the soul' – ideas which found further expression in the travels of a generation of Romantic poets (1796: Letter III). The idea that the sublime in nature was worth seeking out was taken in new directions by the American 19th-century philosopher and travel writer Henry Thoreau. In his book *Walden*, Thoreau observed: '[W]e are earnest to explore and learn all things, we require that all things be mysterious and unexplorable, that land and sea be infinitely wild, unsurveyed and unfathomed by us ... We can never have enough of Nature' (Thoreau, 1854: 440–56). But whereas the Romantic philosophers emphasized travel to see great natural wonders, Thoreau focused on a simpler objective: discovering in nature a sense of the sacred and thereafter seeking unity with this. As such, one did not need to travel to the ends of the earth to find the sublime, for the balm of the natural world could normally be found much closer to home.

Travel for self-knowledge

Such a focus on the experience of travel is reflected in a third benefit that has occupied more recent philosophers: the opportunity that travel offers for better knowing oneself. Something of this was already recognized by the 16th-century French philosopher and man of letters Michel de Montaigne, who made no apologies for his enjoyment of travelling for pleasure and curiosity. In his *Essays* he explained that 'this great world of ours is the mirror in which we must gaze to come to know ourselves', and advised his reader that 'travel seems to be an enriching experience' since it 'keeps our souls constantly exercised by confronting them with things new and unknown' (1993: 167–77 and 1101). The idea that travel can foster self-knowledge took particular life in German philosophy from the late 18th century onwards through thinkers such as Goethe, Schiller and Novalis. For philosophers such as Goethe, a focus on personal spirituality and emotional development became linked with the idea of *Der Wanderer* (loosely translated as 'the wanderer'): a figure who seeks to make their own way in life and is transformed by the experience of the journey. For the wanderer, the destination is less important than the travelling, which gradually brings self-awareness through reflection on one's own desires or yearning (*sehnsucht*) (see Cusack, 2008). These powerful concepts resonated in German philosophy and literature, and it is no surprise that the German language has generated a lexicon of travel-related terms such as *wanderlust* (desire for roaming) or *fernweh* (a painful longing to see distant places) which have no direct equivalent in English. This sense of the self-knowledge gained from travel was explained well by the German-American philosopher Hannah Arendt, who wrote that: 'loving life is easy when you are abroad. When no one knows you and you hold your life in your hands all alone, you are more master of yourself than at any other time' (1974: 71).

Figure 4.3: *The Wanderer Above the Sea of Fog*, **by Caspar David Friedrich (c 1818)**

The wanderer, who seeks to make his/her own way in life by encountering the beautiful, dangerous, and unknown. This romantic ideal is represented in this painting, *The Wanderer Above the Sea of Fog* (c 1818) by the German romantic painter Caspar David Friedrich.

Travel for sociability

If travel offers opportunities for self-exploration, it also provides an excuse for sociability, which many philosophers have recognized as one of the most fundamental of human instincts. Cultivating this desire for sociability can be achieved through travel, to the benefit of the mind.

As Montaigne argued in his *Essays*, 'frequent commerce with the world can be an astonishing source of light for a man's judgment', before going on to praise Socrates for 'having embraced the universal world as his City, scattered his acquaintances, his fellowship and his affections throughout the whole human race' (1993: 176). In the modern age, the rise of urban living has provided a remarkable environment for sociable wandering, a concept captured in the French idea of the *flâneur* – an urban stroller or saunterer. The notion of the *flâneur* developed in the 19th century as a type of Parisian figure wandering the streets, but the concept included not only participation in the social life of the city, but also a role as an observer of others, thereby understanding better one's social environment through casual travel. The importance of this kind of travel was highlighted by the philosopher Walter Benjamin, whose *Arcades Project* explored modern urban life, and who saw the *flâneur* as capturing something of the essence of modern existence through the figure's aimless wandering and observation (1999: 435). More prosaically, travel for social reasons is also tied to commerce and the need to sell our goods and services to the widest audience. George Santanyana included the merchant as one of his four archetypes of traveller for this reason, while more recently there has been interest in how globalization has forced artists to become increasingly mobile. The Russian philosopher Boris Groys has astutely observed: 'All active participants in today's cultural world are now expected to offer their productive output to a global audience, to be prepared to be constantly on the move ... a life spent in transit like this bound up with equal degrees of hope and fear' (2008: 105).

Travel as liberation

A fifth core motivation for travel, which has received attention from modern thinkers, is the possibility for it to provide a sense of liberation for the traveller. On this basis, travel provides benefits by helping people to escape oppressive conditions or the parameters imposed by their home society. The sense of freedom that can result from travelling to new places and environments was recognized by philosopher Friedrich Nietzsche, who would write about how refreshingly 'un-German' he found the cities of the Mediterranean, and explained how distance could help in the process of self-liberation and becoming. Nietzsche's ideas have been embraced by the contemporary philosopher Frédéric Gros, who has explored the process of 'self-liberation' that he believes comes from walking, which allows the traveller to 'throw off the yoke of routine' and become 'disentangled from the web of exchanges' we have in normal life (2014: 3–5 and 11–27). This sense of liberation can be profound. As the French thinker Simone de Beauvoir discovered when she travelled alone to the US for the first time: 'I feel I'm leaving my life behind. I don't know if it will be through anger or hope, but something is going to be revealed – a world so full, so rich and so unexpected that I have the extraordinary adventure of becoming different of me' (2000: 3). Travel can also offer liberation from oppression. In the 19th century, London became an oasis for freethinking revolutionary philosophers such as Karl Marx, who had faced persecution in Cologne and Paris. More recently, the African-American thinker Angela Davis found travel to be a means of escaping from her experience of racial segregation in the southern US. Moving to France as a student she immersed herself in a new language and travelling, finding in these some relief from the conditions she had experienced in Mississippi. Although the reality did not always match the expectation, Davis was travelling in the footsteps of other African-American thinkers such as Richard Wright, who found cosmopolitan Paris a liberating change from the world of his upbringing (see Kaplan, 2013: 145–56).

The drawbacks of travel: philosophical insights

While the beneficial reasons that drive us to travel have attracted widespread consideration, thinkers have also brought insights to the other side of the equation. Sometimes we travel for the wrong reasons, or in ways that are counter-productive, or fail to recognize the hardships associated with travel and discover ourselves in a worse place than where we started. Travel today is incomparably more straightforward than it was in the ancient world, and yet few do not despair when caged with a rowdy stag party on a budget flight, or when struggling for air on a packed commuter train, or if stuck for hours in a road jam. The philosopher George Santanyana recognized the hardships of travel when he wrote: 'Few of us ever forget the connection between "travel" and "travail," and I know that I travel in large part in search of hardship – both my own, which I want to feel, and others', which I need to see' (1968: 5–17). In this case, however, the difficulties of travel are part of the attraction, and indeed are seen as character building. Others have been less sure that the costs, hardships and struggles of travel really do justify the ends. Blaise Pascal, for example, was a fierce critic of aimless distractions and wrote: 'I have discovered that the sole cause of humankind's unhappiness stems from one thing alone, that they cannot stay quietly in their own room' (1976). One of the most entertaining critiques in this fashion was made by Xavier de Maistre, brother of the French counter-revolutionary philosopher Joseph de Maistre. In a delightful short book entitled *A Voyage Around My Room* (first published in French in 1794) Xavier took aim at the pompous travel narratives of his age, with an autobiographical account of being imprisoned in his room for six weeks. His 'travels' involved flights of the imagination and contemplation on the vistas that he saw and found while venturing around his miniature kingdom. Xavier praised this journey as having cost 'neither trouble nor money', and commended it to the frail and infirm, who could enjoy the 'comfort' of this new mode of travelling without fear of 'bleak winds or change of weather' (1871: 1–6). In some ways, the book was far ahead of its time, for it seems an ideal companion to COVID-19-induced lockdowns. Yet there was a more serious message behind Xavier's jesting, which drew attention to the way in which the greatest benefits of travel are ultimately related to the mindset of the traveller, and as such need not involve venturing far from home.

Why does travel often leave us disappointed? As we have already seen, the ancient Stoics argued that the problem was usually found with the traveller, who would wrongly imagine that travel could provide an escape from more fundamental problems. If we travel to escape ourselves, philosophers such as Seneca argued, we are on a doomed quest, for what is really required is a change of mindset or character, not a change of venue. Such insights have continued to be explored by more modern philosophers. Those such as Albert Camus

Figure 4.4: Illustration from Xavier de Maestre's *A Journey Round My Room*

The opening illustration from Xavier de Maistre's book (English edition of 1871) which details his 'voyage' of contemplation around his room.

recognized that one could not escape the self in travel: 'there is no pleasure in travelling, and I look upon it more as an occasion for spiritual testing', he observed, 'travel, which is like a greater and graver science, brings us back to ourselves' (1998: 12–15). The American transcendentalist philosopher Ralph Emerson used such insights to produce a thorough critique of why people travel. A significant part of his 1841 essay 'Self-Reliance' was devoted to exposing the follies of those who idealized travel. Like the Stoics, Emerson was not necessarily opposed to travel if the objectives were truly educational, or 'for the purposes of art, of study, of benevolence'. His objection was rather to criticize those 'who travel to be amused' or the one who 'travels away from himself' in search of a cure for unhappiness. Such a person 'carries ruins to ruins', argued Emerson, and would discover, in his famous phrase, that 'travelling is a fool's paradise'. Emerson's attack on his contemporaries for their obsession with travelling and *wanderlust* was controversial, and he was forced to defend himself in one of his later essays 'On Culture'. 'I have been quoted as saying captious things about travel, but I mean to do justice', he pleaded, 'I think that there is a restlessness in our people which argues want of character'. The gist of his argument was that we should carefully consider what motives are really driving us to travel. Since we carry ourselves with us on our journeys we must focus first on improving ourselves rather than trying to escape our problems. Moreover, the danger with the desire for wandering is that it tends to locate all our troubles in that place we call home, leaving us adrift and homeless, rather than finding value and wonder wherever we actually are. Recognizing this situation can actually make us better travellers and reduce the disappointments on our journeys. It was on this basis that Emerson argued 'the soul is no traveller, the wise man stays at home', since by mastering himself when business really does 'call him from his house, or into foreign lands, he is at home still', and with such self-reliance one can 'visit cities and men like a sovereign, and not like an interloper or valet' (1841; 1860).

While Emerson focused on the motivations of the individual, other thinkers have taken a broader view of the social complications of our demand for travel. For some, travel is seen as a counterproductive urge, which can result in worse outcomes than had we never left home. One criticism of travel motivations comes from a nativist perspective: a viewpoint that suggests that travelling too much can loosen those social ties that bind us to a community. Something of this is discussed by Kris Beuret and Roger Hall in Chapter 6 'The Sociological Perspective', using Durkheim's idea that humans need to feel integrated within a social collective reality. A linkage with too much travel can be found in the thought of the German philosopher Martin Heidegger, who was interested in the concept of *dasein*, or 'authentic being', and what it meant to live an authentic life. Heidegger expanded the idea of *autochthony*, a foundation in the soil and roots of a place, such that authentic existence unfolds as a 'co-happening' within a community. On this viewpoint, individuals experience a fulfilled life through working together in order to develop mutually a common heritage. For Heidegger, one needed be at home in one's community, and not on the road, to experience this. Therefore, by pushing a person outside of home and community, he saw travel as inauthentic and believed it would contribute to heightened anxiety (see Shepherd, 2015). More recently, travel has come under increasing attack from philosophers who emphasize the damaging externalities it can generate, whether social or environmental, and have asked whether there is a moral obligation to reduce travel. The ethical dimensions of travel are worth exploring further.

Travel rights and wrongs: the morality of movement

If travel brings both benefits and drawbacks, what can be said about the rights and wrongs, or the ethics of travel? One of the main branches of philosophy is the examination of virtue and ethics, including the moral dimension of human decisions, and what constitutes good conduct. Given the range of benefits that travel brings, it is not surprising that many thinkers have linked movement with liberty, and constituted it as a natural or human right. In the ancient world, the idea of liberty of movement was contrasted with that of slavery; the Stoic Epictetus, for example, defined freedom as meaning 'I go wherever I wish, I come from whence I wish'. In the early modern period, philosophers such as the Spaniard Francisco de Vitoria and Dutch jurist Hugo Grotius, argued that the right to travel was a natural law, and part of the fundamental nature and dignity of being human. These ideas were developed further by thinkers such as John Locke and Thomas Jefferson, who argued that the freedom to travel, and especially to leave and emigrate from one's country, were natural rights. The power of this concept was later seen in the drafting of the United Nations Declaration of Human Rights (UNHR), Article 13 of which contains the following two clauses:

(1) Everyone has the right to freedom of movement and residence within the borders of each state.

(2) Everyone has the right to leave any country, including his own, and to return to his country.

The inclusion of this article in 1948 owed much to the experiences of World War II, during which Nazi Germany and other totalitarian states had interfered with freedom of movement and emigration in order to undertake persecutions. It was no surprise that authoritarian governments such as the USSR opposed the inclusion of this article in the UNHR on the grounds that it interfered with state sovereignty; these objections were, however, outvoted by the majority of national delegations that represented more open societies (see McAdam, 2011). More recently, the right of freedom of movement has become a central pillar of the European Union (EU), which was also the first modern body to introduce the legal concept of a transnational citizenship across its member states.

The right to travel and the principles of free movement are cherished by many, and are often viewed as important for extending opportunities for self-advancement. It is clear from earlier chapters that movement can be an essential part of wellbeing and our physical and mental health. But how far does such a right to travel extend? We have experienced with the COVID-19 pandemic that freedom of movement sometimes has to be curtailed due to a health crisis; other legitimate reasons for constraining travel might include warfare, or to prevent someone escaping justice, as thinkers such as Grotius acknowledged. Even in such cases, however, libertarian thinkers have pushed back against any limitations to travel. Furthermore, a basic right to travel has been extended recently by bodies such as the UN World Tourism Organization to include a 'right to tourism': an idea that has also encouraged EU officials to consider subsidising vacations for the young, elderly and poor. However, a number of thinkers have pointed out that rights also entail responsibilities, and the damage caused by too much tourism creates moral problems, including identifying what the duties of travellers are and who defines these. Criticisms have also focused on such leisure travel being limited to an affluent and mobile class, restricting the holders of this right to a wealthy subset of people (see Tremblay-Huet, 2017).

As the external environmental and social problems generated by too much travel have become clearer, some philosophers have recently explored whether there is a moral case for reducing our travel. Calculations by philosopher John Nolt (2011) have indicated that the average American is responsible, through their greenhouse gas emissions (of which travel forms a large part), for the suffering or death of two future people, while others such as Rob Hales and Kellee Caton (2017) have identified a 'flyer's dilemma' in terms of balancing the various moral issues that are faced when travelling by air due to its environmental impact. Some have tried to use a utilitarian framework (i.e. the greatest good to the greatest number) to assess these moral challenges, or to think about how travelling well can align with the Aristotelian ideal of living well or virtuously. Reconciling the various moral aspects of travel is not straightforward, since it is difficult to calculate the relative moral weight of these aspects, or to balance them against the benefits travel brings, such as improvements to mental wellbeing. Some philosophers such as Luke Elson (2018) have criticized the consequentialist view of travel, in which only the direct outcomes matter, since this can lead to absolutist conclusions such as forgoing travel altogether. Others, such as Jim Butcher (2009), have argued that too little moral weight is given to the economic benefits arising from commercial travel, which can potentially bring good outcomes, such as reducing poverty through stimulating local economic growth.

Perhaps the most insightful approach, however, taken by thinkers on the morality of travel is that which focuses not so much on *whether* we travel as on *how* we can travel better. Given the environmental and social negatives that can arise from travel, this often means careful thinking about how we can travel in more sustainable and responsible ways. The thinker Irena Ateljevic (2009) has been at the forefront of these attempts, arguing for a 'transmodern' approach to travel, in which our travel choices recognize our global interdependence, both human and environmental. On this framework, better travel means sustainable travel, in terms of mitigating the environmental impacts of our movement, and socially responsible travel, which aims to ensure that travel both respects and results in positive outcomes for those people and cultures who host visitors. A further emphasis in discussions on the morality of travel has been to shift our focus away from distance and speed (ie the quantity of travel) and towards time (ie the quality of travel). Slower travel often involves healthier and more sustainable modes, such as walking, cycling or sailing, as well as allowing experiences to unfold in a more relaxed and less constrained way (in this respect it has some affinities to the concept of the wanderer explored earlier in this chapter). The moral advantages of slow travel have been extolled by the thinker and travel writer Pico Iyer, who has praised the benefits of exploring stillness. 'In an age of acceleration',

Iyer has suggested, 'going at human speed suddenly begins to look like sanity and freedom' (2014; 2015).

Conclusion

Several key themes have emerged from this brief tour through philosophical insights on travel. In the ancient world, a key linkage was made between travel and thinking and learning, as well as the importance of understanding what motivates our journeys. We have seen that travel can bring a range of benefits for the traveller, from knowledge and self-understanding, to opportunities for sociability and wonder, and even liberation from oppression. At the same time, it is clear that travel can be unfulfilling for a range of reasons, often related to misplaced expectations or a failure to understand why we set out in the first place. Today, the philosophical questions about why we travel have never been more apparent, in an age where we have come to consider travel both as a human right, and also as potentially morally wrong in those cases where it contributes towards destruction of the wider environment or those very places and peoples we set out to see. Few thinkers have suggested that we stop travel altogether, such is the centrality of movement to living a fulfilled life and to our human identity. But their encouragement for us all to think more deeply about how we can travel better is a fitting challenge for the 21st century.

References

Arendt, H. (1974) *Rahel Varnhagen: the Life of a Jewish Woman*, trans Richard and Clara Winston, New York: Harvest/HBJ.

Ateljevic, I. (2009) 'Transmodernity: Remaking Our (Tourism) World?', in J. Tribe (ed) *Philosophical Issues in Tourism*, Bristol: Channel View Publications, pp 278–300.

Bacon, F. (1985) 'Of Travel', in J. Pitcher (ed) *The Essays*, London: Penguin, pp. 113–14.

Benjamin, W. (1999) *The Arcades Project*, Cambridge, MA and London: The Belknapp Press of Harvard University Press.

Burke, E. (1757) *A Philosophical Inquiry into the Origin of our Ideas of the Sublime and Beautiful*, London: R. and J. Dodsley.

Butcher, J (2009) 'Against Ethical Tourism', in J. Tribe (ed) *Philosophical Issues in Tourism*, Bristol: Channel View Publications, pp 244–60. Chapters 12–15 in this book are also relevant to the discussion.

Camus, A. (1998) *Notebooks 1935–51*, New York: Marlowe & Co, pp 12–15.

Cicero, M. T. (2001) *De Finibus (On the Ends of Good and Evil)*, Book V, 86, ed Julia Annas, Cambridge: Cambridge University Press, p 146.

Craig, M. and Casey, E. (2018) 'Thinking in Transit', in R. Scapp and B. Seitz (eds), *Philosophy, Travel and Place: Being in Transit,* Cham: Springer Nature Switzerland AG, pp 51–67.

Cusack, A. (2008) *The Wanderer in Nineteenth-Century German Literature*, Rochester, NY: Camden House.

de Beauvoir, S. (2000) *America Day by Day,* Oakland, CA: University of California Press, entry for January 25 1947.

de Montaigne, M. (1993) 'On Educating Children' and 'On Vanity', in *The Complete Essays,* trans. M.A. Screech, London: Penguin, pp. 176–77 and 1101.

de Maistre, X. (1871) *A Journey Round my Room* (originally *Voyage autour de ma chambre* [1794]), trans. H. Atwell, London: Longmans, pp 1–6

Elson, L. (2018) 'How a moral philosopher justifies his carbon footprint', *The Conversation*, 27 July.

Emerson, R. W. (1841) 'Self Reliance' and (1860) 'On Culture' (1860) in M. Oliver (ed) (2000) *The Essential Writings of Ralph Waldo Emerson*, New York: Random House, pp 132–53 and 642–62.

Gros, F. (2014) *A Philosophy of Walking*, London: Verso.

Groys, B. (2008) *Art Power*, Cambridge, MA: MIT Press.

Hales, R. and Caton, K. (2017) 'Proximity ethics, climate change and the flyer's dilemma: ethical negotiations of the hypermobile traveller', *Tourist Studies*, 17: 94–113.

Iyer, P. (2014) *The Art of Stillness: Adventures in Going Nowhere*, London: Simon & Schuster/TED.

Iyer, P. (2015) 'The art of slow travel', *The Guardian*, 17 January.

Kant, I. (1790) *Critique of Judgment*, Berlin and Libau: Lagarde und Friederich.

Kaplan, A. (2013) *Dreaming in French: the Paris years of Jacqueline Bouvier Kennedy, Susan Sontag and Angela Davis*, Chicago, IL: University of Chicago Press.

McAdam, J. (2011) 'An intellectual history of freedom of movement in international law: the right to leave as personal liberty', *Melbourne Journal of International Law*, 12: 1–31.

Montiglio, S. (2005) *Wandering in Ancient Greek Culture*, Chicago, IL: University of Chicago Press.

Nivala, A. (2016) 'Catastrophic Revolution and the rise of Romantic Bildung', in H. Nivala, A. Salmi and J. Sarjala (eds) *Travelling Notions of Culture in early Nineteenth-Century Europe*, Abingdon, Oxon: Routledge, pp 19–37.

Nolt, J. (2011) 'How harmful are the average American's greenhouse gas emissions?', *Ethics, Policy and Environment*, 14: 3–10.

Pascal, B (1976) *Pensées*, trans A. J. Krailsheimer, New York: Penguin, 67, Pensée 136 (139).

Rousseau, J. J. (2003) 'On the Uses of Travel', in *Emile*, trans W. H. Payne, Amherst, NY: Prometheus Books.

Santayana, G. (1968) 'The Philosophy of Travel', in D. Cory (ed) *The Birth of Reason and other Essays*, New York: Columbia University Press, pp 5–17.

Seneca (2015) *Letters on Ethics: to Lucilius*, Letter 28, 1–3, and Letter 104, 19, trans M Graver and A A Long, Chicago, IL: University of Chicago Press.

Shepherd, R. J. (2015) 'Why Heidegger did not travel: existential angst, authenticity and tourist experiences', in *Annals of Tourism Research*, 52: 60–71.

Stephens, W. O. (2007) 'The Providential Tourist: Epictetus on How a Stoic Travels', in E. Hoppe and R. Weed (eds) *Ancient Greek to Asian Philosophy*, Athens, Greece: Athens Institute for Educations and Research, pp 127–40.

Thoreau, H. (1854) *Walden; or, Life in the Woods*, ch XVII Spring, in J. S. Cramer (2012) (ed) *The Portable Thoreau*, Publisher: London: Penguin, pp 440–56.

Tremblay-Huet, S. (2017) 'A right to tourism – and the duty of hosting the leisure class', *Völkerrechtsblog*, 6 November.

Twain, M. (2003) *The Innocents Abroad or, The New Pilgrims' Progress*, London: Random House (f.p. 1869) Conclusion, pp 490–4.

Whitfield, P. (2011) *Travel: A Literary History*, Oxford: Bodleian Library, p 2.

Wollstonecraft, M. (1796) *Letters Written During a Short Residence in Sweden, Norway and Denmark*, London: J. Johnson, Letters III and XIII.

Xiang, O. (2014) 'Detachment and Reunion: Travel and Human Presence in Landscape', in H.-G. Moeller and A.K. Whitbread (eds), *Landscape and Travelling East and West: A Philosophical Journey*, London: Bloomsbury, pp 81–94.

5

The Economics of Travel: It's Not the Destination, It's the Journey

Matthew Dillon and Alexander Jan

Taking the train out of town for a weekend away can be such a pleasure. In this case I am taking my children to see my sister and her family in Leeds: a well-rehearsed event. The journey that has become a ritual. There are encounters with some familiar characters along the way. The commuter, on her way home, limbering up to get off at the next stop; it cannot come quickly enough. Then there are two men, both in suits. No doubt they have been in meetings in the city all day. From the look on their faces, and the liquid lunch stacked on the table from the buffet car, it looks like it was all worth it. Another deal closed. And, through the whining of the train's electric motors, it is possible to pick out the sound of another young family, squabbling over crisps and sweets. I wonder if they are making a similar pilgrimage to ours? Friends or relatives at the opposite end of the country.

In the seat across and opposite, a man in his 20s is staring out of the window, wearing a rugby shirt. This weekend the international game is on. He does his best to shut out the noise from the youngsters. Someone else has the same idea. She has hidden herself away in one of those unlucky seats where you cannot quite see out of the window, where she is staring into her phone. Everyone is on their way to or back from *somewhere*. This what economists refer to somewhat dryly as a 'derived demand'; our act of travelling is borne from a desire to be somewhere purposeful at the end of the journey. It begs the question as to who would travel for its own sake? Surely any rational human being would only travel to get to work, to meet suppliers and clients, to visit loved ones, to attend sports fixtures, or to access some other essential, valuable or enjoyable activity?

Well up to a point. This is partly why the study of economics is important for understanding travel behaviour and motivations, why economics has come to play a significant role in informing decisions about transport investments, and why successive UK governments have claimed – at least until recently – to have had economic growth at the heart of their transport policies. Good transport provides people with access to jobs, to a wide range of services and leisure activities. It allows people to get swiftly home to their loved ones at the end of the day. It provides businesses access to wider labour markets, and to other companies to do business. And people are willing to pay for access to all these things. Around 14 per cent of total household spend is spent on transport; ahead of housing and power it is, on average, the single highest category of families' outgoings in the UK.

And that is only half of the story. The UK government adds a further £25 billion of spending on transport every year. Improvements in the quality and capacity of transport are often requested to boost growth and tackle a whole host of society's ills. The call for more investment in trains, roads, trams, tubes and a variety of other 'modes' can be heard in London, the north of England, and throughout the country. Politicians are often instinctively drawn towards cutting ribbons; hard hats at the ready; high visibility jackets to the fore. And they are on to something – at least in economic terms. Venables et al (2014) suggested that effective transport systems, if invested in alongside other sectors, could underpin as much as ten per cent of all future UK economic growth. While all that might well be true, there is, even today, something relaxing, enjoyable – even exhilarating – about the glide of a new train or the flow of a new road. Travel surely can and does hold value in its own right. The restrictions on our movement in spring and summer 2020 as a result of the COVID-19 crisis, and the pressure to get us moving again, has – if anything – reinforced this.

As well as taking a more objective view on why people choose to travel to get from one place to another, this chapter digs a little deeper into whether we enjoy (or 'gain utility from', as an economist might say) the destination, and travel for its own sake. By taking an economics perspective on the question of why people travel, it looks at how travel motivations are perhaps governed by a combination of rewards at the end of the journey and other rational economic factors, as well as a wider range of human elements that influence travel behaviour. There are time budgets, human habits and natural daily rhythms, against the background of societal norms on our attitudes to the climate, and to each other. Understanding these might mean that we can find ways to drive the sorts of travel behaviour that help create benefits for us as a society. But first, let us look at the more conventional reasons why people might leave the house.

Travel as a derived demand

Economics textbooks explain that when people buy items they derive a certain utility from the consumption of these goods. So, for example, if I purchase a subscription to a paid TV content provider, then it will be in anticipation of gaining some pleasure from watching a box-set on a Saturday evening. These goods have a certain value, and this reveals itself in our willingness to pay for them. We call this value the benefit of the goods. The overall demand for the goods is a combination of their desirability, coupled with the audience's willingness to pay. These in turn are driven by the quality of the goods in question, their cost, the price of related goods (such as, in this case, a rival TV subscription, or the price of cinema tickets) as well as the disposable income levels of potential consumers.

Historically, transport has been treated as a derived demand product, meaning that people are using it primarily – perhaps solely – to access work or goods or services. This would make travel demand heavily dependent on the benefits that are accrued as a result of arriving at one's destination. Why on earth would anyone want to board a train before dawn on a winter's morning, if not because they want to get to work? For that matter, why is the same train packed full of other people wanting to do exactly that? It follows that the number of people willing to travel into a major city in the morning peak will be related to the quality, value and abundance of work opportunities. The demand for a holiday will be nearly all about the desirability of the destination. Business travellers will be more likely to make a trip if a potentially large deal awaits.

Of course, all of this has a significant economic value. The salary from a well-paid job will normally significantly outweigh the cost of a year's motoring, or of an annual season ticket. Leisure and tourism is the world's single largest industry. And a key component of successful businesses are employee visits to suppliers, to clients, and to training courses.

Figure 5.1: Journey purposes (England, 2018)

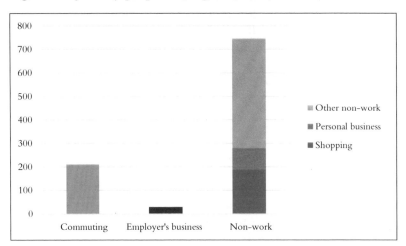

This chart shows the average number of trips per person per year by journey purpose in England in 2018. Commuting, which includes travel for work and education, is the most popular single purpose but overall most trips were for non-work reasons (National Travel Survey, 2017/18, Table 0403).

There is perhaps no better illustration of travel as a derived demand than what the transport industry calls journey purposes. When transport professionals wish to estimate the demand for the network, the users are initially allocated to three different groups. This is not done according to their demographic characteristics, whether they visit the buffet car, or even the distance travelled, but according to the things that they want to do at either end. Commuters are those accessing employment and education services. Business travellers are those who are travelling on their employer's time, often to meet potential suppliers, collaborators and customers. Non-work related purposes include holidays, visits to friends and family, trips to the supermarket, and less-looked-forward-to personal business appointments such as healthcare. In England, somewhat surprisingly, business travel on behalf of our employers is rare, and most of our transport journeys are made outside of a work context, with commuting and shopping being the most popular purposes of travel (see Figure 5.1).

Economists suggest that a desire to reach and consume a better quality or quantity of work, business and leisure opportunities would lead to greater demands being placed on the transport network. And this, broadly speaking, holds true. In the UK, London is by far the most popular city to commute to because of the sheer range of employment opportunities it offers. Furthermore, individuals are willing to travel

Figure 5.2: Commuting distance and time by income (England)

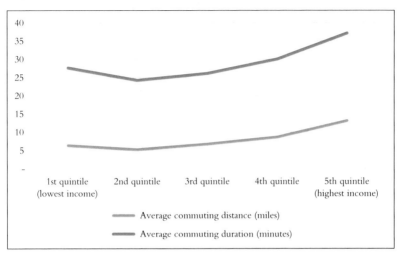

As this graph of data from England shows, workers on the highest incomes tend to travel further to their place of work, and for a longer time, than those on lower incomes (National Travel Survey, 2017/18).

for much longer to access higher-paid jobs: higher-income workers commute for 30 per cent longer, and over twice as far, as lower-income workers, as shown in Figure 5.2.

Inspiring destinations

This derived demand argument also works for leisure journeys – sometimes at extreme distances. People appear to be willing to travel for many hours for a once-in-a-lifetime trip to Florida's Disneyland, the Egyptian pyramids, or the Eiffel Tower. But often they are quite content with a shorter trip to get some fresh air – maybe for a mile or two – for a more prosaic visit to the local park.

People often travel great distances for leisure purposes for a feeling of foreign-ness which goes beyond the quality of the attractions at each location. Humans have a fondness for adventure, for experiencing different cultures, tasting different food, and even using different money and language. All of this helps us to take our minds to a place away from our everyday lives, often giving us new challenges in the process, and allowing us to take on a different identity as a result. It makes sense that we are willing to pay for these experiences. There may be fabulous theatres, art galleries or shops near to where we live.

But many with the money are willing to pay much more to experience the same in a different setting.

Simply being away from home can be a positive experience in itself. It is good for our mental health, allows us to return to our everyday lives refreshed, perhaps a little wiser, having gained new and different perspectives. This is not just something that individuals acknowledge – businesses place a value on getting their staff out of the office for a day or two. A change of venue creates a different dynamic. 'Changing the scenery' trumps the sometimes hefty cost of 'lost' working time, hotels, dinners and, of course, the drinking.

From an economics perspective, innovation often happens when we are inspired by different experiences, and combine them with something more familiar. This is why we find that many writers set their novels in cities that they have visited on holiday. Fusion cuisine happens when chefs mix exotic tastes with established ones. And many entrepreneurs' ideas are hatched when they are far away from the office.

The economic argument behind all of this is that it is worth our while to travel. We will travel further, if we have better work opportunities, more time to relax, greater choice of customers and suppliers, and access to higher quality or unique leisure opportunities.

These key travel drivers also hold true for many types of once-in-a-lifetime journeys such as migration to a new country and moving house. What would be the point in moving a great distance if one did not expect one's life to be better at the other end? The better the opportunity, the further we are willing to travel. And, of course, immigration offers a special type of incentive to contribute to the economy. It is no accident that a whole host of companies, from Google to Goldman Sachs, from Kraft to Colgate, were founded by immigrants. People born outside the US are more than twice as likely as Americans to start a business there. Some of this is due to the need to work hard to make ends meet in a new country when arriving without connections (and often without cash). But a substantial part is due to immigrants taking an idea that has worked well at home, adding a twist from their recipient country, and deriving a better business product as a result. Moving to a new setting can be truly inspirational. As well as hard work.

Are we nearly there yet?

It follows that with all the value at the end of the journey, rather than noticing any intrinsic benefit to travel, many people would prefer to pay to avoid it, and would rather travel for a shorter period, or for someone else to do it for them. And given the choice, most rational individuals would prefer to get to their destination more quickly. That is why, of course, many higher speed transport services charge higher prices than their slower counterparts. And when, following in-service announcements of delays, few travellers are rejoicing; most are probably scowling. When a journey time becomes unpredictable, that can make things even worse. The M6 toll road in the West Midlands, which offers a congestion-free alternative to the M6 through Birmingham, relies on this behavioural trait to generate income from its arguably higher-end tariffs.

So quite often we would rather not travel – especially when it is not enjoyable – and we would much rather devote the time to other, more worthwhile, opportunities. And it is possible to place a value on this. In 2015, research by Arup, for the UK Department for Transport, suggested that for our non-work trips, citizens are willing to pay just over £5 for every hour that can be cut off a journey. The value for in-work trips is even greater at £18 per hour.[1] And these values of time are important. They drive almost all government investment in transport by making an economic case based on providing people with time to spend doing worthwhile things that do not involve travel at all. That is, faster routes to work (so more time at home), less time between business appointments and more time to undertake leisure activities. Our faith in them has underwritten pretty much every major project in transport for the last 50 years, from the completion of the motorway system, to the planned high-speed rail network.

This can seem somewhat paradoxical. If travelling has a value, how can reducing the time that we spend doing it also be important? And despite the value of travel time savings, why do almost all of us still choose to move around?

Travel time budgets

Throughout history, people have travelled for around one hour per day, a figure that has become known as 'Marchetti's constant'. Of course, how we have moved about has changed over time, with walking giving way to travelling by horse, to the age of the motor car, and the aeroplane, meaning that this hour has been getting us further and further. Zahavi (1979), the originator of the travel time budgets theory in the 1970s, asserted that humans tend to maximize the distance they can travel within the constraints of time and money. This impressively elegant theory has managed to hold true through the ages and is remarkably constant throughout the world.

Figure 5.3: Travel time per day (England)

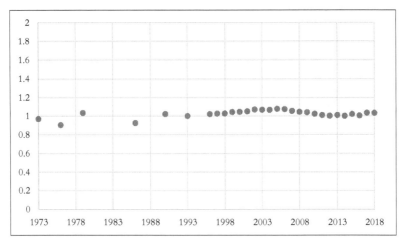

This graph, of the average number of hours spent travelling each day in England (before 1989, Great Britain), shows remarkable constancy at an average of 1 hour: a result that can also be found across the world and throughout history (National Travel Survey, 2017/18, Table 0101).

It is important to note that the hour is an average figure, and can change from person to person, vary over time, and be different in one location than in another. Zahavi found that poorer residents in developing countries, where average speeds were slow, devoted an average of an hour and a half to daily travel, and two hours in some cities, whereas in the UK, Figure 5.2 showed that the better-off are more likely to commute for longer periods.

Nevertheless, this simple law has had a profound effect on the shape and size of our cities and our built environment: the one-hour rule has defined the size of settlements since before the industrial revolution (see Chapter 13 'Placemaking and Travel'). As transport has become faster, the places where we choose to live and work have grown in size and become further apart. Our settlements have gone from being walkable – at most a mile in diameter – in the middle ages, to several miles and more across with the coming of the railways and the motor car in the 19th and 20th centuries. And in certain parts of the world, such as China, the advent of higher speed rail creates the possibility of the megalopolis. The prospect of a hyperloop system could take this to the next level.

How do we make sense of this in economic terms? The 19th-century economist Gossen suggested that the additional utility derived from the acquisition of additional goods decreases for increasing consumption. This means that the more we consume something, the less pleasure we derive from each bite. For travel, that suggests that despite the benefits that come with it, we would not expect anyone to travel for ever, as the returns would diminish the more we undertake. The one hour a day average is also limited for the regular traveller by biological constraints rather than economic ones. There are considerations such as daylight, fatigue, a need for rest, sleep and mealtimes. Travel time is perhaps the remains of the day when other, essential – as well as pleasurable – daily activities have been accounted for. Caring responsibilities are also important. Preparing meals and bathing others takes up time. That is partly why many people give up jobs in distant locations when they have children.

This hypothesis means that when governments (or others) invest in transport infrastructure, they are perhaps not necessarily creating more work and leisure time for passengers as the travel time savings theory would suggest – at least not over the long term. They may ultimately be providing the opportunity for people to live further from where they work and play, and encouraging long-distance commuting, with its negative environmental consequences, and the more desirable benefits to employers to recruit from wider labour pools and for individuals to have better access to more facilities.

David Metz, a former chief scientific advisor to the UK's Department for Transport, has said that giving employers better access to workers is perhaps the largest category of benefit from a transport scheme, and that – notwithstanding our temptation to travel to do the same things elsewhere – access to more amenities is of only marginal value when these amenities are replicable. He argues that the value of access is much higher if the facility is rare or unique such as a central business district, a major airport, a unique landmark, or a beautiful coastline. All of this suggests that transport schemes that open up new employment or leisure opportunities, by bringing them within the one-hour-a-day travel time budget, may be worth more than those that provide benefits over much longer or shorter distances.

Inspiring journeys

But not all travel behaviour is explainable by the derived demand theory. Even those who advocate purely for derived demand would observe that some travel has as its primary purpose a direct rather than a derived benefit. Most obviously, many people use active modes such as walking, running and cycling for physical and mental health purposes. Walking is the UK's most popular recreation activity. Every week, around half of the British adult population walk either entirely for pleasure or because they value the activity of travelling, rather than the specific journey purpose associated with it. Around eight per cent of adults cycle at least once a week for similar reasons. Motivations for these types of journeys are as simple as getting out of the house, accessing daylight, the chance of meeting a neighbour, or using it as an opportunity to enjoy the company of others.

It is telling that many governments exempted walking, jogging, cycling, and other forms of exercise from the spring 2020 COVID-19 restrictions on movement because it was felt that the positive impact on people's physical and mental health outweighed the risk of further spread of the virus. And in countries that endured more stringent lockdowns, leaving the house to exercise was among the first of the restrictions to be lifted. Furthermore, recent research suggests that the benefits of active travel are not limited to personal wellbeing but can serve a secondary purpose: there are indications that conversations can be more productive outdoors, with natural environments allowing people to listen and respond accordingly, and that social interactions are enhanced when they are made in this way.[2]

Valuing the impact of participating in these so-called active modes of transport is something that economists have tended to struggle with. Firstly, they have attempted to value the physical health impacts of walking and cycling by looking at the impact that improved physical fitness has upon extending life expectancy, as it reduces the chance of a life-impacting illness. But they do this on the basis of people's willingness to pay. UK government and World Health Organization guidance estimates that cycling as a young adult can be worth £200 per annum in increased life expectancy. That is valuable information for policy makers but may not resonate with the general population.[3] And it is hard to imagine it as a real-life response to the question 'why are you going out on your bike today?'

In 2008 Metz made an alternative attempt to estimate the benefits of an active travel journey by suggesting that a recreational walk starting and finishing at home would bring total physical and mental benefits broadly equal to the time taken. If we use the value of travel time savings to estimate this (noting that Metz himself is not a fan of this method), then a half-hour recreational walk would be worth just over £2.50 to the average person exercising. Walking this distance every day would be worth almost £1,000 each year. While this substantially outweighs the cost of a new pair of trainers, it does not quite seem to go far enough in terms of the broader sense of value and enjoyment that walking can bring. It also implies a linearity of benefit, that a ten-mile walk is ten times more valuable than a one-mile walk, and that a walk today is equally valuable whether I walked yesterday, or if I have not left the house for a fortnight.

Elsewhere, many use motorized transport as a form of leisure by 'going out for a drive' or taking the scenic route. Heritage railways, pleasure flights, boating firms, ski resorts and even theme park rides all charge for the pleasure of movement, often in novel surroundings, and in these cases travel is not seen as an inconvenience or a cost to avoid as the derived demand and value of travel time theories would suggest. The high level of willingness to pay for a thrilling ride demonstrates how these forms of travel have transitioned into attractions in their own right. And these examples perhaps provide some clues as to why moving around is such a draw for humans: the pleasurable sensation of movement, a sensation of speed, a feeling of being in control (or almost out-of-control), a feeling of discovery and adventure, of being able to take in passing scenery for mile after mile. Not surprisingly, these more positive characteristics of the act of travelling have found their way into popular culture through advertising, the travelogue, the road movie genre, and are celebrated in countless hit songs ('Come Fly With Me', 'On the Road Again', and 'Born to Be Wild', to name but a few).

Long solo journeys can be a time for self-contemplation – almost meditation – often accompanied by a musical soundtrack that seems to take on extra meaning. Travel can provide valuable thinking time precisely because it is often agendaless. These sorts of experiences can prove economically valuable; many business ideas have been dreamt up while in motion. And the highly successful Harry Potter franchise was apparently conceived whilst J. K. Rowling was on a delayed train between Manchester and London.

Of course, a journey by air – particularly a long haul one ideally towards the front of the plane – can often be pleasurable. In his book *Skyfaring* (2015), pilot Mark Vanhoenaker celebrates the surreal experience of sipping drinks in civilized settings at 37,000 feet while looking down towards a landscape that appears to be part of a distant world. Of all the means by which to move around, aircraft can offer those with the resources an exceptional sense of splendid isolation. They form part of an imagined, privileged, almost abstract world, that becomes even more mystical in the hours of darkness. A cocooned place to be waited on, away from our daily lives that somehow exists many thousands of miles away in a rapidly retreating time zone.

Alain de Botton's book *The Art of Travel* (2003) identifies how the whole journey has a role to play in achieving this special mental state. For those going on holiday, the anticipation of the journey ahead, and the heightened senses as a result, mean that the airport wait is often celebrated as a special occasion by many travellers, complete with treats such as a meal, drinks, and other indulgences that might otherwise not be made.

This all sounds like a rather romantic view. And it is. In some countries, and for many budget travellers, air travel may be no more than a flying bus service with all the stresses and strains that delays, congestion, routine and fatigue can offer the traveller. Not all travel experiences are like this.

Some writers, including Hupkes (1982) and Salomon and Mokhtarian (1998; 2001) have attempted to distinguish between the intrinsic utility of travel itself, and the additional benefits of the activities that can be undertaken while travelling. For example, many car drivers use their time to have in-depth conversations with their captive passengers. On the train, business travellers can prepare for the meetings ahead, do some additional work, or catch up with colleagues. For many school trips, the most fun part of the day is the coach journey. For commuters, the journey itself can book-end the day, allowing time to assimilate thoughts, to transition between work and home life. In British culture, peak-hour trains are often close to silent. It is as if they have become the place for a collective act of reflection, sandwiched between homes and work.

This need not necessarily be productive time. Research by Arup and Future Thinking for HS2 Ltd in 2016 suggested that after 'reading', the most common activity on long rail journeys was 'gazing out of the window' and 'relaxing'. 'People-watching' and, interestingly, 'sleeping' were also popular activities (see Figure 5.4).

This concept of having time that can be well-spent is well-known in the travel industry. Customers do not like queuing for planes because they cannot use the time wisely. But they do not mind an extra few minutes on board with a movie. And in some cases they are willing to pay for the privilege of speedy boarding, which does nothing to shorten the journey, but does increase the amount of useable time when travelling (and provide certainty of an overhead locker). Even when they have a purpose to the trip, many people choose to move more slowly, perhaps to prolong some of the pleasure of more civilized travelling. Despite taking longer and often costing more, almost one-third of travellers prefer to travel by rail between London and Scotland, rather than air, and the proportion is increasing as environmental awareness does. As Rudyard Kipling, once said, 'transport is civilisation'.

Figure 5.4: Customer activities during rail journeys

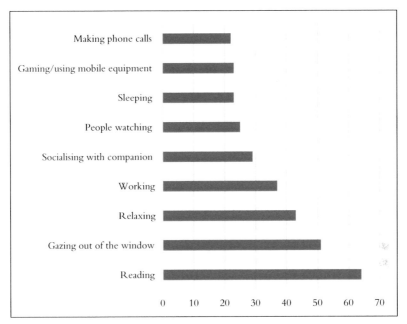

This chart shows activities reported as being undertaken by customers on long distance rail journeys (per cent of customers reporting) (Arup/Future Thinking for HS2 Ltd (2016)).

Back on that train to Leeds, as I look around once more, its again obvious to me that as well as going somewhere, everyone is in fact doing something. Our commuter appears to be finishing off the last of her work-related emails. The businessmen are using the time to have a gossip about their colleagues. Arguments aside, the young family are enjoying spending some quality time together. And our friend in the rugby shirt is no doubt rehearsing how best to tease his friends that are supporting the other side.

Valuing the travel experience

Can economics help us to place a value on both the pleasure gained from movement, and benefits of the activities that are carried out, for the different modes of travel? Lumsdon and Page (2004) suggested that metro rail and bus services, particularly in cities, have low value (presumably because of the lack of surety of a seat, having to make way for others to enter or leave the vehicle at frequent intervals, and the frequent lack of views out of the window); that taxis, if taken while on holiday, could have a higher value if the driver was deemed to be engaging, or if the scenery was appealing; and that walking and cycling were deemed to have the highest intrinsic value.

Perhaps the destination affects the value of the journey as well. Jumping on the same train must surely feel different if it is a chance to meet your lover rather than your first day back at work.

Nevertheless, the average daily travel time budget has not increased above one hour despite the intrinsic and wider benefits of travel. Perhaps the desire to read, listen to music, do work, read and look out of the window is somehow limited by attention spans, and more active travel is limited by exhaustion. Too much travel appears to substantially erode the intrinsic benefits it can create. This is backed up by research from the UK Office of National Statistics in 2014, that noted that after 30 minutes of travel time, anxiety levels increased for people using car, bus or train.

Back on my weekend away, as my train eases towards its final stop, I can see impatience and expectation emerging among my fellow travellers. Phones are put away and people have begun looking at their watches impatiently. One or two people are yawning. The laughter from earlier on has been replaced by silence, breath is exhaled as the train pauses just a fraction too long outside Leeds station. The novelty of travel has been replaced by a mixture of monotony and fatigue. People are ready to get off and do something else.

So perhaps the old saying about 'it's not the destination, it's the journey' is somewhat correct. Travel does have an intrinsic value. Up to a point.

The economic downsides of travel

So far we have focussed on what individuals gain from travel, and what benefits flow to employers from allowing their people to move around in working hours. There are also spill-over impacts on those who might not be travelling at all. Since the 1950s economists have recognized that travelling more often, and for greater distances, may generate costs not only for fellow travellers (congestion and overcrowding) but for those who experience the noise, pollution, accidents and severance (being cut off by a main road) that transport might generate.

Right now the economic benefits of travel outweigh the disbenefits. But our estimates for the negative impacts seems to be getting more severe each year: poor air quality is the largest environmental risk to public health in the UK, and is estimated to cause 64,000 excess deaths annually.[4] Climate change is perhaps the most threatening issue facing the world today, potentially affecting the entire global population, many of whom are far from the source of emissions, and may be several years in the future. Transport is now responsible for one-quarter of global carbon generation and is the fastest-growing sector.

This is why while, on the one hand, governments invest in infrastructure, on the other, they try to minimize some of the negative impacts – what economists would call the externalities of transport. This might be through road user charging on busy networks, fees for parking, overnight bans on aircraft take-offs and landings, plus fuel taxes and restrictions on higher emission vehicles. These have the added benefit of generating revenue that can be used to offset general taxation burden, or spent on programmes designed to offset the harm being generated. However, it is perhaps fair to say that not all of these externalities are internalized, and, as a result, the price signals passed to the consumer sometimes encourage what we might deem 'bad' behaviour. Think of the bargain basement flights that offer a carbon-intensive journey of several hundred miles for less than the price of a round of drinks.

Despite aviation being the fastest source of carbon emissions, there is no tax on aircraft fuel, largely because it would be impossible for governments to implement unilaterally – they have yet to find a way around the prospect of the pilot simply filling up at the other end. In the UK, a policy to increase fuel duty above the rate of inflation, to discourage car use, was shelved after a few years, once it was found to be a significant vote-loser. And in France, the *gilets jaunes* protesters successfully overcame a similar plan to increase the price of diesel in 2018. Sometimes even economists admit that in a democracy, the will of the people must prevail. And sometimes people do not behave entirely rationally, as we will find out in the next section.

Why do we *really* travel? A behavioural economics perspective

It is in our culture to travel away for a week or two each summer. Much of Europe slows down during August, schools are on holiday and, while the days of complete factory shutdowns are behind us, many workplaces encourage employees to take a chunky period of annual leave in the summer months. It is not unreasonable to say that going away during this period is a societal expectation. We also get to impress our friends with stories of our trip when we return home. Are these the real reasons that we tend to travel for our summer holiday?

A few years ago a friend recalled how an acquaintance booked a hotel less than a mile from their home for a week's annual holiday. Free from the familiarity of their domestic surroundings, they were able to see their city as a tourist would, undertaking activities that they had only ever thought to do when hosting out-of-towners. The evenings were spent eating out at local restaurants and attending local theatres, without any temptation to spend the time washing clothes, tackle domestic clutter, or attempt other household chores. And perhaps best of all, on their last day they were able to pack up and be at home in a few minutes, rather than needing to spend hours travelling, with a threat of crowding, cancellations or delay.

Why is this particular type of stay-cation not more popular? Partly because after the first time it might become rather tedious. There is a desire for the alien and unfamiliar. But also it appears that many people prefer to travel further for holiday-type leisure. It is possible that a key reason we travel is because everyone expects us to. And so when we do go away, we are able to meet those expectations, and increase our likeability in a social group. British tourists who have never visited the beautiful mountains of Scotland may visit similarly beautiful mountains in New Zealand. And part of it is also down to what economists call 'conspicuous consumption', that is, the purchase of goods purely to display one's wealth; to be able to trump friends, family and colleagues with one's more exciting, further afield tales of adventure and trekking. A long-haul holiday that piques just a little envy in one's closest pals, is more likely to be remembered as such by those that took it. And of course, the means of travel itself plays a role in this: many first-class air travellers would surely admit that a share of the fare goes on bragging rights, and a degree of self-identification.

Whereas classical economics would subscribe to the theory that travel must have an intrinsic or derived utility in order to motivate people to undertake it, behavioural economics, popularized by Thaler and Sunstein's *Nudge* (2008), accounts for the fact that human beings are often less rational than that.

We do not exactly have whirring algorithms in our heads that finely balance up the costs versus enjoyment of each possible holiday destination, or every time we see a job advert. Neither do most normal human beings undertake cost–benefit analysis on what to do every weekend. We pick up on the ideas of our friends, relatives and neighbours. We tend to be a bit more stuck in our ways, and perhaps a bit more clumsy in our decision-making than many economists would suggest. Or perhaps we are just being creative, spontaneous and responsive to the ideas and influences of others in how and when we choose to move around. Of course this means that people tend to do what other people are doing. So if everyone else is driving, we do it too. Once our peers start using the train instead, we will too.

As humans, we also tend to form habits that can be difficult to break. We are creatures of routine. We will often eat out at the same set of local restaurants. We will have a favoured dress sense. We are much more likely not to opt out of something than to opt in. Within transport, we have a well-worn route for many of our regular journeys and we perhaps rarely look at the alternatives. When was the last time you asked a journey planner to find a new route from home to your place of work? Switching the mode of transport is even rarer, perhaps because it would require changes to the morning routine, additional preparation, and ongoing concentration during the journey itself that would erode some of the in-travel benefits described earlier. These mental transaction costs have to be overcome in order for the individual to make a change – however rational that change might be from a financial or time-based perspective.

We are often in the mood for different things at different times. People tend to be most likely to plan a holiday, or change workplace, in the month of January as it is in the middle of winter, and after the Christmas break. Expensive duty free is available after we have dealt with the stresses and strains of airport security and have time to kill. In this way, travel behaviour can be influenced and influence other habits by tempting or coaxing people when they are more likely to accede. Some airport owners suggest that when encouraging people to access their facility by sustainable means, an offer of low-cost public transport two weeks before they fly is likely be to the best time. That is the moment when they will be thinking about the journey and when the time elapsed from the original booking is sufficient for them to divorce the two transactions.

In essence, the behavioural framework is powerful. It gives us a new paradigm to add to that of derived demand, and the intrinsic value of the act of travelling itself. The answer to the question of 'why travel?' becomes 'because I have always travelled, because everybody else does, and because it's easy'.

The future

Using the behavioural framework is a key part of adjusting some of the 'bad' behaviour we encountered a moment ago, so that we can make travel more sustainable. The significant influence that others have over our travel habits shows how we can use cultural and social pressure to change travel behaviour to take better account of climate change. Already, accumulating long-distance loyalty points for certain forms of travel is in danger of going out of fashion. New, more environmentally conscious social norms are being established as the spectre of global warming and climate disaster haunts middle-class dining tables up and down the land. In some circles, travelling by train to foreign destinations gains the kudos that a long-haul flight might have done a generation ago. The culture of *flygskam*, or flight shame, which started in Sweden, and has now spread to other parts of the world, has had an impact on travel behaviour, and may continue to dampen the recovery of air travel, at least among those in rich countries who have already experienced the privilege of flying. *Flygskam* was cited as one of the factors in the four per cent annual decrease in the volume of passengers travelling through Sweden's airports in 2018, compared with 2017.

We are now beginning to travel less frequently, as new technology means that many of our commuting, leisure and shopping trips are transferring online, a process that was accelerated during the COVID-19 pandemic. The implications of this are twofold. Firstly, that the trips that are left must be longer, of a higher economic value, somehow more worthwhile to us than the ones that we are choosing not to make. In this respect it is worth noting that while we are no longer travelling as much to go shopping, or to see family and friends, Marchetti's constant is holding true, and we are banking the time saved in our daily hour to travel further on holiday. We can see where our priorities are.

Secondly, our shops and our employers are having to work harder to get us to leave home. We have already seen the high street decline as a shopping destination, and now that video-conferencing is embedded, fewer people are travelling into work each day, fewer are attending face-to-face meetings, and so firms are less willing to pay for swish offices in the centres of our cities.

In spite of this, if the events surrounding the COVID-19 pandemic have taught us anything, it is that many jobs cannot be done remotely at all. Even for those that can, a conference call cannot yet replace in-person interaction, either in a social, or in a work context. Research has shown us that face-to-face meetings are more productive, more positive, and are much more effective at co-creation. Meetings are better managed. Deals are more likely to be done. Working alongside colleagues allows for networking, for the randomness of chance moments and for water-cooler moments that are hard to replicate online. Social relationships are able to be maintained by online contact, but it is much rarer for them to be created virtually. And watching the match on television cannot compete with being there in person.

New high-speed transport modes, Marchetti's constant, an increase in leisure time from automation, and our own deeply embedded culture suggest that we will each be travelling even further, on average, 50 years from now.

So does that get us any closer to estimating the economic value of travel? The potential $8.8 trillion downturn (Park et al, 2020) that was partly due to lockdown restrictions is perhaps one of our best estimates of the GDP value of travel. It seems that even with new technology, our economy depends on experiencing human contact, and the more interactions we have, the more transactions we have. But even this figure is perhaps understated, as it excludes the significant wellbeing benefits that we reap for ourselves. We have seen that the destination and the journey itself can both be purposeful and pleasurable, allowing contemplation, such that we seem to have an innate requirement to move for a certain amount of time each day, in the same way that we need a certain number of hours' worth of sleep. And so at the deeply personal level, journeying, and experiencing things first-hand, will continue to bring significant benefits for the foreseeable future. Just ask any one of my fellow passengers to Leeds.

Notes

1 https://assets.publishing.service.gov.uk/government/uploads/system/uploads/attachment_data/file/470229/vtts-phase-2-report-non-technical-summary-issue-august-2015.pdf

2 https://assets.publishing.service.gov.uk/government/uploads/system/uploads/attachment_data/file/821842/walking-and-cycling-statistics-2018-accessible.pdf and www.manchester.ac.uk/discover/news/conversations-are-a-walk-in-the-park/

3 https://assets.publishing.service.gov.uk/government/uploads/system/uploads/attachment_data/file/805253/tag-4.1-social-impact-appraisal.pdf

4 https://inews.co.uk/news/health/air-pollution-kills-64000-people-in-the-uk-every-year-80393

References

de Botton, A. (2003) *The Art of Travel,* London: Penguin

Hupkes, G. (1982) 'The law of constant travel time and trip rates', *Futures*, 14: 38–46, 10.1016/0016-3287(82)90070-2.

Lumsdon, L. and Page, S. (eds) (2004) *Tourism and Transport.* London: Routledge, https://doi.org/10.4324/9780080519401

Metz, D. (2008) 'The myth of travel time saving', *Transport Reviews,* 28:3, 321–36, DOI: 10.1080/01441640701642348.

Mokhtarian, P. L. and Salomon, I. (2001) 'How derived is the demand for travel? Some conceptual and measurement considerations', *Transportation Research Part A,* 35(8): 695–719.

Office for National Statistics (2014) *Measuring National Well-being, Commuting and Personal Well-being, 2014* https://webarchive. nationalarchives.gov.uk/20151014110242/http://www.ons.gov.uk/ ons/rel/wellbeing/measuring-national-well-being/commuting-and-personal-well-being--2014/index.html

Park, C.-Y., Villafuerte, J., Abiad, A., Narayanan, B., Banzon, E., Samson, J., Aftab, A. and Tayag, M.C. (2020) 'An updated assessment of the economic impact of COVID-19', *Asian Development Bank Briefs*, 133, May, www.adb.org/sites/default/files/publication/ 604206/adb-brief-133-updated-economic-impact-covid-19.pdf

Salomon, I. and Mokhtarian, P.L. (1998) 'What happens when mobility-inclined market segments face accessibility-enhancing policies?' *Transportation Research Part D: Transport and Environment*, 3(3): 129–40.

Thaler, R. H. and Sunstein, C. R. (2008) *Nudge: Improving Decisions about Health, Wealth, and Happiness*, New Haven, CT: Yale University Press.

Vanhoenaker, M. (2015) *Skyfaring: A Journey With a Pilot*, London: Chatto & Windus.

Venables, A., Overman, H., Laird, J. (2014) *Transport Investment and Economic Performance: Implications for Project Appraisal.* www. gov.uk/government/collections/transport-appraisal-and-strategic-modelling-tasm-research-reports

Zahavi, Y. (1979) 'UMOT' Project. Prepared for US Department of Transportation, Washington, DC and Ministry of Transport, Federal Republic of Germany, Bonn. Rept DOTRSPA-DPB-20-79-3, August.

PART II

Travel for Exploration and Knowing Ourselves

6

Why Travel? The Sociological Perspective

Kris Beuret and Roger Hall

Introduction

In spite of the fact that travel, even to the ends of the earth, has become increasingly routine and involving a much broader spectrum of society, it remains the case that there are mysteries at the heart of it. Differences in the patterns and amount of travel between social groups are of particular interest to sociologists and not simply related to income or wealth but to perception and attitudes. There are many historic examples of taboos against travel by sea, for example the *Kala Pani* (meaning 'black water') which is a taboo in Hindu culture that proscribes against travelling over the ocean. When invited to attend the coronation of King Edward VII in 1902 in London, Madho Singh, Maharajah of Jaipur, overcame this proscription by carrying 8,000 litres of water from the Ganges in his ship.[1] There were similar sea taboos in the Ming dynasty of China where the Confucian bureaucrats forbade overseas travel, Korea was known as the Hermit Kingdom at one time and Tokugawa Japan had also banned overseas travel. On a personal level too, insularity has always had its vocal champions. Sir Thomas Beecham boasted that he had seen a great deal of the world but did not think much of it. Samuel Johnson showed some interest in seeing the Giants' Causeway but had no desire to travel to see it: 'Good enough to see but not good enough to go to see' (Boswell, 1811). In the same spirit Philip Larkin rarely left Hull and if he were urged to see the pyramids or the like would be tempted only if it could be wrapped up in a day. Perhaps the most reduced travel boast belonged to the comedian Peter Cook when nominating his favourite trip as being that to his newsagent and back again.

Reasonable caution you might think but it does raise the question of why people high and low have always been drawn to travel. One set of urges could be labelled cultural, including faith itself, as various ideologies provide a legitimating framework for travel. One of the key cultural appeals of travel lies in seeking a balance between the exotic and the familiar. Escape of various sorts is another drive. This can range from the gap year experiences of college students to refugees in fear of their lives. Lifestyle or role demands point to a third set of explanations. The dull experience of commuting or the unavoidable demands of changing demographics each exert a pull over the need to travel.

Theme one: culture and travel

Perversely, one of the drivers for travel is the need to understand one's own identity. A fundamental thought process while travelling is to measure the culture of others against your own. This even applies to travel to different regions of the same country but is more marked beyond national or language boundaries.

Of course, none of this urge to seek out new experiences is totally open-ended or spontaneous. A sophisticated marketing industry exists and builds on sociological concepts to target the different reference groups. Apart from the pressures of age, gender, income and education there is the crucial influence of holiday companies, television drama and soap operas. The media are increasingly exercising direct responsibility over travel choice. This will mean a more subtle segmenting of the target audience – age groups, families versus couples, background and taste – and a greater variation in the product – duration, side-trips, customized events, self-catering and so forth.

Central to this process lies the spread of relevant information. Some of this is a two-step flow which sociological research has established as one of the most telling modes of communication (Katz and Lazarsfeld, 1955). The message comes indirectly to the potential traveller from a friend, a relative or some other trusted source. It is powerful because it is (apparently) disinterested. Advertising attempts to replicate this by disguising the intent behind the message. A whole regime of advertorials, influencers, customer ratings and social media videos blurs the line between advert and documentary. Presumably the modern scepticism that has eroded most of the simple faith we had in authority figures in the media, the law, and medical practice now encompasses the travel business.

Travel and political values

The way in which political values are formed is complex. In the past sociologists explained voting patterns by social background, employment and residence. For example in the UK, Parkin (1974) showed how the propensity to vote for the Labour Party increased in proportion to the extent to which people were located in all three working-class contexts, namely family, occupation and residential area. Others explained working class Conservative voters in a similar way in terms of having greater contact with other social groups (McKenzie and Silver, 1969). Most such analysis was carried out in the 1960s at a time when the industrial structure was characterized by large manufacturing with associated council estates. Middle class people as owner-occupiers were also located and employed in separate locations and white-collar employment. Few people of either group went overseas for holidays. Thus, political reference groups and voting patterns were relatively stable.

Since this time the UK has become far more diverse and a much higher proportion of its citizens engage with people born overseas and have international experiences. There have been numerous social changes, including:

- increased immigration levels[2]
- new service sector and more diverse employment replacing traditional manufacturing and industry-based communities
- sale of council houses – increasing home ownership and the private rental sector
- more diverse and cosmopolitan urban centres
- expansion of higher education
- more media channels extending globally and in real time
- more travel to other countries
- larger political groupings – EU, NATO.

The political impact of these changes has been significant. How we vote is no longer simple to predict or explain. We know so much more about other lives, not just in our own country but worldwide, and travel either virtual or physical is an influencing factor. Indeed, one of the drivers for travel is the need to understand one's own individual and group identity in this new world with so many more uncertainties and choices.

However, such experience does not predict the attitudes that emerge. Indeed, it has been suggested that travel can lead to 'two ideal type' reactions. Namely the creation of either a global or a nationally focused perspective, both of which cut across traditional party lines. In his book *The Road to Somewhere: The Populist Revolt and the Future of Politics*, David Goodhart (2017) divides society into two groups (see table).

'Somewheres' and 'anywheres'

Somewheres (estimated 50% of the British population)	Anywheres (25% of the British population)
People whose identity is based on a strong sense of place and attachment to the community where they come from.	People whose identity is tied to achievements and this is associated with an open and diverse society.

The 'anywheres' have higher levels of education especially since university education encourages movement away from home at the stage of forming social and political views and these are likely to be reinforced by travelling and working abroad. In contrast the 'somewheres' are more likely to stay in their community where their identity is reinforced. The remaining 25 per cent Goodhart calls 'inbetweeners'.

This division has been further explored in terms of the growing number of people who work in the global economy. Often employed by multinational companies and with highly portable skills, their lifestyle is based on a lifetime level of mobility half way between temporary mobility and permanent migration (Bell and Ward, 2000). This lifestyle results in a sense of not belonging to only one single location but for this reason also values ease of physical mobility – the truly 'anywheres'.

Not surprisingly these theses have been applied to voting with many traditional left/right patterns changing and much discussion of what this means. From the perspective of travel it could be argued that exposure to other cultures would broaden the perspectives of the 'somewheres' and create more tolerance to our increasingly diverse society. Conversely, policies such as encouraging attendance at local universities, working from home, shopping locally or taking more holidays in the UK could reinforce a sense of community and cohesion.

Rick Steves, in *Travel as a Political Act* (2015), takes the travel experience in a different direction as something that can only be understood less as confirmation than reinterpretation. His approach could be said to emphasize the role of travel in focusing on the consensual rather than the

Figure 6.1a: Backpackers in a busy city

Figure 6.1b: Cruise port, St Maarten, Caribbean

'Independent' vs cruise tourism. Travel by 'gap year' students is increasing year on year – current UK estimates three million – this form of travel encourages contact with local cultures. Cruises are also increasing – this form of travel encourages people of the same nationality and culture to travel together with less contact with local cultures.

combative. For example, Steves suggests that the experience of travelling to Palestine and Israel can lead to seeing the situation less as a persistent cold war but as a subtle chess game. On the same basis Steves argues that getting a handle on complex issues, such as understanding Iranian politics, can come only from travel. Similarly, the attempt by different societies to get a grip on the drugs problem is best understood at first hand. Thus, the Dutch approach to the open sale and consumption of cannabis by the same token should not be seen as one end of a spectrum running from total tolerance to prohibition. Rather experience of Amsterdam would show that cannabis is both tolerated but highly regulated. Alternatively, the traveller to Arizona would experience a decriminalized market-led approach to recreational drugs.

In conclusion, a core tenet of the sociological approach is the need for cultural identity and a sense of belonging. It includes the beliefs that people hold about reality and the impact of this on values and behaviour. Some of the classic sociological theorists such as Émile Durkheim (1951) went further in explaining how high rates of suicide are related to a lack of shared social norms, which can cause the breakdown of those bonds which tie an individual to a community. This phenomenon, which Durkheim called 'anomie' (normlessness), could lead to a dysfunctional state of mind and an inability to integrate with a person's social world, due to the absence of a collective reality. For Durkheim religion enabled the growth of this collective reality but more recently a broader view has developed based on the sharing of culture enabled by mass communications. Travel is also an important influencer on this need for a shared culture, but it is still unclear how the influence of travel plays out. Does exposure to other cultures lead to cultural dilution or does it strengthen awareness of the difference between cultures?

Theme two: travel as escape or attraction: push and pull factors

Global movements of people across history demonstrate a number of explanations: some reflecting external dangers and some internal compulsions. In other words motivations may be due to *escaping from* or alternatively *moving towards* and often an element of both. Sometimes this might involve spiritual journeys such as religious conversion or personal changes such as divorce. But there are also many examples of wider physical movements of whole communities, such as the movement of Muslim and Hindu populations at the time of Indian independence, which resulted in the displacement of around 14 million people along religious lines, and up to two million deaths. On a more positive note, emigration is frequently motivated by a desire for freedom or economic improvement. The movement of a half a million Irish to America during the potato famine of the 1840s is a good example of escape from (starvation) and moving towards (economic opportunity).

Thus, in many instances escape is ambiguous. For example, as discussed below, how does sex tourism fit within this theme of escape? Is it a sort of 'escapism' on the part of tourists while in contrast those that provide such sexual needs cannot escape? And is this definition different to escape for fear of life by those who might be persecuted for their sexual preferences or religious or political beliefs? Clearly the concept of 'escape' is a broad one.

However, in all cases the question 'why travel?' remains pertinent. Cost–benefit analysis would emphasize the level of risk and uncertainty at stake but the high volume of travel for both inward and outward migration suggests that rational weighing of pros and cons scarcely scratches the surface. Some model of a limited rationality seems more plausible (see Chapter 5 'The Economics of Travel' for more on this).

Social identities and travel

Race, religion, sexual identity, social status and caste disadvantages may be resolved by travel and relocation. Internal migration within nations has always been a feature of economic and social change, carrying with it familiar challenges of accommodation, schooling, health and so on. Between 1910 and 1970 approximately seven million citizens of the southern US, variously persecuted minorities and/or economic migrants, moved to the industrial heartlands of the north. More recently the tide has turned and the movement is in the reverse direction as the 'rust bucket' north loses swathes of population to the south and west. The question of why travel in this case is better expressed as 'what is the alternative?' Similar population movements are apparent in the UK with significant numbers of people moving region. Excluding those moving to the UK from another country, around 1.4 million (including students) travelled to a new region in 2016 and around 140,000 people changed both region and employer. Interestingly, in recent years a key trend is from London to elsewhere in the south and the south east (Clarke, 2017).

Nevertheless, when immigration from other countries is taken into account the population of London is now over eight million. Cities in particular are places where young people want to be and they are increasingly accepting reduced living space and giving up car ownership in favour of all-night buses and tubes to achieve this (SRA, 2015).

Much of this is spontaneous and unplanned and involves travel systems as playing catch-up with wider social phenomena. Both north–south and rural–urban drift are involved. Sometimes this is pronounced enough to inspire permanent road and rail links. A rail journey from the north east to the south west of England passes through a cluster of university towns, emphasizing that travel is as much bound up with the university experience as curriculum is. It is a reminder too of how far the university calendar is associated with phases of travel and the movement of undergraduates in many cases from small communities to larger ones and the return journey at the end of term. The sheer growth in student numbers and the relative brevity of the student year has or ought to have clear repercussions for urban transport systems.

Social mobility

Sometimes social mobility can be achieved only by spatial flight and this is not just about moving for work. Travel to enable social mobility can take a variety of forms and can accompany downward as well as upward movement. In each case it may involve cutting the bonds of kinship and social background.

For many working class families in the UK moving out of cities was a way of escaping from areas of monolithic council estates to first generational home ownership and a move up the class scale: 'When my own family moved from Bethnal Green to Surrey my gran left behind was told not to write her address on parcels she sent us in case neighbours found out we were from the East End' (author's diary). Even today many socially mobile people who have perfected standard English speech revert to their local accents when returning to visit their hometown: "I had a South Lancashire accent and my mother wanted me to get on in the world so she sent me to elocution lessons."[3] Perhaps such social distinctions are less important in this day and age although there is much evidence that social background is still a constraint on opportunity as evidenced by the continued domination of people from elite backgrounds in top jobs and higher income levels. Moving away both physically and culturally from a working class community is still seen by many as a prerequisite to breaking through the class barrier.

The suburban lifestyle

For some the move to suburbia is a way of achieving a new way of life. Much has been written about the impact of this on gender roles with men commuting to the cities, and suburbs in the daytime populated by women and children. A key book that influenced the women's movement in the 1960s was Betty Friedan's *The Feminine Mystique* (1963), which described the impact of the suburban lifestyle, free from the drudgery of housework and city problems, yet isolating and disempowering: 'The green lawns and big corner lots were isolating, the housework seemed to expand to fill the time available. All that was covered up in a kitchen conspiracy of denial so instead the problem was with the mystique of waxed floors and perfectly applied lipstick.' Today motives for moving to the suburbs are more varied ranging through affordability, the search for better secondary schools, so-called 'white flight' and even avoiding constraints on driving such as the inner-city congestion charges.

But there are also push factors related to impacts of political decisions such as privatization, which reverses the trend towards the public provision of merit goods, like housing and building land, and turns them over to private organizations with knock-on travel effects. For example, the right to buy council houses (previously owned by the public sector and rented on the basis of social need) has led to an increase in property prices and a reduction in low-cost housing in city centres and in turn dispersion of lower income groups to the outskirts. To some extent cities in the UK, with their mosaic of social classes, tend to counter the outward march of low-income residents, but as property prices become ever higher those left behind in social housing tend to be socially isolated with high rates of crime and social problems.

This need to move for cheaper housing is particularly apparent in developing countries where poorer people who have service jobs in city centres such as Rio de Janeiro may spend up to four hours each day travelling. In other cases, such as Detroit, the reverse occurs with the middle class moved out to the security and lifestyle of the suburbs. In both cases, travel increases albeit for commuting to white-collar jobs in the city or for blue-collar jobs in the city centre service sector. But such movements are not purely economic: there is also an element of social selection. In the UK, the East End white working class favoured moving out to Essex, and orthodox Jews are establishing communities in Canvey Island while maintaining close links with their original community in north London, including by establishing a dedicated minibus service between the original and the new community.

Sex, sexuality

One of the drivers for travel as escape relates to legal, social and religious constraints around gender, sexuality and sexual behaviours. Sex tourism and political flight have strong moral connotations. This can work in both directions. In the 1960s Joe Orton and other homosexuals travelled to north Africa and now the UK accepts asylum seekers from countries around the world where homosexuality is not only illegal but a capital offence. Nevertheless, sex can feature as a prime travel magnet to third world countries whereby a majority of travel for sexual purposes is by males from developed countries to destinations like Thailand, Kenya, India and Vietnam. However, as taboos are broken women as well as men can be involved, with a growing practice of older women seeking younger male partners in developing nations. McPhee notes that one of the central challenges to curbing sex tourism is the differing laws and norms regarding normal sexual behaviour in sending and receiving countries. Sex tourism also has economic implications for all nations involved and is often encouraged by the tourist industry of poorer countries as an important source of income from Western tourists (McPhee, 2014).

Obviously, there is an exploitative side to all of this and many women and children find themselves caught up in international trafficking. There is nothing particularly new in this trade but global figures of approximately 29 million worldwide – legal and illegal – shows it to be a growing aspect of semi-legitimate travel.

Mass migration

A great deal of migration stems from wider decisions made in other parts of the world. Wars and deprivations due to famine in particular can spur desperate attempts to secure economic and personal wellbeing. In the 20th century the huge disruptions of two world wars caused mass migrations on an unprecedented scale. In the UK, the decades following World War II have seen a large increase in immigration. The British Nationality Act of 1948 provided inadvertently the rationale for possible millions to seek residence in the UK. Likewise, the EU legitimized a massive movement of citizens mainly into western Europe. Most recently wars in the Middle East and Afghanistan have led to unprecedented growth in numbers of asylum claims and economic migration. Clearly transport has facilitated such travel although legal constraints still result in migrants taking desperate safety risks.

Nowadays, movement from western Europe outwards, though not inconsiderable, hardly matches the main flows of immigration. But a century ago, Europeans left in their millions. Many of the great diasporas of the past into the US, Canada and Australasia were into destinations of great expanses of lower population density and, despite some host resentment and opposition, continue at various volumes to this day. For over a million people between 1945 and 1972, the 'ten pound pom' offer to emigrate to Australia was a clear step up from the grim post-World War II economic climate and hierarchical social class structure of the UK. Some of the movement in either direction is perceived as temporary, some as permanent – with many ending up with different priorities: "I always intended to go back to London after a few years but then I met my future wife and that was forty years ago" (diary of author's family member).

Wider movements of people are often bracketed under the twin labels of refugees and asylum seekers. An asylum seeker is someone who is seeking international protection but whose claim for refugee status has not yet been determined. In contrast, a refugee is someone who has been recognized under the 1951 Convention relating to the status of refugees to be a refugee. Migrants, in contrast, are travelling for economic reasons – but distinctions are hazy. For example, many people travelling to the US from Central America can be seen as asylum seekers rather than migrants since they are escaping crime and persecution.

Some of this movement involving millions of displaced people comprises both cross-border and internal migration. A more complicated process than simply the journey from undeveloped to developed world; refugees comprise the latest instalment of global movements that can be traced back centuries in northern and southern Europe and the Americas among others. Currently Turkey and Pakistan, not western Europe or the US, are the biggest recipients of refugees and asylum seekers, taking most migrants especially from Syria and Afghanistan (which has been the largest source of displaced people over the last 40 years).[4] In 2019 there were 70.9 million displaced people worldwide and annually some 3.5 million refugees will attempt to achieve the contested status of asylum seekers.[5]

This 'refugee roulette' tends to encompass arrivals from Africa, Asia, and Latin America into Europe, Australasia and North America. The majority are fleeing from persecution, wars and economic catastrophe but some will be economic migrants, typified by an urge to seek a better life in more affluent nations. While the United Nations High Commission for Refugees (UNHCR) and many legal frameworks do distinguish clearly between refugees and migrants, these concepts can be contentious – especially for those whose lives may depend on the category they are assigned.

A new motivation predicted to be of increasing importance in the future is that climate change will force huge population movements

Figure 6.2: Immigrants arriving in New York City (1887)

Immigrants Arriving in New York City, 1887 Engraving

Migration, both towards a better life and away from danger, has had profound impacts on societies across the globe.

as low-lying areas become flooded and temperatures in southern areas render vast areas uninhabitable.

To conclude, there are complex reasons for migration both within and between countries and indeed such movements are the very essence of the story of mankind. As our understanding of DNA develops, the extent of previous migration is becoming apparent. So for example, a third of the over 30 million visitors to Britain each year will contact relatives and friends who live here and others will be interested in tracking down their heritage and ancestors. And there is no doubt that the speed, ease and lower cost of modern systems of transport have made it easier to escape, to return and for those left behind to expect to be visited.

Theme three: why travel and the life cycle

Travel as a means of tapping into cultural identity was discussed in section one and travel as escape from physical and psychological pressures was covered as a second theme. What remains is to tie the travel instinct to particular stages of the life cycle. Generation factors are inevitably central to this. Different travel experiences fit in with the needs and tastes of various age groups. Footloose adolescents and young adults are apt to be relatively adventurous, defining travel not simply as destinations with inherent charms but as open-ended. Applying the Donald Rumsfeld concept, they are tempted to view travel as entailing known unknowns with a sketchy set of expectations apt to be blown away by events. They are replicating the experiences of the explorers of yore like Vasco da Gama and Columbus, having only a rudimentary notion of the world but willing to risk it. In contrast, older travellers tend to prefer more certainty and comfort.

Travel and personal development

One thing we have a greater understanding of today is the importance of physical mobility on the development of very young children. The Sure Start programme based on the model of the similar US Headstart Programme, was set up to address the disadvantage of under fives through the improvement of childcare, early education, health and family support, with an emphasis on outreach and community development. Since many of the children had never travelled beyond their neighbourhoods, outings to broaden experiences were a key feature of the initiative. In 2010, robust research demonstrated significant positive effects of the programme including better physical health for children (NESST, 2010). The value of travel to childhood development is also recognized by school visits programmes, which have expanded rapidly in recent years leading to concerns that those whose parents cannot afford to pay are disadvantaged. Recent research has shown that a third of London's children have never been to the countryside (Natural England, 2017). Certainly, the experience of children who travel beyond their comfort zone to outdoor activity centres is overwhelmingly positive (King's College, 2011). Yet one of the worrying trends is for children to spend more time indoors using electronic devices and social media. This is particularly noticeable during the summer holidays and there is growing evidence that it is resulting in a decline of outdoor play with associated increases in obesity and mental health problems (Beuret, 2016). And not only this but deeper impacts follow such as lack of spatial skills and associated poorer mathematical ability. The Children's Commissioner (2018) has continually raised this problem and they and other experts are calling for national guidelines on the use of screens.

At the other end of the age scale, the reasons for encouraging travel by older people is especially important. Physical exercise has a more beneficial effect on older people in delaying brain shrinkage than mental exercise, and the social contact that goes with it is a crucial

Figure 6.3: Children playing outdoors (L) and child using digital device while travelling (R)

Outdoor activity is an essential element of developing spatial and mathmatical skills. There is growing evidence that children who spend more than two hours a day on screens develop thinking and language skills more slowly.

aspect of avoiding social exclusion: "The day an older person decides to keep their slippers on and stay in is the beginning of dependency."[6] One of the difficulties here is that older people find the transition from car to public transport daunting but the provision of free or concessionary travel on public transport is a great catalyst. For longer journeys, older travellers will tend to eschew car trips and favour train and coach outings, not to mention the growth of the cruise market. For couples the romance of each other's company might have petered out and the fresh conversations with strangers by land, sea or air can be oddly comforting. Travel will be welcomed as an alternative to staying at home with its tired routines. Apart from improved longevity, the increasing accessibility of transport systems has also freed far more disabled and elderly people to travel to the extent that this group is now an important part of the travel market. For example, over half the tourists visiting the Caribbean have some form of disability. Of course, at the other end of the income scale many elderly or disabled people are socially excluded largely due to low income and, for this group, but others as well, the design of the local walking environment is crucial in enabling travel. As we explore in Chapter 13 'Placemaking and Travel', planners are becoming increasingly aware of such needs, including longer road crossing times, the design of seating and wider issues such as security and visibility in the design of public space.

In recent years travel has also been recognized as a way of combatting loneliness and isolation for all age groups and some transport providers are using publicity and design to encourage social interaction. Examples are buses in Brighton and Hove badged as 'chatty buses', which feature a table badged as a place for people who are happy to talk to each other to sit. The company has partnered with Brighton community group Impetus to connect more people and help reduce loneliness as part of the Campaign to End Loneliness. Chatty Bus ambassadors distribute 'happy to chat' badges and talk about how buses can help reduce social isolation.[7] A similar campaign has been introduced by London Transport and a cross party commission published a report advocating new approaches to tackle the problem (Jo Cox Commission on Loneliness, 2017).

Travel and changing family structure

A core subject of study for social scientists is the family. Early studies in the East End of London contrasted the close residential proximity of different generations typical of the working class family with the smaller nuclear family of the middle class (Young and Willmott, 1961). Later research suggested that this picture is outdated and that due to geographical mobility, lower birth rates and increased longevity the typical family is now three or even four generational but with smaller numbers within each generation – the so-called 'beanpole family' (Brannen, 2003), who co-operate with each other even though physically living apart and who maintain contact via cars, public transport, air travel and social media.

Travel and equality

There is no doubt that there are vast differences in access to transport both between the developed and developing worlds as well as within nations (Banister, 2019). This issue of equality (and the related problem of transport related social exclusion [Lucas, 2019]) has attracted a growing body of research and literature which in turn has been built into transport policies. Clearly travel opportunities enable a wider choice of jobs, education and social activity, which most people would accept as a good reason to travel. But there are other aspects of equality that impact on lifestyles such as status. The car industry has long understood that car ownership is not just about getting from A to B and this is reflected in styling, marketing and consumer identity. Compared to investments and even residence, travel status is more demonstrable to others and this is not just in terms of having a Rolls Royce or travelling first class. There is also a plethora of specialist travel groups – car, motorbike, cycling, sailing, flying – who all see travel as an identifier and vast sums are spent on pursuing such activities (Alam, 2020).

But, of course, not everyone can express themselves via travel choices and many find their lives constrained by the lack of opportunities to travel either through cost, lack of infrastructure or disability. Some people must therefore spend huge amounts of unproductive time in accessing activities; for example there are people who live in South African townships whose walking journey to work takes longer than the hours they spend at work. Others simply fail to make the journeys they need, leading to multiple disadvantage or poverty due to lack of access to employment, health, education or social connectivity. In the UK the rich make about 30 per cent more trips than the poor by the main modes of transport apart from bus. In terms of distance, the differences are even greater, with a huge imbalance between the minority of frequent flyers and the rest of the population – most of whom have never flown. The impact of these differences is detrimental not only in terms of job opportunity but for wider experiences such as access to the countryside and wider retail, health and education choices (Banister, 2019; Lucas, 2011). Currently such access is distributed largely by price, which inevitably creates inequality even when mitigated by elements of subsidy. In contrast, there is growing interest in alternative strategies such as rationing or traffic exclusion, which would reduce inequality where applied to all while also tackling global warming.

The occupational treadmill

Travel as a correlate of occupation takes various forms (as also described in Chapter 12 'Technology and Travel'). Travel can involve commuting, in-work related travel or driving as a job.

Commuting is a feature of daily travel for many both within and between urban centres. National capitals tend to be a magnet for job seekers, and cities such as London or Beijing, regardless of the occasional blip, have a vast capacity for job creation mainly in white-collar and professional sectors and the service sectors that support these. As we saw earlier, commuting has its own dynamic partly shaped by the interplay between time and distance. Mental maps of feasible travel distances increasingly linked to house prices will continue to change depending not only on rail capacity but also a willingness to spend the time usefully since the train is increasingly equipped with IT to enable work during travel. Some have even raised the concern that highspeed rail links may be detrimental to this growing practice: 'Forty minutes to Birmingham is too quick – I could barely have time to get my computer out' (HS2, public engagement research for *Environmental Impact Analysis*, SRA (2015)). Although the great wave of home working has yet to break out, it does represent a potential challenge to established travel patterns especially since the experience of COVID-19 lockdown (as discussed further in Chapter 12 'Technology and Travel'). Location has a powerful effect on job choice and vice versa. There tends to be a tension between either locating close to work or close to relatives involving some extensive commuting. There is growing evidence that people miss the buzz and interaction of the workplace and even when working from home find themselves looking for reasons to go out locally.

Travel for work is a second category and despite video conferencing this is still a significant aspect of the travel mix. Occupations such as sales, care working or decorating still involve travel (usually driving with equipment or products), and rail and air providers still depend on business travel revenue (around a third of international tourism is classed as business travel by the World Tourism Organization). There is something about conferences and face-to-face meetings that do not seem to be replaced by virtual or electronic communications, although this may change due to climate change or global health threats.

Driving as a job is a third category. Many driving occupations have a strong occupational culture, which both attracts and feeds the desire to travel. Working with vehicles including vans, taxis, buses, planes and even cycle couriers, tend to attract people who enjoy travel and the relative autonomy that accompanies their working environment. Perhaps the socially indeterminate nature of driving jobs is part of the attraction aside from the fact that such jobs combine the twin benefits of reasonable pay and wide availability. However, for others in the gig economy working as low-paid couriers or in food delivery, conditions and motivation are less positive.

Conclusion: social science and travel

To conclude this discussion of 'why travel?' from the sociological perspective, it is clear that travel is essential to achieve our human need for both self and group identity. In spite of ever-advancing techniques of electronic communication and concern about climate change, direct interaction with other cultures and fellow humans, and ultimately

Figure 6.4: Food delivery by bicycle courier

Travel as work: Deliveries to households have grown in recent years.

the hug of a friend or relative, is what makes our complex social and political world viable. But whether this answers the question of travel as a tutor of tolerance remains unclear. Travel has undoubtedly enabled understanding, acceptance or even celebration of complexity across cultures, and more broadly the march of human progress. On the downside it can lead to the destruction of traditional cultures and intolerance of differences. More likely the findings of this chapter make a claim for immersion in the issues discussed in this book as part of wider understanding as against simply explaining travel as a practical method of getting from A to B.

Notes

[1] www.thehindu.com/society/history-and-culture/when-the-ganges-came-to-london/article24994242.e

[2] The proportion of the population born outside of the UK has grown from around 4 per cent in 1951 to around 13 per cent in 2011: www.ons.gov.uk/peoplepopulationandcommunity/populationandmigration/internationalmigration/articles/immigrationpatternsofnonukbornpopulationsinenglandandwalesin2011/2013-12-17

[3] www.bbc.co.uk/news/uk-politics-16744393

[4] www.un.org/en/sections/issues-depth/refugees/

[5] www.unhcr.org/uk/figures-at-a-glance.html

[6] Ann Frye speaking at Transport Associates Network Conference 2013.

[7] www.brightonandhoveindependent.co.uk/news/people/chatty-bus-comes-to-brighton-to-combat-loneliness-and-isolation-1-8789984

Suggestions for further reading

Travels with a Donkey in the Cevennes Robert Louis Stevenson (1862)

Off the Beaten Tracks: Three Centuries of Women Travellers National Portrait Gallery (2004)

Billy Liar Keith Waterhouse (1959)

The Grapes of Wrath John Steinbeck (1939)

Walk! A Celebration of Striding Out Colin Speakman (2011)

English Journey J. B. Priestley (1934)

Freedom to Go: After the Motor Age Colin Ward (1991)

Untouchables: My Family's Triumphant Escape from India's Caste System Narendra Jadhay (2007)

The Idle Traveller Dan Kieran (2012)

References

Alam, Y. (2020) *Race, Taste, Class and Cars*, Bristol: Policy Press.

Banister, D. (2019) *Inequality in Transport,* Marcham, Oxfordshire: Alexandrine Press.

Bell, M. and Ward, G. (2000) 'Comparing permanent migration with temporary mobility', *Tourism Geographies*, 2(1): 97–107.

Beuret, K. (2016) *Children and Travel,* ITC Paper No 9, www.theitc.org.uk/wp-content/uploads/2016/04/ITC-Occasional-Paper-9-Children-and-Travel-April-2016-1.pdf

Boswell, J. (1811) *The Life of Samuel Johnson, LLD*, New York: Everyman's Library (Knopf). (This book follows Malone's 6th edition, 1811. Knopf does not claim copyright.)

Brannen, J. (2003) 'The age of beanpole families', Sociological Review, November.

Children's Commissioner for England (2018) *Playing Out,* www.childrenscommissioner.gov.uk/publication/playing-out/

Clarke, S. (2017) *Get a Move On?* London: Resolution Foundation.

Durkheim, E. (1951) *Suicide: A Study in Sociology* Glencoe, trans J. A. Spaulding and G. Simpson, Illinois: The Free Press of Glencoe.

Friedan, B (1963) *The Feminine Mystique*, New York: W.W. Norton

Goodhart, D. (2017) *The Road to Somewhere: The Populist Revolt and the Future of Politics*, London: Hurst Publishers.

Jo Cox Commission on Loneliness (2017) *A Call to Action.* London: Jo Cox Foundation.

Katz, E. and Lazarsfeld, P. (1955) *Personal Influence,* New York: New York Free Press.

Kings College, London (2011) *Understanding the Diverse Benefits of Learning in Natural Environments*. Commissioned by Natural England, York: Natural England.

Lucas, K. (2011) 'Transport and Social Exclusion: Where Are We Now?', in M. Grieco and J. Urry (eds) *Mobilities: New Perspectives on Transport and Society* Surrey, UK: Ashgate Publishing Limited, pp 223–44.

Lucas, K. (2019) 'A new evolution for transport-related social exclusion research?', *Journal of Transport Geography*, 81(C) https://doi.org/10.1016/j.jtrangeo.2019.102529

McKenzie, R. and Silver, A. (1969) *Angels in Marble: Working Class Conservatives in Urban England,* London: Heinemann.

McPhee D. (2014) 'Sex Offending and Sex Tourism: Problems, Policy and Challenges', in: K. McCartan (ed) *Responding to Sexual Offending,* Palgrave Studies in Risk, Crime and Society, London: Palgrave Macmillan.

National Evaluation of Sure Start Team (NESST) (2010) *The Impact of Sure Start Local Programmes on 5 Year Olds and Their Families,* November, London: Department of Education.

Natural England (2017) *Monitor of Engagement with the Natural Environment: Developing a Method to Measure Nature Connection Across the English Population (Adults and Children)*, York: Natural England, fig 11, p 10.

Parkin, F. (1974) *The Social Analysis of Class Structure,* London: Tavistock Publications.

Social Research Associates (SRA) (2015) *On the Move: Exploring Attitudes to Road and Rail Travel in Britain*, London: Independent Transport Commission.

Steves, R. (2015) *Travel as a Political Act,* New York: Hachette.

Young, M. and Willmott, P. (1961) *Family and Kinship in East London,* London: Routledge and Kegan Paul.

7

Religious and Spiritual Travel

Alison Kuznets

We are pilgrims, our life is a long walk or journey from
earth to Heaven. (Vincent van Gogh)

These words, written by Vincent van Gogh for a Sunday sermon he
delivered in 1876, express a ubiquitous metaphor, found across times,
cultures and religions: that of life as a journey – and one with a spiritual
purpose. In the Christian scriptures, this comparison is found in Jesus's
Sermon on the Mount, in which Christ explained that 'narrow is the
gate and difficult the road that leads to life' (Matthew 7:13–14). The
great Hindu mystic Swami Sivananda spent many of his early years
as a wandering mendicant and credited this with developing spiritual
and mental strength. 'Life is a pilgrimage', he later said, and 'the wise
man does not rest by wayside inns, but marches direct to the illimitable
domain of eternal bliss, his ultimate destination.'

   This chapter explores the question: what can a study of spiritual travel
tell us about the wider human motivations for travel? Travel plays a
central role in all major religions both in practice and conceptually –
and not only as a metaphor for a spiritual life. Travel can be found both
at the core of religious narratives and also as an important religious
practice, whether it be pilgrimage, mission, or a weekly journey to a
place of worship. If we take a moment to glance at the numbers, this
importance starts to become clear. There are an estimated 200 million
journeys of pilgrimage made every year (perhaps considerably more,
according to the Alliance of Religions and Conservation and the UN
World Tourism Organization). Many of these are people travelling
within their own country but a considerable (and probably increasing)

Figure 7.1: Statue of Gandhi walking, Chennai, India

Travel as a spiritual exercise: life as a journey. This image depicts a statue of a famous spiritual, religious and even political walker, Mahatma Gandhi.

number are international journeys. If we add to this the number of missionaries travelling the world to spread their message (again, difficult to estimate but in the low millions every year), let alone the number of people displaced due to religious persecution (which arguably runs into tens of millions), we can see that travel for religious purposes has been – and remains – a force shaping the history of nations and the spiritual and physical lives of billions of individuals.

In this chapter, I explore why travel has developed such an important religious role, and ask what this tells us about the centrality of travel to human psychological and cultural life. I look first at how travel is used within the metaphors, teachings and foundational stories of religions, before looking at four major religious motivations for travel: pilgrimage; 'holy war'; missionary travel; and flight from persecution.

Travel as allegory

The concept of travel is at the heart of many religious stories and beliefs. Travel is used not only as an allegory of life, but also for perhaps the most fundamental and uncertain journey for many religious believers: namely the journey after death into the next world. This has been the case since very early civilizations. Ancient Egyptian tombs and texts depict the journey that the deceased had to make through the realm of the dead to where their heart was weighed, and their ultimate fate decided. The Ancient Greeks described the passage across the river that all souls have to cross into the realm of Hades, be they bound for heavenly Elysium or hellish Tartarus. Perhaps the human spirit does not cease to travel even when it has moved on from life on earth.

Many religions trace their origins through the travels of their founding figures. Some were actual travels – as in the case of Muhammad's travels around Arabia and to Yemen, and Jesus's years of wandering. Others were journeys in the mind – as was the case with Buddha's 'awakening' following lengthy meditation under the Bodhi Tree (although prior to that he had led an itinerant life, wandering for seven years). Some journeys were born of necessity: Jesus's flight with his parents into Egypt, or the exile of Abraham. Others were undertaken in order to reflect on faith in solitude: for example, Jesus's 40 days in the wilderness and St Jerome's sojourns in the desert of Chalcis.

Travel appears to have been integral to many religions from their very inception, with these religious tales recognizing the power of travel to change both the traveller and the places and people among whom they move. This is perhaps not surprising if we consider the role of travel deep in the past of humanity (see Chapter 2 'Biological

Perspectives on Travel') and the fact that spiritual feeling seems to have emerged in humans along with symbolic and linguistic abilities, long before settled societies (Lieberman, 1991). As Christian author Charles Foster puts it: 'The anthropological and divine norm, remember, is to travel' (2010: 94).

Travel as religious practice

The interweaving of travel and religion is also clear when we look at the important role travel plays in the religious life of believers. Travel for religious purposes can broadly be grouped into three categories. Travel as worship (most notably pilgrimage) in which believers show their devotion and become closer to their god(s) both at their destination and – importantly – through the process of the journey itself. Travel as mission; to spread the word and find new followers (also seen as an act of worship in itself). And travel to escape persecution; to keep one's self and one's religion intact by transplanting to new lands. By exploring these diverse, but widely shared, religious motivations we can gain an insight into the deeper importance of travel to humans on a psychological, cultural and spiritual level.

Pilgrimage

Pilgrimage has been of great importance in many religions across the millennia and remains so today, motivating hundreds of millions of journeys each year. The origin of the term in English can be traced to the Latin word *peregrinus*, used to designate a wanderer or foreigner who is undertaking a special journey, the *peregrinatio*. Pilgrimage stretches across the world both geographically and doctrinally; in fact, pilgrimage has been a central part of nearly all faiths since their beginnings. Destinations for pilgrimage are varied in nature, ranging from sacred rivers and mountains, to temples, tombs and sites of miracles and holy relics.

In Judaism, it had been traditional to make a pilgrimage to the Temple in Jerusalem on the occasion of their three major festivals of Pesach, Shavuot and Sukkot, until the Temple was destroyed by the Romans in 70 AD. The Western Wall in Jerusalem continues to be a major pilgrimage site for Jews with an estimated eight million visits each year. The sites of Jesus's life and death, and those of Christian martyrs, had drawn pilgrims since the beginnings of the Christian faith, and especially from the 4th century when the emperor Constantine sacralized many sites to form the 'Holy Land'. In Medieval Europe, pilgrimage became immensely popular (some estimate that it rivalled the wool trade in economic importance (Bell and Dale, 2011)) and pilgrimage sites proliferated to include Rome, Canterbury, Walsingham and Santiago de Compostela. Today, many millions of Christian pilgrims visit these sites and those established on more recent miracles, such as the healing waters at Lourdes in France, and the Basilica of Our Lady of Guadalupe in Mexico (which receives an estimated 20 million pilgrims per year). In the Islamic faith, pilgrimages had started in the years immediately following the life and teachings of Muhammad, echoing the pilgrimage taken by the Prophet himself. Today, around three million pilgrims make the Hajj each year, and the journey forms one of the central five pillars of the faith.

Pilgrimage has been a core religious activity in cultures more ancient even than some of these Abrahamic religions. The shores of the Ganges and other great rivers have drawn Hindu worshippers from a very early date and today they attract perhaps more than ever – with an estimated 70 million pilgrims attending the 2013 Kumbh Mela. In the classical world, pilgrims travelled to Delphi and Olympia. Buddhist pilgrims have long travelled to worship at temples with holy relics and, particularly, at the four main sites that Gautama Buddha himself identified as worthy of pilgrimage: the places of his birth, enlightenment, first teaching and death (in the 4th century BCE). Within Daoism, a Chinese philosophical tradition, pilgrims journey to present offerings of incense to sacred mountains, which are seen as the dwelling place of gods and the embodiment of the perfect harmony of Yang and Yin. These Daoist pilgrimages are recorded from at least the 4th century, and over the course of the next few hundred years the establishment of mountain temples generated a 'sacred geography' in which 'pilgrimage to the sacred mountains … became a symbolic journey through the universe' (Renard, 2002: 187). Indeed, the 'Dao' of 'Daoism' means way, road, channel or path. The most eminent of the five sacred Dao mountains, Mount Tai, in Shandong Province China, has been a site of pilgrimage for thousands of years; it is said that 72 emperors of different dynasties made pilgrimage there, and today the mountain continues to draw an estimated half million pilgrims every year.[1]

The desire to travel and to visit holy places seems to be a near-universal drive within religious faiths. Why should this be? As with all travel, there seem to be two main aspects to pilgrimage: the journey and the destination. These two elements, although greatly entangled, both hold their own rewards (and dangers) for the spiritual traveller.

Figure 7.2a: Mount Tai, Shandong Province, China

Figure 7.2b: Masjid al-Haram, Saudi Arabia, during the Hajj

Pilgrimage has been a motivator for travel since before ancient times and continues today in ever greater numbers. Destinations include natural features, such as the Daoist sacred Mount Tai; and sites associated with holy figures, such as the Sacred Mosque in Mecca.

The journey

> 'The feet of the wanderer are like the flower ... his soul growing and reaping the fruit; and all his sins are destroyed by his fatigues in wandering. Therefore wander.' (Aitareya Brahmana)

These words, from an ancient Indian sacred hymn, illustrate the feeling underlying many pilgrimages – the desire to unburden the pilgrim from their wrongdoings, and the ability of travel to perform this release. This unburdening is a part of the pilgrim's desire to better know their true selves and thus to have a closer relationship with their god or gods. The famous Socratic maxim written over the entrance to the Ancient Greek pilgrimage site of Delphi is still oft-quoted: 'Know thyself.' For many religious travellers it is the journey itself that enables this self-knowledge. 'The abrasion of the road rubs away some of the stuff that cakes onto us all', says Christian writer Charles Foster (2010: 92), echoing a common sentiment about the transformative power of removing oneself from the everyday and ordinary, and just keeping moving. According to Bruce Chatwin, in the Islamic Sufi practice of *Siyahat,* or errance, 'the action or rhythm of walking is used as a technique for dissolving the attachments of the world and allowing men to lose themselves in God' (1987: 179). These reflections seem to suggest that travel is a state of mind as well as a state of motion, and, moreover, that the physical state of motion can induce this renewed state of mind.

For some pilgrims, this act of unburdening and cleansing the soul on the journey is augmented by the way in which they travel, specifically by the hardships they endure which can be increased by their rituals of travel, for example the practice of walking barefoot, or crawling. Within medieval Europe, penitential pilgrimages formed part of the justice system; people of all ranks in society might be condemned to exorcize their crimes by making a punitive pilgrimage. The severity of the sentence was often compounded by the insistence that the pilgrim should wear a hair shirt, or carry some special burden: murderers, for instance, sometimes had to make their journey wearing a belt constructed from the sword blade with which they had committed their crime, others may have walked on their knees, or been scourged at monasteries on their route.

For many other pilgrims, part of the transformative process of the journey has been the act of meeting and travelling with others – often complete strangers outside their normal social experience. Chaucer's lively band of pilgrims in *The Canterbury Tales* illustrate the social nature of many pilgrimages. Foster, whose book urges modern Christians to go on pilgrimage, views this sociability as an essential part of meeting Jesus on the road: 'A pilgrimage is a journey to the ultimate *otherness*. Navigating there will be a lot easier if you travel in a shoal of othernesses' (2010: 177).

The destination

While most religious traditions recognize the power of the journey itself, there is nearly always a destination for that journey – a place where one might encounter and come closer to god. The great Persian poet and Sufi mystic Rumi suggested: 'Pilgrimage to the place of the wise is to find escape from the flame of separateness.' Others have also spoken of this idea of becoming one with god by being in a special place: for example Sikh scriptures state: 'He who bathes here [in the sacred pool at Amritsar]' will find a 'mystical union with God' (Kavita, 1984).

These destinations, these holy places that enable a greater connection with god, are usually believed to be a site of theological importance: the birth place of a founding figure, the site of a miracle, or (as Rumi indicates) a place where holy or wise figures lived. Many pilgrimage destinations contain objects believed to be sacred: relics of a holy person or event, which by viewing or touching, allow pilgrims to be closer to god, to receive absolution for their sins, or to be healed of physical or mental ailments. This is true across many faiths, not least within Christianity, especially during the Middle Ages when trade in relics reached a feverish pitch and each relic in Rome had been granted by papal decree its own strength of indulgence (praying in front of or touching each relic could provide a defined amount of time off purgatory). Relics of Muhammad are venerated by many Muslims; particularly sacred are those housed at Topkapi Palace in Istanbul: Muhammad's cloak, swords, a tooth and a hair from his beard. Sacred relics of Buddha (Sarira) and Buddhist spiritual masters are housed in temples across Asia and even some in the US, including teeth, bones and mysterious crystalline objects found in the cremated ashes of leading monks. There is a strong attraction, for followers of many religions, to touch and be in the physical presence of such relics; perhaps reflecting the importance that we humans place on the sense of touch as a form of connection and a way of strengthening relationships. (see Chapter 2 'Biological Perspectives on Travel' and Chapter 3 'Travel and the Mind'). However, the worship of relics is not without its spiritual critics: within many religions there are strands that decry such practices as idolatrous, looking externally to the material world when salvation should come from within. It is thought that Martin Luther's experience of relic-worship acted as a decisive turning point in his beliefs on reformation of the Church.

The action of stepping in the footprints of a founding figure has a powerful meaning across many traditions: 'Let us worship where his feet have stood' says the Christian Psalm 132; and during the Hajj, pilgrims tread in the footsteps of Muhammad, who in turn was treading the path of Abraham. Such 'footprint worship' may also provide, as historian Eric J. Leed argues, a means for individuals and religions to legitimate and authenticate their traditions and beliefs, making them seem more real by placing them within a physical reality: 'thus does the grounding and "siting" of myth demonstrate its truth and objectivity' (1991: 145).

Even those who believe god to be in everything, often believe certain places to be closer to the sacred or spirit world: early Celtic Christians termed these 'thin places'. This conception of certain places holding a connection to something 'other worldly' or 'the sublime' can be found within non-religious thought too. As Alain de Botton points out in discussing the rise of Romanticism in the late 18th century: 'It is no coincidence that Western attraction to sublime landscapes developed at precisely the moment traditional beliefs in God began to wane ... The landscapes offered an emotional connection to a greater power' (2003: 171).

It is not just the destination itself, but the acts undertaken there that are important in many pilgrimages. These rituals are many and varied, from the offering of incense, foods and sacrifices to bathing in sacred waters and formalized prayers. Many religions require the pilgrim to be ritually cleansed – physically and often spiritually too, through acts of celibacy, abstinence and austerity – before entering the sacred site and encountering the holy. Some pilgrimage customs involve ritualized forms of travel; for example, Catholics may ascend the Scala Santa on their knees; and, during the Hajj, pilgrims walk seven times around the sacred Kaaba and walk or run seven times between the hills of Safah and Marwa (re-enacting Abraham's wife's desperate search for water).

Performing these acts in the company of other pilgrims – often thousands of other people – is itself a profound part of many pilgrimage experiences. The powerful psychological drivers to conform to group behaviour and the emotional benefits of partaking in shared rituals have been well documented by psychologists (Fiske, 2004); similarly, many pilgrims attest to the importance of shared experience. Within Islam, the Hajj is believed to be not only a demonstration of individual submission to Allah, but also an expression of the solidarity and unity of all Muslims. This intention is translated into real changes in attitudes: research shows that Hajjis (those who have completed the Hajj) express increased belief in peace, equality and harmony among Islamic sects, ethnic groups and non-Muslims (Clingingsmith et al, 2009). And civil rights leader Malcolm X (1964) claimed, after his experience of the Hajj, that 'on this pilgrimage, what I have seen, and experienced, has forced me to rearrange much of my thought patterns previously held [about harmony between different races].' By sharing ritualized experiences with others, the spiritual power of the pilgrimage is increased, perhaps resulting in a closer unity not only with god but also with other humans.

Challenges and contradictions in pilgrimage

'Unworthy' motivations

There are many other motives that people may have for making pilgrimages, some of which might seem far from the spiritual considerations above. But as with any human undertaking, motives may have many layers, intertwined and sometimes inseparable. Whether the passengers on medieval Venetian ships crossing from Europe to the Holy Land were pilgrims funding their voyage by selling cloth, or merchants gaining safe passage under the guise of pilgrimage, may have been difficult for even those travellers themselves to define. Likewise, the desire for adventure, to see the sights and to return with tales to tell, have long been recognized as potential motives for pilgrimage: as early as the 4th century, St Augustine had denounced such travelling for curiosity's sake as 'an interruption and distraction from our prayers'.

Criticism of these more 'worldly' motivations highlights a view that is common to many religious thinkers: that travel in itself is not sufficient, but when undertaken with heart and mind appropriately focused, the process of travel enables the traveller to be transformed in some way – to be cleansed of sins or to become closer to god. As the immensely popular 19th-century preacher Charles Spurgeon (1885) explained: 'A company of pilgrims who had left their hearts at home would be no better than a caravan of carcasses, quite unfit to blend with living saints in adoring the living God.'

Staying still: the 'inner journey'

'All pilgrimages should be stopped', declared Martin Luther in 1520, arguing that they 'give countless occasions to commit sin and to despise God's commandments'. Similar sentiments – although often less vehemently stated – have echoed down the ages and across different traditions. To some, the road threatens distractions and dangers for the soul. Within Confucianism (a philosophic-religious tradition originating in China around 500 BCE) pilgrimage is generally discouraged and has been seen as 'a threat to the stability of society' as it encourages people to abandon their responsibilities, and bands of wandering pilgrims might upset the social order of places they journeyed to (Renard, 2002). Not travelling – the act of staying at home, remaining faithful by honouring one's responsibilities and, importantly, by seeking god through contemplation and prayer – forms an important duty for many religious believers, counterbalancing the drive to go on pilgrimage. The 11th-century Sufi Mystic Abu Said explained his reasoning for not performing Hajj as follows:

> It is no great matter that you should tread under your feet a thousand miles of ground in order to visit a stone house. The true man of God sits where he is, and the celestial House (bayt al-ma'mūr) comes several times in a day and night to visit him and perform the circumambulation above his head.[2]

Some of the most devoted followers of many faiths (for example monks, nuns and hermits) often give up the ability to travel and instead live a life of confinement. Monks have been living in seclusion on Mount Athos in northern Greece since the 1st century AD. Many young Christian pilgrims and students of all nationalities (although all are men, for women are not allowed) make the difficult journey to this monastic enclave to experience the atmosphere of dedication and unworldliness that pervades the peninsula; but the monks themselves, who have often lived there for the greater part of their lives, hardly – if ever – leave the sacred peninsula. Such places may be travel objectives for some, but for those who have chosen that way of life, they offer a place away from the distractions of the world that travel can bring; such isolation perhaps allows the spirit to travel rather than the body.

And here is an important point: that many who talk of staying still physically, still talk of a journey – an 'inner journey' of the heart, spirit or mind. The transformative power of travel is recognized by such adherents: the journey that the spirit makes in coming closer to god. As we have seen, pilgrimage involves not just physical movement but an inward intention too. Perhaps for some believers such an inward journey can be made by staying still; but it seems that for many, it is the act of physical travel that helps give them 'new eyes' and an opened heart.

Protecting god's creation

Modern pilgrims are coming up against another challenge to the appropriateness of pilgrimage, one that has practical, ethical and theological elements: pilgrimages are damaging the local and global environment. With increasing global population (an estimated 90 per cent of whom are religious), and the increasing availability of cheap, often international, transport options, the number of pilgrims seems to be growing. Such large-scale movement of people has devastating environmental impacts, both in terms of the carbon produced in transporting them and the impacts on pilgrimage sites and host areas (see also Chapter 14 'Travel's Place in the Environment'). For example, Mecca, being located in a desert ecosystem, suffers particularly from water stress; air pollution also exceeds recommended safe levels during the pilgrimage. Muslim journalist Ruqaya Izzidien advised:

> [P]ilgrims – particularly those who live far from Saudi Arabia – should consider the ecological damage caused every time they fly several thousand miles to Mecca. The Muslim Prophet only completed Hajj once and if a single trip was adequate for him, it should be sufficient to those who wish to mirror him.[3]

Such a concern becomes particularly pressing to many (would-be) pilgrims when interpreted in the light of their religious beliefs about care for the environment: there is an imperative within many religions to look after the Earth, as part of god's creation, as well as wanting to protect the holy site itself. Pope Francis has stated that: 'A Christian who does not protect creation, who does not let it grow, is a Christian who does not care about the work of God; that work that was born from the love of God for us.' With these sorts of concerns in mind, some religious believers are trying to raise awareness in their communities and to work together with those of other faiths to address how to make pilgrimage more environmentally sustainable (for example the Green Pilgrimage Network). Pilgrimage, with its roots deep in the origins of human religious belief, is thus ever evolving as the world changes; but the basic urge to travel, and the transformative power of those journeys, remains the same.

Travel for 'holy war'

A less pacific motivation for religious travel is the act of 'holy war'. Such action has been sanctioned across various faiths throughout history, often with the aim of converting non-believers or establishing religious supremacy over a territory. These wars are frequently championed by religious leaders and can offer some form of spiritual reward to those involved. An early example can be seen in the campaigns of Muhammad, the prophet of Islam, and his followers. From 622 CE Muhammad engaged in a number of military campaigns to subdue the tribes of Arabia and establish the supremacy of Islam in the region. In the following decades his followers conquered most of the Middle East and north Africa in order to establish a caliphate: an Islamic state under the leadership of a *caliph* – a leader who claimed to be a successor of Muhammad. During the classical era of Islam one of the meanings of *jihad*, or religious struggle, was in a military sense to fight the unbelievers, and some theorists argued this was an obligation on Muslim leaders (see Bonner, 2006; Khadduri, 1955; Lewis, 1993). A fighter engaged in *jihad* was termed a *mujahid* (plural: *mujahideen*), and associated with this concept was a belief that one who died engaging in *jihad al-sayf* (*jihad* of the sword) would become a martyr, or *shahid*, and was thereby promised travel to that greatest of all locations – paradise.[4] In the modern era, the interpretation of *jihad* as a form of holy war has undergone a revival among hardline Islamists, and *mujahideen* may travel great distances to foreign lands in order to pursue this quest.

The medieval crusades, a series of wars sanctioned by the Roman Church in the 11th–13th centuries, were considered at the time as a form of armed pilgrimage to recover Jerusalem. Although to modern minds the two types of religious travel may seem quite distinct, the same term *peregrinatio* was used for both activities throughout the 11th and 12th centuries. And many of the personal motivations for undertaking armed or unarmed pilgrimage were the same, whether those were spiritual considerations (such as absolution of sins and performance of an act of devotion), or more 'worldly' aims (like desire for adventure, economic gain, or social status). Protection of Christian pilgrimage routes and sacred sites within the 'Holy Land' was one of the key motivating factors behind the Roman Church's call for a crusade against the Islamic leaders who controlled that area. While the factors driving the crusades were complex (often involving the power politics of the elites), pilgrimage and crusade were both enmeshed within the same religious beliefs and were carried out within the same geographical spaces.[5] Whatever the motivations for holy wars, as with all violent conflict they result in great human suffering and often entail the enforced travel of refugees fleeing for their lives.

Travel for holy war can, therefore, be seen as related not only to pilgrimage but also to the other types of religious travel that I will explore in the remaining pages of this chapter: the act of spreading the faith to non-believers (missionary travel) and the enforced travel of those who must escape wars of persecution.

Missionary travel: spreading the word

Another strong motivation for travel in major religions has been missionary activity: the spreading of the faith among different peoples, sometimes accompanied by practical assistance to host communities but other times by violence and forced conversion. Missionary activity has been particularly prominent in Christianity, where Jesus Christ

Figure 7.3: *John Wesley preaching to native American Indians* (engraving)

The urge to 'spread the faith' has been a motivating factor in many millions of missionary journeys, including the travels of English evangelist John Wesley in the 1730s. Missionary travel has spread faiths across the globe, but has also played a role in colonial expansion and the destruction of other cultures.

commanded his followers to make disciples in all nations (Matthew 28:19–20); and in Islam, where Dawah or the 'invitation' to Islam was practised by Muhammad and his followers. Buddhism has also been 'a missionary religion' since its beginning, with Buddha telling his disciples:

> Go ye forth for the good of the many, for the welfare of the many, out of compassion for the world. Let no two of you go in the same direction, teach the Dhamma that is beautiful in the beginning, middle and end, expound both the spirit and the letter of the holy life completely fulfilled, perfectly pure.[6]

The Bahá'í faith is a small but fast growing religion whose numbers have risen to 7.3 million since the religion's foundation in the late 19th century. This impressive increase has much to do with its effective 'pioneering' (they prefer this term to 'missionary', which they feel implies bribery and coercion rather than the 'teaching' they aim for). Although some religions, most notably Judaism, generally oppose missionary activity, many religions today embrace societies that promote the spread of their faith and writings, even those not thought of traditionally as missionary in nature, including Hinduism, Sikhism and Jainism.

It is difficult to find numbers for missionary activity across all religions but in 2005 an estimated 1.6 million Christians went on short-term mission trips (an average of eight days) from the US. In addition, some estimates suggest there are nearly half a million long-term Christian missionaries around the world, about a quarter of whom are from the US (followed by Brazil and South Korea).[7] Although the US sends the most missionaries abroad of any country, many other countries have active missionary organizations of different faiths sending people to travel and settle abroad, and within their own country, for the short or long term. Within Islam, it is estimated that the Saudi government has spent around US$45 billion funding mosques and schools around the world as part of its Dawah activities. The Ahmadiyya sect (who believe themselves to be Muslim, although they are not accepted by some Islamic authorities), has active missionary programmes, particularly in Africa, with an estimated 1,800 missionaries worldwide, all of whom have graduated from Ahmadiyya university missionary training. In total, it seems, there may be a few million people travelling every year for the purposes of religious mission.

Missionary travel has also been a shaping force throughout history, whether in centrally organized or state-supported missionary drives, or in the individual activities of wandering monks and trades people. Christian missionaries spread their religion around the Mediterranean, throughout western Europe and the Middle East by 600 AD. Merchants and missionaries travelling along the silk roads helped carry religions east and west, taking Buddhism from India to China and, later, Nestorian Christianity and then Islam into central Asia and China. Arab traders and missionaries also took Islam as far as Zanzibar and Indonesia by the 13th century. From the 16th century Catholic, and later Protestant, missionaries began converting native peoples in the Americas. Across the centuries different empires conquered other peoples with the aim of not only possessing lands but also of converting those conquered peoples to their religion. As T. W. Arnold described it in his history of missionary Islam:

> In the history of the Christian church missionary activity is seen to be intermittent, and an age of apostolic fervour may be succeeded by a period of apathy and indifference, or persecution and forced conversion may take the place of the preaching of the Word; so likewise does the propaganda of Islam in various epochs of Muhammadan history ebb and flow. (1913: 8)

Such periods of zeal and persecution often brought great human suffering, and sometimes the loss of whole cultures, particularly of native tribes in the Pacific Islands and across the Americas through the action of Christian missionaries (Lewis, 1989).

Motivations

The motivations for missionary travel spring from several sources. In religions whose founding figures urged their followers to spread the faith, the motivation seems at first a simple one – to obey that command and thus obey and worship their God. But a brief look at historical and contemporary missionary activity paints a more complex picture. At an institutional level, missionary activities have sometimes been used to promote political and economic interests. In the 19th century, British missionaries took control of many islands of the South Pacific, bringing them under de facto British control. In the decades following World War II, there was, according to Norman Lewis (1989), 'the second great historical upsurge of missionary activity' mainly due to political and technological opportunities opening up Latin America to US Protestant missionaries. Many of these missionaries held the millennial belief that by converting people of all nations they were hastening the end of days and thus bringing about the Kingdom of God. But to achieve this end they sometimes worked with the support of dictatorships, loggers and mining companies in clearing native peoples they had converted from their land, and introducing them to low-paid wage labour, destroying their traditional way of life in the process.

Not all missionary activities have such negative consequences of course, and the motivations of many missionaries include the desire to help those less fortunate in a practical as well as spiritual way. Organizations such as the Alliance for Excellence in Short-term Mission, are reforming the ways short-term Christian missions are carried out with the aim that missionaries work effectively and sensitively with host communities to bring about lasting benefits, not just good feelings for the missionaries. Missionary publications abound with advice for would-be missionaries. One such article lists seven reasons to go on mission, including 'expanding the Kingdom of Jesus' and 'encountering God's heart' as well as more secular and psychological motivations, such as expanding your limited perspective, overcoming your fears, and making you more grateful for what you have (ie seeing your own life more clearly through contrast with something 'other') – all motivations that might be found in a blog extolling the benefits of secular travel. An individual may have many concurrent motivations encouraging them to go on mission, from a desire to escape home, to seek adventure and pursue a purpose, as well as more overtly 'spiritual' reasons such as working towards their own salvation and saving the souls of others. For young men of the Church of the Latter Day Saints (LDS, often known as Mormons), two years of full-time proselytizing mission is expected and, although not a requirement for continuance within the church, it is seen by many as a 'rite of passage'. This strong social pressure has resulted in a large body of missionaries worldwide: over 67,000 LDS missionaries in 399 missions in 2019.[8]

Escape from religious persecution

Throughout human history, flight from religious persecution has driven many away from their own homelands, some in search of basic safety and others to find new and more liberating horizons. The very idea of enforced travel is at the foundations of the Abrahamic religions – which together number over half of the world's population as their followers – starting with the exile of Adam and Eve. The concept of exile runs

Figure 7.4: Camp for Yazidi refugees, Iraq

Over the course of human history, countless millions have been forced to leave their homes in fear of religious persecution. Here a woman walks through the Sharya camp in Iraq set up for Yazidi people fleeing Islamic State group militants.

throughout the narratives of these religions and in the mindsets and cultural understandings of its followers. Abraham was urged by God to leave his homeland in search of the Promised Land; the Israelites were enslaved in Egypt and later exiled in Babylon. Perhaps the most classic image of all such enforced – if temporary – emigration in Christianity is the flight of the Holy Family (so often depicted in Christian art) from Bethlehem to Egypt to avoid Herod's massacre.

Travels of exile (and return) have had far-reaching consequences. For example, the Pilgrim Fathers and other early European settlers in North America came there – often at great personal danger and hardship – to attain the freedom to worship as they liked, and to govern themselves; and ideas of freedom of religious belief were built into the First Amendment of the US Constitution. Such spiritual motivation was frequently mixed with more mundane considerations, such as economic advantage or opportunity, and came at great spiritual and physical cost to the native peoples already living in the Americas.

For every emigrant motivated by a desire for spiritual freedom, there have also been many motivated by the even sharper need to escape positive religious or ethnic persecution. Examples are, sadly, to be found throughout the world both historically and today. Jewish peoples have suffered due to religious intolerance throughout their history: in 70 CE they were expelled from Jerusalem by the Romans and throughout the centuries their diaspora has been subjected to a series of pogroms or persecutions in Russia and Europe, with the 20th century witnessing the horrors of the Holocaust. A great many conflicts over the centuries have had religious aspects to them, even if religion was not their sole cause, and where these conflicts occur many people have been forced to flee for their lives across countries and continents. Examples from the 20th century alone are numerous, including the Christian Armenian genocide by the Ottoman caliphate, persecution of religious groups in Communist China and the USSR, violence between Hindus and Muslims as they moved across the newly-formed India/Pakistan frontier following independence in 1947, and religious persecution in the Balkans during the Yugoslav conflicts of the 1990s. The 21st century continues to see huge numbers of people displaced by religious violence and intolerance between those of different religions and sects: the troubles faced by Muslim Uighurs and Tibetan Buddhists in China, Rohingya Muslims and Hindus in Myanmar, and by Christians and different sects of Muslims across the Middle East are just a few examples. According to research by the Pew Centre, religious intolerance by governments and social hostilities involving religion are not decreasing, and the rise of nationalist parties may cause yet more religious conflict, and the enforced flight of people that comes with it.[9]

Religiously-affiliated persecutions and enforced displacement have changed the fate of individuals and nations, creating diaspora across the world of people of different faiths, impacting both the travellers, those left behind and people in the new lands. In the case of Judaism, such persecution and enforced flight has been reacted against in the form of Aliyah (the immigration of Jews from the diaspora to the land of Israel), an anti-diaspora movement which, following the Nazi atrocities in Europe, resulted in the formation of the state of Israel in 1948. As with many other large-scale movements of people, this has had resounding impacts on regional and global politics.

Conclusion

From the wanderings of Buddha, to the Old Testament tales of Moses's 40 years in the desert, travel is at the centre of the foundations and narratives of religions across the world. Indeed, to some believers their god is a travelling god, and they must travel in his footsteps, along the path he has shown — metaphorically and, in the case of some pilgrimages, physically also. Travel is also a religious practice of immense importance to many believers. Pilgrimage offers the promise of an encounter with god, a refreshing and cleansing of the soul. Missionary travel, commanded by the founders of some religions, enables missionaries to honour their god and save the souls of others. Enforced travel is also central to the stories of many religions and escape from religious persecution has driven many millions of people away from their homelands to the far corners of the world. Movement on such a large scale has shaped the histories of nations and empires, the results writ-large of the experiences of millions of individuals in all their variations from spiritual rapture to grief and pain.

With all these depths and complexities of motivations that religious travel illuminates, it is plain to see that travel is a great deal more than just getting from A to B. Far from being an activity that people wish to minimize, the journey is something that humans seek out as a process that will transform them spiritually. The destination is, of course, crucial too, and what those religious travellers seek is not something that can be replaced digitally: a direct encounter with a holy place or sacred object; the opportunity to spread the truth of their religion by living among other communities; or even a safe place to live and practise their own religion. Religious traditions have long recognized the power of travel to enlighten and transform; perhaps it is time that this perception of travel was adopted more broadly.

Notes

[1] www.pilgrimroutes.com/walks-of-interest/tai-shan-pilgrimage.aspx
[2] www.ibnarabisociety.org/articles/mystics-kaba.html#ftn5
[3] www.aljazeera.com/indepth/opinion/2011/03/20113221445229564.html
[4] This concept is explained in the Qur'an Suras 3 (169–70) and 9 (111), and more fully in the Hadith, *Sahid al-Bukhari*, 4:52:49, 4:52:54, 4:54:72, 5:59:318.
[5] www.britannica.com/event/Crusades/The-First-Crusade-and-the-establishment-of-the-Latin-states#ref392334
[6] www.buddhanet.net/e-learning/dharmadata/fdd31.htm
[7] According to the Center for the Study of Global Christianity (CSGC) at Gordon-Conwell Theological Seminary.
[8] https://newsroom.churchofjesuschrist.org/topic/missionary-program
[9] www.pewforum.org/2018/06/21/global-uptick-in-government-restrictions-on-religion-in-2016/

References

Arnold, T. W. (1913) *The Preaching of Islam*, London: Constable.

Bell, A. R. and Dale, R. S. (2011) 'The medieval pilgrimage business', *Enterprise and Society*, 12 (3): 601–27. doi: 10.1093/es/khr014.

Bonner, M. (2006) *Jihad in Islamic History: Doctrines and Practice*, Princeton, NJ: Princeton University Press.

de Botton, A. (2003) *The Art of Travel*, London: Penguin Books.

Chatwin, B. (1987) *The Songlines*, London: Jonathan Cape.

Clingingsmith, D., Khwaja, A. I. and Kremer, M. (2009) 'Estimating the impact of the Hajj: religion and tolerance in Islam's global gathering', *The Quarterly Journal of Economics*, 124 (3): 1133–70. doi:10.1162/qjec.2009.124.3.1133.

Fiske, S. T. (2004). *Social Beings: A Core Motives Approach to Social Psychology*, Hoboken, NJ: Wiley.

Foster, C. (2010) *The Sacred Journey*, Nashville, TN: Thomas Nelson.

Kavita, M. P. (1984) [6], quoted in W. H. Mcleod (ed) *Textual Sources for the Study of Sikhism*, Manchester: Manchester Univ Press, p 28.

Khadduri, M. (1955) *War and Peace in the Law of Islam*, Baltimore, MD: The Johns Hopkins Press.

Leed, Eric J. (1991) *The Mind of the Traveler*, New York: Basic Books.

Lewis, B. (1993) *Islam and the West*, Oxford: Oxford University Press.

Lewis, N. (1989) *The Missionaries*, New York: McGraw-Hill Companies.

Lieberman, P. (1991) *Uniquely Human*. Cambridge, MA: Harvard University Press.

Renard, J. (2002) *101 Questions Answered on Confucianism, Daoism and Shintoism*. Mahwah, NJ: Paulist Press.

Spurgeon, C. (1885) *Treasury of David* (Psalm 84:5). London: London Metropolitan Tabernacle.

X. M. (El-Hajj Malik El-Shabazz) (1964) *Letter from Mecca*. Available: https://www.malcolm-x.org/docs/let_mecca.htm

8

Travel in Art and Literature

Alison Kuznets and Matthew Niblett

Introduction

Travel lies at the heart of many of our creative enterprises – so much so that it is difficult to imagine much of our greatest art or literature without the concept of movement. In this chapter we illustrate the deep and mutually influencing relationship between travel and art (in its broadest sense): how our artistic creations have been influenced by travel, and how travel has been shaped and inspired by art. Travel enables interchange of ideas, inspiring aesthetic trends and new art forms. Travel also provides a core motif or metaphor around which we tell stories and make sense of the world: from the great epics of ancient times, to science fiction and modern travel tales of self-discovery. And travel assists the creative process itself: providing the artist with inspiration and freedom.

The links between artistic endeavour and travel are fundamental. Both seem to be instinctive behaviours, linked closely with creativity. As explained in earlier chapters (Chapter 2 'Biological Perspectives on Travel', Chapter 3 'Travel and the Mind' and Chapter 4 'Philosophy and Travel'), travel – even the *idea* of travel – can increase our creative thinking. Both travel and creativity are linked with 'novelty' and 'challenge' (two concepts of huge importance within the development of art), which are good for our brains: in the short term they make us feel good, and in the long term they make our brains healthier. This chapter, then, builds on a relationship between travel and creativity that has biological foundations, and that has been noted and used by people since at least the Ancient philosophers. Writer Paul Theroux claims: 'The nearest thing to writing a novel is travelling in a strange country. Travel is a creative act – not simply loafing and inviting your soul, but feeding the imagination, accounting for each fresh wonder, memorizing and moving on' (1985: 140).

The approach of this chapter is necessarily a specific and personal one. We have chosen to explore the links between artistic endeavour and travel by first examining the language we use: metaphors and idioms in speech and writing. We then look at how travel has inspired the creation of artistic works, and shaped the form of those creations: artistic movements, aesthetic trends, and the development of different literary and art forms. This is a two-way process in that artistic creations have themselves inspired many to travel, to step in the footsteps of the creators and to see those places for themselves. We explore the links between travel and creativity, as described by many artists and writers. And, lastly, we examine some of the travel-related themes found within oral and folk traditions, literature, films and visual arts.

Travel forms a core motif in a great many artistic works, particularly within the stories we tell in verbal and written form. The ubiquity of travel as an important theme in literature has led Peter Hulme, Emeritus Professor of Travel Writing at University of Essex, to declare that 'there is almost no statuesque literature' (cited in Youngs, 2013: 4). Others agree: for example, Professor Jan Borm defines 'travel writing' as any text dealing with the theme of a journey (2004: 13–26); and novelist Michael Mewshaw claims that 'All writing is travel writing – even if the journey is entirely inward through the obscure bends and elbows of the mind, or even if it's an intimate exploration of a body.'[1] In this chapter we will take this broad view, exploring the important roles that the idea of 'travel' plays within art and literature, beyond the conventional travel genre. We will examine how authors and artists use 'travel' within their works to introduce new ideas and sensations, and to help us to understand ourselves and the world around us.

From the vast canon of world art and literature, it has been necessary to draw some boundaries aiming, at best, to skim across time periods and genres in this short chapter. The main focus, given our native language and European home, is on literature and cinematography in English, and visual art from the Western world. For reasons of space we have not been able to delve into the realm of sculpture or textile art, music, dance, and only cursorily into poetry and oral traditions; neither have we touched on journalism and the 'foreign correspondent'. There is much more that could be said were we able to cast the net wider; but we hope that the examples and themes drawn out below illustrate the fundamental relationships between travel and artistic work; and provide fruitful insights for a better understanding of human travel.

Travel and language: a 'metaphor we live by'

The origins of the word 'travel' in English reveal that the concept has held changing meanings. In Old English the verb for travelling was *faran*, related to the modern German verb *fahren*, and reflected in some modern English words such as 'ferry', which today retains positive and active connotations. Sometime in the middle ages, however, *faran* was replaced in English usage with the word *travailen*, which was derived from the Old French *travail*, meaning to work, toil, suffer or expend painful effort. Etymologists have suggested that the French concept had an even more painful origin in the Latin term, *tripaliare*, meaning an instrument of torture! So the establishment of the word 'travel' in English, curiously for a concept so central to human existence, appears to be related to the difficult and tormenting experience of travelling in medieval times. Perhaps travellers today, when faced with airline delays or traffic queues, might reflect that the very word travel is a reminder that journeys are not always easy.

The concept has, however, had a profound influence on the language we use. According to Professor Percy Adams, 'Travelling is one of the oldest and largest clusters of metaphors in any language' (1983: 270). Adams lists examples: from the scriptures, in which 'life is a pilgrimage and those who pass through it are sojourners'; and Dante, who writes that he was 'midway on the journey of life'; to Scudery in the 1650s, writing how 'lovers wish to sail past rocks and sands that wreck true love'. These metaphors persist in everyday language today. We talk of our life as a journey, describe a need for change as 'itchy feet' or 'restlessness', or tell someone not to 'rock the boat' in a difficult situation. At an important decision point we are 'at a crossroads' needing to 'choose which path to take': perhaps we should 'forge our own path' or 'take the road less travelled'. All manner of processes are linked to a journey: life, birth, death, careers, love, arguments, recovery from injury or trauma, and thought processes. As Adams indicates, this is true in languages beyond the anglophone world. For example, in French *Y aller par quatre chemins* (to get there by four paths), means avoiding the core of the subject in a discussion; and in Russian *Галопом по Европам* (galloping across Europe) means to do something hastily or haphazardly.

Figure 8.1: *The Gulf Stream*, **by Winslow Homer (1899)**

This painting, by American artist Winslow Homer, depicts a strong sense of the 'travail' aspects of sea travel. Created shortly after the death of his father, many have interpreted the work as an expression of the artist's sense of mortality.

This use of metaphor in speaking and writing is more than just 'rhetorical flourish'. According to cognitive psychologists Lakoff and Johnson, 'our ordinary conceptual system, in terms of which we both think and act, is fundamentally metaphorical in nature' (1980: 3). If this view is correct, then the ubiquity of the travel metaphor indicates that much of our thought, action and language is shaped by our idea of travel. To borrow Lakoff and Johnson's phrase, travel is a 'metaphor we live by'.

Travel inspiring artistic creativity, and art inspiring travel

Development of artistic forms

Travel, particularly that which involves encounters with new landscapes and cultures, has had a powerful influence on the development and style of many different artistic forms. In turn these have helped to define aesthetic tastes and cultural trends. The Grand Tour beloved of European aristocratic travellers, for instance, with its emphasis on visiting sites from Roman and Greek antiquity, helped to foster an obsession with classical forms and ideas from the 17th century onwards. This in turn was reflected in the artistic achievements of the period, through the works of artists such as Claude Lorrain and Nicolas Poussin, whose neoclassical paintings using idealistic forms from classical civilization were widely considered the height of taste and fashion. In the 18th century, an increase in travel and trade between east Asia and Europe encouraged a fashion for artistic creations that reflected what Europeans believed were Chinese or Japanese motifs. The obsession with *chinoiserie* ranged from artists such as the Rococo painter Francois Boucher, to architecture and garden design – Sir William Chambers's pagoda at Kew Gardens and Catherine the Great's Chinese Village are good examples – to the decorative arts including ceramics and furniture. Interest in the Middle East during the 19th century, following Napoleon's invasion of Egypt, led to an orientalist turn in European art, with themes from lands of the Ottoman empire featuring widely in the art of popular painters such as Eugene Delacroix, William Holman Hunt and John Frederick Lewis. The use of such themes could be used to shock and challenge viewers: Jean-August-Dominique Ingres's *The Turkish Bath* (1862) was notorious for its eroticism and challenge to conventional rules on perspective, such that it was suppressed until 1905 when it influenced a new generation of artists including a young Pablo Picasso. The ability to instil in one's audience a sense of places and cultures far away was crucial for the impact and effect of such artistic creations.

The interest in travel and movement has influenced painters and visual artists in various ways. In China, the depiction of natural landscapes had a long pedigree, related to the Taoist belief in the sacred nature of places such as mountains and waterfalls. The Shan Shui artistic school often depicted meandering pathways, rivers, and a threshold destination at the end of the path, often a mountain. Scroll paintings, such as the revered *Along the River During the Qingming Festival* by the 12th-century artist Zhang Zeduan, could also depict narratives and travelling peoples in a way that foreshadows later cinematic forms. In European art, the growth in personal travel during the 17th and 18th centuries led to a new genre based on painting views of famous urban scenes, known as *vedute*, which travellers could take home with them as a souvenir and reminder of their visit. The centre of this activity was Venice, led by artists such as Canaletto, Guardi and Michele Marieschi, whose skill at capturing the life and architecture of the city made their works enormously popular. Canaletto later was lured to England where he painted many classic scenes of London, while other *vedutistas* emerged catering for tourists in Rome and Paris.

In the 19th century, impressionistic painters began to explore not only new themes associated with speed and movement, but also moved

Figure 8.2: *Entrance to the Grand Canal from the Molo, Venice,* **by Canaletto (1742/44)**

This depicts a *vedute*, or view, of Venice, painted by Canaletto. Such images were popular with English travellers on The Grand Tour.

away from realism to create a stronger sense of the feelings that particular places or modes of travel aroused. J. M. W. Turner's *Rain, Steam and Speed* (1844), in which a locomotive emerges out of a blur of mist and smoke, provided a startling illustration of how technology was transforming our sense of velocity, while later French impressionists, such as Claude Monet and Camille Pissarro, depicted urban landscapes in London and Paris in a radically different way to the realistic scenes of the *vedute*. Modern art has also had its occasional obsessions with speed, movement and the thrill of travel. The futurist movement in Italy aimed to celebrate 'a new beauty, the beauty of speed' (Marinetti, 1909), and artists in this school tried to depict something of the energy, dynamism and rush associated with modern living. The British Vorticist movement took this further, with artists such as David Bomberg and Wyndham Lewis depicting motion and the frenetic pace of modernity through bold and jagged lines drawing the eye into the centre of their canvas. The true modern heirs of the *vedute*, however, are probably photographic artists: the works of landscape photographers such as Ansel Adams, Cath Simard and Michael Kenna have brought distant wild places into the homes and hearts of many would-be travellers.

Figure 8.3: *The Tetons and the Snake River,* **by Ansel Adams (1942)**

The photographs of Ansel Adams, such as this taken in Grand Teton National Park, Wyoming, reflect an experience of nature and the wild as sublime and spiritual.

Development of literary forms

Travel has also had a central role in the development of literary forms. In his essay 'Anywhere Out of the World', the author and critic Nicholas Delbanco argues that all writing is travel writing. 'The common denominator of the *Odyssey* and *Pilgrim's Progress, The Canterbury Tales* and *The Divine Comedy'* Delbanco suggests, 'is near-constant motion.' On this basis, the writer is almost always taking the reader on a journey. Even if an author is confined or imprisoned, Delbanco makes the case that 'each and all of them are travel writers in the largest sense: I have been there, witnessed it, and am come alone to tell thee what I saw' (2005: 57–74).

In the dramatic arts, early actors would form travelling companies of players, often performing folk tales of quests or re-enacting key journeys from the Bible, from the nativity to the passion story. During the renaissance of English theatre through the Elizabethan period, playwrights would frequently locate their plays overseas. Shakespeare set about three-quarters of his plays in foreign lands, in locations from Denmark to Spain to Syria, although his favourite was

Italy. Intriguingly, he probably never visited any of these places, yet he understood the fascination of his audience with far-away settings, with Italy in particular having a compelling reputation for passion, violence and high culture. Travelling is also a central theme in many of Shakespeare's plays, particularly by sea, including the shipwrecks that form key parts of the plot in *Twelfth Night* and *The Tempest*, Hamlet's ill-fated voyage to England, or the sea battles that feature in *Othello* and *Anthony and Cleopatra* (Maquerlot and Willems, 1996). The stage, although static, provides a remarkable place for the imagination to wander.

Perhaps the literary form with the deepest connection to travel has been the novel. Percy Adams, in his *Travel Literature and the Evolution of the Novel* (1983), shows how the novel came into being in the early modern period, and the ways in which travel accounts and discussions influenced early novelists. If one looks at the early development of the form and its characters, from Cervantes's knight errant in *Don Quixote* (1605–15) to Daniel Defoe's castaway in *Robinson Crusoe* (1719) or Jonathan Swift's gentleman adventurer in *Gulliver's Travels* (1726) it is striking how often travel and wandering are used as a form of satire or to help illustrate personal development. During the later 18th century, travel became a central motif in a new form of fiction, the Gothic romance, in which the supernatural and wanderings allowed the imagination to run riot. Ann Radcliffe's popular novel *The Mysteries of Udolpho* (1794), which strongly influenced Jane Austen among others, explored the misadventures of a heroine who travels through untamed landscapes in France and Italy. Even Austen illuminated the plots of her 'novels of manners' by contrasting life in different parts of England, although the landscapes featured here are usually less 'wild'. Frequent country walks and outings enable Austen's heroines to have chance encounters as well as the opportunity to think, showing us the transformative power of travel, in narrative and emotional terms (Solnit, 2014). Later Gothic novels, notably Mary Shelley's *Frankenstein* (1818) and Bram Stoker's *Dracula* (1897) also involve travel through strange and wild landscapes in search of knowledge and the supernatural. This phenomenon was not limited to European literature: some critics have argued that the Japanese novel derives from their tradition of travel diaries, such as those produced by the 17th-century poet Matsuo Bashō, most notably *The Narrow Road to the Interior*: an account of his dangerous journey on foot across Edo-era Japan (Adams, 1983: 37).

Travel themes provide a powerful opportunity to explore human psychology and offer a counterpoint to and a critique of society at home. Joseph Conrad, for example, used long voyages and journeys in novels such as *Heart of Darkness*, *Lord Jim* and *Nostromo* to create an extraordinary sense of how danger, mystery and the unknowable can affect the human mind. In the 20th century, travel has also been used by novelists to provide a deeper sense of the complications of globalization and inter-continental migration. The Nobel laureate V. S. Naipaul saw himself as both a novelist and a travel writer, and used the various settings of his novels in the Caribbean, Africa and South America to explore the legacies of empire. Naipaul blurs the lines between fiction and travel narrative: in the view of Percy Adams, Naipaul's 'novels are travel books' and his 'récits de voyage are novels'.

Science fiction is a genre highly reliant on travel narratives. From the pen (or rather keyboard) of authors from H. G. Wells to Douglas Adams and Liu Cixin, novels that involve interstellar encounters have proven some of the most popular in modern fiction. The mass appeal of this genre perhaps is due to its ability to provide new avenues for journeys across space and time, far beyond our own world, while at the same time plugging into the rapid pace of scientific and technological change that we are all experiencing.

Development of cinematography

In the early 20th century moving pictures created a new artistic form and provided a fresh way to convey the idea of travel. The very nature of film had motion at its core and allowed directors to add a visual dimension to those stories they wished to tell. Some of the earliest films were travelogues, bringing the sights of faraway places to a new audience, while the era of silent film ensured that there would be a strong emphasis on visual movement to compensate for the lack of sound. The slapstick comedies of Buster Keaton or the swashbuckling action films of Douglas Fairbanks are good examples, but even in more recent films the recurring themes of car chases, aircraft dogfights or train journeys are testament to the ability of film to convey the thrill of movement. The ability to take the audience to new worlds has also been a strong influence in the history of film. Sometimes this has been developed through science fiction films, with classic examples being Stanley Kubrick's *2001: A Space Odyssey* (1968) or Andrei Tarkovsky's *Solaris* (1972); others have modified depictions of travel from great novels, such as Francis Ford Coppola's translation of Joseph Conrad's *Heart of Darkness* from the Congo to the jungles of Vietnam in *Apocalypse Now* (1979). Film has also provided an artistic outlet to depict some of the travel motivations explored elsewhere in this volume, whether that be pilgrimage, as in Emilio Estevez's *The Way* (2010), which shows the *camino* to Santiago de Compostela; the adventurer's quest, as in Ang Lee's *Crouching Tiger, Hidden Dragon* (2000); or the concept of wanderlust, depicted in films such as Walter Salles's *The Motorcycle Diaries* (2004) or Sean Penn's *Into the Wild* (2007).

Travel and the creative impulse

Many artists and writers have found they need to travel to undertake their creative work. The author Suzanne Joinson has written that, for her, travel is 'a compulsion, like a tic, like a bad habit'. She explains that the reason why travel is so compelling is because 'stories involve movement of one sort or another: a linking of memory, a series of events, a chain of internal shifts, and a negotiation between faraway and home' (2016). Even when writers are not physically travelling, they often describe the process of creation as a form of travel. The Chilean Nobel laureate Pablo Neruda, himself a veteran traveller who spent many years outside his own country, explained this mysterious process succinctly: 'when I'm writing, I'm far away; and when I've come back, I've gone'. This relationship is also evident in the careers of writers and artists, for example Robert Louis Stevenson, whose journeys to France, America and the South Pacific have been shown to correlate with important turning points in the evolution of his narrative style (Zulli, 2014).

For artists, the ability to move and paint outside became an important consideration in the nineteenth century with the development of the field easel. The interest in painting outdoors, *en plein air*, was particularly important for the French Barbizon school and later the impressionists, and artists like John Singer Sargent (1856–1925). They believed that natural light and the ability to witness and depict various weather conditions was a major benefit for their craft. Other artists travelled further afield and found inspiration in the places they visited. The French romantic painter Eugène Delacroix travelled widely in north Africa and was entranced by what he found, resulting in over 100 works of art based on the life of the people he witnessed. Later, the post-impressionist artist Paul Gauguin found his muse in the South Pacific island of Tahiti, the setting for many of his most audacious and distinctive paintings.

Art inspiring travel

If travel has been a major inspiration for artistic creation, it is also clear that works of art, literature and film have acted as a key motivation

Figure 8.4: *An Out-of-Doors Study*, **by John Singer Sargent (1889)**

Artists such as Sargent (himself a widely travelled expatriate American), felt that it benefited their art to travel and paint outdoors *en plein air*. This image depicts Sargent's friend, French artist Paul Helleu, painting at Fladbury, in the Cotswolds.

for their readers and viewers to make journeys to destinations beyond just the famous art galleries. Today, cultural tourism has become a major international business. In part, this is because the world of a book, film or great work of art can help to drive the experience of a traveller, led by the imaginative desire to escape what is often a mundane reality. The phenomenon of literary tourism has been described as a form of secular pilgrimage, seeking out not a saint but the inspiration that drove a particular artist or writer. Long-distance walks have been created for such purposes, such as the Thomas Hardy Way in Dorset, or the Robert Louis Stevenson Trail, which follows the 12-day hill-trek described in Stevenson's *Travels with a Donkey through the Cévennes* (1879). The Van Gogh trail in St-Rémy-de-Provence winds through the arid Provençal countryside, with its silver-leafed olive trees and twisted cypresses, encouraging the traveller to sense the special qualities of the landscape reflected in Van Gogh's celebrated works.

Perhaps the artistic form that today generates the most travel, however, is film, aided by the ability of cinematographers to promote the visual beauty of places and landscapes. New Zealand, which was the location for Peter Jackson's *Lord of the Rings* trilogy (2001–03), saw a 40 per cent increase in tourism in the five years after the first film's release, while the New Zealand tourist board adopted the film-inspired slogan 'Home of Middle Earth'. Other locations which have seen a rise in travellers as a result of film productions include Lyme Park, the setting for Pemberley in the BBC's 1995 adaptation of *Pride and Prejudice*; the Austrian village of Hallstatt, reputedly the inspiration for the fairytale town Arendelle in the Disney film *Frozen* (2013); and the Greek island of Skiathos, the setting for the hit film *Mamma Mia!* (2008). Many such travellers seem to be partaking in a peculiar blurring of the boundaries between reality and fantasy: such destinations are often more important to them as a reflection of the imagination inspired by the film, than as a real place independent of being a cinematic location.

Travel themes within the arts

The journey stands as a metaphor for, or allegory of, life and death in many art works, (often strongly influenced by religious texts, which commonly use this theme – see Chapter 7 'Religious and Spiritual Travel'). Author Jonathan Raban even describes the ideal of a journey as 'a miniature scale-model life'.[2] One of the most famous and influential examples of travel as an allegory for life is John Bunyan's *The Pilgrim's Progress* (1678), which describes the journey of 'everyman' Christian, from his hometown, the City of Destruction ('this world'), to the Celestial City' ('that which is to come'), facing difficulties and temptations along the way. In these works travel plays an important role beyond narrative impetus, standing as a symbol or vehicle for other themes and issues, as we will examine in the following section.

Hardship and the spiritual journey

Suffering is a feature of many depictions of travel in art and literature (reflecting the etymological origins of travel). *The Odyssey,* one of the most formative texts in Western literature, depicts travel as a state of hardship, with sufferings inflicted by vengeful and capricious higher powers (see Chapter 9 'Why People Travel: An Anthropological View'). In medieval literature too, particularly in literature of the Crusades, 'suffering and striving, mental and physical are constant themes' (Whitfield, 2011: 20). Journeys of loss and alienation are also a feature of many stories: Shakespeare uses the idea of travel to illustrate decline and dystopia, most evidently in *King Lear*; and in Conrad's *Heart of Darkness* the brutality and isolation of the Congolese setting has a profound effect on Marlow – the visitor.

In some of these stories, this suffering is purposeless, no spiritual enlightenment is gained, no great truths are revealed; and this may hint at a particular view of life itself, in which suffering is inevitable and without spiritual purpose. English professor Dan Vogel suggests a classification system for the many types of travel that appear across literature. Among these is 'the odyssey', a tale of travel in which 'the physical movement itself has no particular ostensible spiritual significance'. As well as Homer's epic, Vogel offers modern examples, including Hemingway's *The Sun Also Rises,* which follows a group of British and American ex-patriates (all of whom have been greatly affected by World War I) as they travel between Paris and Spain in the 1920s. In Vogel's view, 'the existential absence of a mission may very well be the author's point in writing the odyssey. The journeying from one group-decided place to another without real motivation signifies the spiritual sterility of the characters in the novel. Thus this odyssey reflects the "lost generation" era of its composition' (1974: 188).

More numerous than the spiritually purposeless odysseys, are the narratives of 'quest': a great journey undertaken with a mission of some moral or spiritual purpose (Vogel 1974). This type of travel narrative is enormously broad and important, encompassing knights, kings, hobbits, shepherd boys, beat poets, gap-year students and disaffected 30-somethings. Quests, whether grand and heroic, or more pedestrian, encompass some sort of inner journey towards better self-knowledge for the protagonist. In his literary history of travel, Peter Whitfield describes this as 'the archetypal paradigm of travel … the conviction that travel is deeply purposeful: as we move through space, we are changed, we discover, and we are transformed' (2011: 38). Ancient texts show us the importance of the quest far back in human history. Gilgamesh, the Bronze Age Sumerian king, questing for eternal life (see Chapter 9 'Why People Travel: An Anthropological View'), Jason and his Argonauts seeking the golden fleece and Hercules voyaging to the western-most limits of the Mediterranean world during his labours.

Sometimes the purpose of these dangerous journeys is the establishment of a new homeland: travel is often a key feature of foundation myths (see Chapter 7 'Religious and Spiritual Travel' and

Chapter 9 'Why People Travel: An Anthropological View'). In the Hebrew Bible, for example, the Exodus tells the founding myth of the Israelites: who are liberated from slavery in Egypt and leave via the parting of the Red Sea, cross the Sinai desert and wander in the wilderness for 40 years before they can enter the land promised to them. This story, argues Whitfield, is about group identity and formation: 'a journey so important that it forged the consciousness of a people… the death of the old life and the awakening of the new' (2011:10). Similarly Virgil's *Aeneid*, describes the 'Long labors, both by sea and land' of Trojan Aeneas and his men, who settled in Italy where he founded Rome.[3] Whitfield maintains this is 'a pagan equivalent of the Exodus story, the myth of the founding of a nation through a great and terrible journey' (2011: 11).

The hero's quest, and the spiritual journey through suffering, continued to be popular themes throughout the pre-Modern period. For example the Anglo-Saxon *Beowulf*, and medieval chivalric romances such as *Gawain and the Green Knight* and Sir Thomas Malory's *Le Morte d'Arthur*. Dante's *Divine Comedy*, one of the key texts of medieval European literature, describes the author's journey beyond the known world into successive spheres of the universe: a journey that involves 'purification through suffering and awakening' (Whitfield, 2011: 38).

Many of the best-selling books and associated films of modern times continue this motif of quest, hardship and self-transformation: for example, Tolkein's *Lord of the Rings* (1954), Paulo Coelho's *The Alchemist* (1988), and even popular Disney animations such as *Moana* (2016). These all fit the archetype of the 'hero's journey'. This idea, popularized by Joseph Campbell, is a narrative pattern found across many myths in which: 'A hero ventures forth from the world of common day into a region of supernatural wonder: fabulous forces are there encountered and a decisive victory is won: the hero comes back from this mysterious adventure with the power to bestow boons on his fellow man' (1949: 23).

The idea of travel as a means of gaining insight and self-knowledge has a long history in the West and East. St Augustine, in the 4th century, was a believer in the importance of travel as a means to reflect on one's self, and counselled that many travellers did not take sufficient care to do so (Whitfield, 2011: 37). The 16th-century *Journey to the West*, considered as one of the four great classical novels of Chinese literature, is an account of a Buddhist monk's pilgrimage to India, a journey of spiritual enlightenment through physical travel (and also a satire on Chinese bureaucracy, a comic adventure story, and a retelling

Figure 8.5: *Sir Galahad – the Quest for the Holy Grail,* **by Arthur Hughes (1870)**

The adventures of King Arthur and his knights have inspired poems, novels, films and paintings, depicting the 'quest' and travel with a spiritual purpose. The pre-Raphaelites, and many of their sympathisers like Arthur Hughes, were particularly fond of these Arthurian themes, often inspired by the poetry of Tennyson.

of many traditional folk tales). Byron believed that 'the great object in life is "to feel that we exist": the three experiences that he believed gave life's richest rewards were gambling, battle and travel'. (Whitfield, 2011: 184).

It has been argued that the emphasis on personal tales of self-discovery has become stronger in modern times, beginning in earnest in the 19th century. According to Whitfield: 'whatever the avowed motive, behind all major travel texts of the century lay the interaction of the self with the outside world, as the European psyche refined itself, seeking knowledge and power, but also self-understanding, through this deliberately sought encounter with the world' (2011: 181). As technological and social change has opened up travel to an ever-wider audience, we see this trend also in the 20th and 21st centuries across travel literature, films, podcasts and blogs, in which the inner journey can be used as a means of critiquing the outer journey. As Colleen McElroy, American poet and author, writes: 'Partly, I travel to discover more about myself. My journeys have taught me that a definition of who I am cannot be mapped on the simple black-and-white limits of stateliness and borders' (1997: ii).

Freedom and self-identity

Travel offers an opportunity for freedom, to escape from the constraints of home, achieve independence, even remake oneself. It is often portrayed as a rite of passage. In Laurie Lee's *As I Walked Out One Midsummer Morning*, the author, aged 19, leaves his small village (and the bucolic life there, depicted in *Cider with Rosie*) and walks across southern England and then Spain. 'I was propelled', writes Lee, 'by the traditional forces that had sent so many generations along this road – by the small tight valley closing in around one, stifling the breath with its mossy mouth, the cottage walls narrowing like the arms of an iron maiden, the local girls whispering 'Marry, and settle down' (1971: 12). Within a few hours of leaving, Lee felt 'I was free. I was affronted by freedom' (1971:13). In his review of the book, Robert Macfarlane writes about Lee's precise style that is 'voluptuous' with details:

> He gathered these details as he walked, and he could not have done so had he not opened himself to the kinds of encounter and perception that travel on foot makes possible. Walking, Lee notes early on, refines awareness: it compels you to 'tread' a landscape 'slowly', to 'smell its different soils' … Lee, like [travel writer] Leigh Fermor, believed in walking not only as a means of motion but also as a means of knowing.[4]

Walking may constitute freedom to these authors, but to many the lure of the open road involves the speed and independence of the motor. Jack Kerouac's *On the Road* became a 'bible to any aspiring bohemian' writes journalist Sean O'Hagan:

> I was given a battered copy by an older friend and, even before I read it, knew that it carried within its pages some deep, abiding truth about youth, freedom and self-determination. *On the Road* instilled in me a belief that, in order to find oneself, one had to throw caution to the wind and travel long distances with no real goal and very little money.[5]

The 1969 box-office hit *Easy Rider* also associates travel with freedom and an opportunity to find a new, more authentic life – albeit one that ends differently than intended. According to film professor Emmanuel Levy, the film was a 'travel poster for a new America, encouraging people to hit the road for themselves in search of an ideal lifestyle. A classic road narrative, *Easy Rider* begins as a hymn to the openness and vastness of the American land, and ends as a tragic vision of the American Dream.'[6]

D. H. Lawrence and Lawrence Durrell are two 20th-century British writers who, according to Lata Marina Varghese, both use travel as means of escape within their works. Dr Varghese argues that in Lawrence's book *Sea and Sardinia* and Durrell's *Sicilian Carousel* 'travel is seen as a metaphor for both discovering one's identity and also in discovering the spirit of the place/landscape.'[7] Indeed many of Lawrence's books reflect the role of both physical and spiritual travel in enabling escape from his early emotional and working class background in a Midlands mining community.

According to Freud, the linking of travel and escape have deep-rooted origins: 'a great part of the pleasure of travel lies in the fulfillment of these early wishes to escape the family and especially the father' (cited in Wise, 2009: 133). Novelist Michael Mewshaw argues that 'travel may be viewed as a rebellious, even a subversive act, part of the process of self-actualization. I travel to define and assert my existential identity. I travel. Therefore I am.'[8]

Understanding the 'other'

A major theme of travel-related art and literature is the importance of improved understanding of the 'other', of people and places perceived to be 'exotic', different or unfamiliar. The purposes for such an understanding, however, can vary widely, including curiosity and wonder, the desire to conquer or exert power, or a better understanding of oneself and home through comparison and contrast.

Many ancient travel accounts, while describing foreign lands and peoples, tend to focus on the superiority of the author's culture and on the idea of conquest. This is apparent in the accounts of the travels of Alexander the Great, and in Caesar's writings about his own campaigns, which are told in a political narrative that portrays himself and Rome as superior. As Whitfield writes: '"I came, I saw, I conquered" is hardly an ideal credo for the travel writer but it surfaces again and again' (2011:10). Similarly the works of Herodotus and Xenophon, from the 5th century BCE, both emphasize the superiority of the Greeks over the peoples described in their works. And accounts written during the 'Age of Discovery' focused on the usefulness of knowledge of the unfamiliar in terms of economic and political dominance and utility to governance 'back home' (see Chapter 9 'Why People Travel: An Anthropological View' and Chapter 11 'Travel as Exploration').

Many travel guidebooks (the earliest known examples date to antiquity: see Chapter 10 'Tourist Travel') aim to help the traveller to fulfil their curiosity, wonder, and education, rather than to promote a sense of superiority or desire to conquer. Those who create art and literature about their travels often develop a deep appreciation for the people, cultures and landscapes they have encountered – an appreciation that they convey powerfully in their work.

Travel-related art and literature can help the development of empathy with others. Some commentators argue that this is one of the most important features of good travel writing, exemplified by authors such as Andrew Solomon and Colin Thubron.[9] Travel and art are both ways of practising and enabling empathy, of trying to put ourselves into the place of another, and therefore better understanding ourselves and our world. A recent multimedia storytelling project called *Migration Trail* uses this link between empathy and travel in an innovative way. Through maps, data, audio and social media, the project tells the (fictionalized) personal stories of migrant journeys across Europe, which can be experienced in real time over a period of ten days, making the audience member a participant. The project aims to increase understanding and empathy around the realities of modern-day migration, beyond what we see in the mass media.[10]

Childhood and travel

Children are an important and eager audience for a great many works of art, literature, musical and oral story-telling – and travel is a core motif in a great number of these works. Folk tales and fairytales often contain an instructive or moral element and are a useful source of knowledge about the beliefs and attitudes of the past, reflecting some of the fears and preoccupations that people once – and sometimes still – hold. In many of these tales, the road is a dangerous place: for some it brings the chance for heroism, for others it highlights vulnerability. Often this difference is gendered. Little Red Riding Hood, for example, is vulnerable travelling through the dangerous forest (saved by a strong man), as are the children Hansel and Gretel (saved by their own cunning). For the prince in *Sleeping Beauty*, however, the journey is filled with peril but marks his heroism and worthiness to marry the princess. These divisions reflect gendered roles in many cultures, whereby the feminine is associated with home and being settled, and the masculine with the public sphere and dynamic forces. Men, particularly rich men, were allowed or encouraged to travel where women were not.

In other folk tales, travel offers the protagonists a chance to improve their lot and move up the social ladder (reflecting the real social mobility associated with travel: see Chapter 6 'Why Travel? The Sociological Perspective'). In the Slavic fairytale *The Journey of the Sun and Moon,* the hero, a poor shepherd, is sent on a seemingly impossible journey by the father of the girl he loves. He is told to find the sun and moon to ask them questions. In the process of the journey the hero gains a vast wealth in riches and knowledge and returns to marry his true love.

It is interesting to see how these stories themselves have travelled. According to the author Jamila Gavin:

> [T]ales would have been carried by people travelling along the trade routes: the silk roads and spice routes, across oceans and continents. These stories were interpreted and re-interpreted to suit the culture in which they found themselves. As Jack Zipes says in his book, *Fairy Tales and the Art of Subversion* (1983), you can follow the process of civilisation in fairy tales. They show us how society used them to establish its own gender and racial stereotypes, and manipulate its own social values.[11]

In many of the most loved works of children's literature, travel is used as a vehicle for exploring child development (many of these books feature evocative illustrations as an integral aspect alongside the text). Lewis Carroll in *Alice in Wonderland* addresses the tension between our childhood needs for independence and anxiety. Travelling alone down the rabbit hole and around the strangeness of another world is intriguing, but it is also reassuring when Alice returns to the security of home. These are familiar themes also in *The Wizard of Oz*: 'there's no place like home' repeats Judy Garland's Dorothy at the end of her adventure, despite her eagerness at the beginning of the film to travel far away 'somewhere over the rainbow'. A similar theme is depicted in Maurice Sendak's *In the Night Kitchen*, which depicts a child's dream journey. According to Sendak the book is the first in a trilogy which he based on child psychological development from *In the Night Kitchen* (toddler) to *Where the Wild Things Are* (pre-school) to *Outside Over There* (pre-adolescent), with all three based around journeys and the tensions between independence and home. For older children, there are many 'coming of age' novels centred on travel, often within imagined worlds of great depth and complexity. Philip Pullman's *His*

Dark Materials books feature profound quests, played across different dimensions and theological worlds, intertwined with the growing up of the child protagonists who must negotiate the boundaries between child and adulthood.

Imagination plays a key role here. Children are hugely creative and works that inspire their imagination through tales of travel have proven immensely successful. Some of the most popular (among adults and children alike) have been within the science fiction genre. One of the most watched films of all time is Steven Spielberg's *ET,* and among the most popular and long-running TV series are *Star Trek* and *Dr Who.* These all have travel as a central theme: ET searching for a way to travel back home across the galaxy; the crew of the Starship *Enterprise* fulfilling their mission 'To explore strange new worlds. To seek out new life and new civilisations. To boldly go where no one has gone before!' and Dr Who travelling through both space *and* time in his/her police box. As well as inspiring the imagination, these shows also enable us to look back at ourselves and learn better who we are and who we want to be, whether as children or adults.

Conclusion

Travel holds a key place in our individual and cultural imaginations, a metaphor that we use in everyday language and in the verbal and visual stories we tell ourselves, helping us to conceive, describe and understand ourselves and the world we live in. It is a 'metaphor we live by'.

We have seen that travel is also linked with the arts in another fundamental way, through creativity. Travel has inspired many artists and writers, providing them with material, and the freedom of thought to create great work. And, equally, artistic works have then inspired others to travel, to seek the source of that beauty or meaning. The novelist Michael Mewshaw describes how his writing and travel relate:

> [T]ravel for me is a kind of writing, ... It is an act of creativity in which the world is an empty page and I'm the pen scrawling looping, recursive lines across a landscape. The goal in each case is the same — insight, joy, euphony, vivid experience, visual excitement, sensuous delight and discovery. Safer than alcohol, cheaper than heroin, it's my method, a la Arthur Rimbaud, of systematically deranging my senses, opening myself up to the new and unexpected.[12]

This link to creativity may even go beyond artistic endeavours and into the subconscious itself. According to the great psychoanalyst Carl Jung, without the experience of travel – either physical or imagined – the scope of dreams would be restricted. With travel, art and even our dreams so intertwined, it seems the answer to 'why travel?' is that it is at our core, culturally and psychologically.

Notes

1   First presented as the plenary address at the 2004 South Central MLA Conference in New Orleans, 28 October 2004. An excerpt is available at: https://rolfpotts.com/travel-writing-and-the-literature-of-travel/
2   www.theguardian.com/books/2016/dec/30/jonathan-raban-author-recovery-stroke-fears-dis-united-states
3   Virgil (1906) 'The Aeneid: book 1', in *The works of Virgil* trans John Dryden (original edition 1697), Oxford: Oxford University Press, line 4.
4   www.theguardian.com/books/2014/jun/20/laurie-lee-centenary-birth-english-travel-writer-walking-robert-macfarlane
5   www.theguardian.com/books/2007/aug/05/fiction.jackkerouac
6   https://emanuellevy.com/review/easy-rider-ideology-politics-and-culture-6/
7   https://www.academia.edu/8507884/Travel_as_a_Metaphor_D_H_Lawrence_and_Lawrence_Durrell
8   www.vagablogging.net/michael-mewshaw-on-the-importance-of-travel-to-literature.html
9   www.theguardian.com/books/2016/sep/25/far-and-away-reporting-from-brink-change-andrew-solomon-review
10 https://www.migrationtrail.com
11 www.bl.uk/childrens-books/articles/fables-and-fairytales-myth-and-reality
12 https://rolfpotts.com/travel-writing-and-the-literature-of-travel/

References

Adams, P. G. (1983) *Travel Literature and the Evolution of the Novel,* Lexington, KY: University of Kentucky Press.

Borm, J. (2004) 'Defining Travel: On the Travel Book, Travel Writing and Terminology', in G. Hooper and T. Youngs (eds), *Perspectives in Travel Writing*, Aldershot: Ashgate.

Campbell, J. (1949) *The Hero with a Thousand Faces,* New York: Pantheon Press.

Delbanco, N. (2005) 'Anywhere Out of the World: Why All Writing Is Travel Writing', in *Anywhere out of the World: Essays on Travel, Writing and Death*, New York: Columbia University Press

Joinson, S. (2016) 'Writing, travelling and the creative act', *Literary Hub*, 4 February, https://lithub.com/writing-traveling-and-the-creative-act/

Lakoff, G. and Johnson, M. (1980) *Metaphors we live by,* Chicago, IL: University of Chicago Press.

Lee, L. (1971) *As I Walked Out One Midsummer Morning*, Middlesex: Penguin Books.

Maquerlot, J.-P. and Willems, M. (eds) (1996) *Travel and Drama in Shakespeare's Time*, Cambridge: Cambridge University Press.

Marinetti, F. (1909) 'Manifeste de Futurisme', *Le Figaro*, February 20, 1909

McElroy, C. (1997) *A Long Way from St. Louie*, Minneapolis, MN: Coffee House Press.

Solnit, R. (2014) *Wanderlust,* London: Granta.

Theroux, P. (1985) *Sunrise with Seamonsters: Travels and Discoveries 1964–84*, Boston, MA: Houghton Mifflin.

Vogel, D. (1974) 'A lexicon rhetoricae for "journey" literature', *College English* 36(2): 185–9.

Whitfield, P. (2011) *Travel: A Literary History,* Oxford: Bodleian Library.

Wise, B. E. (2009) 'The Cosmopolitanism of William Alexander Percy', in C. Thompson Friend (ed) *Southern Masculinity,* Athens, GA: University of Georgia Press.

Youngs, T. (2013*) The Cambridge Introduction to Travel Writing,* Cambridge: Cambridge University Press.

Zulli, T. (2014) 'Changing authorial perspectives in R.L. Stevenson's pacific travel narratives', 11(2) *E-rea.* doi.org/10.4000/erea.3887.

9

Why People Travel: An Anthropological View

Tom Selwyn[1]

Foundations

Why do humans travel? What are the motivations behind this fundamental behaviour? These are questions that have been explored in various guises within a wide range of anthropological studies, from early analyses of ancient myths to ethnographies of both traditional and contemporary peoples (cf Selwyn, 2018). An anthropological approach, for the purposes of this chapter, entails the examination of cases from many different cultures (spread temporally and geographically) in order to draw insights, both specific and general, to understand better why humans travel.

There is an overall assumption underpinning the chapter, namely that a good way to approach the subject of why people travel from an anthropological point of view is to build upon two foundations: ethnography and myth. We need, in other words, to base our generalizations on solid empirical observation and description, on the one hand, awareness of directly and/or indirectly associated symbolism, imagery, fantasy and myth, on the other. In what follows, therefore, the intention is to present a blend of the ethnographic and mythological. Both speak to different aspects of reality while both are closely intertwined and interrelated.

Figure 9.1: Trobriand Islands, Papua New Guinea

Traditional fishing vessels of the Trobriand Islands (possibly made by the descendants of Malinowski's Argonauts of the western Pacific) lie on the beach, whilst a cruise ship sails in the background bringing tourists to shore.

In case of doubt or scepticism about the place of myth, fantasy, and so on in our scheme of things, Roland Dufour's (1977) proposal might be helpful:

> According to the humanities, the myth is neither falsity, nor fable, nor fiction. If the 'logos' is reasoning, the 'mythos' is the irrational part of human thought. Myth is neither pure imagination nor pure intellect, but a faculty for intuitive grasping of invisible, even sacred and transcendent realities. Nestled in the collective unconscious, the myth is beyond history.

The point being that if we want to get into 'motivation' of why people travel there are various ways to do it – including looking into the unconscious motivations revealed in myth.

The examples that follow in this chapter are therefore taken both from myths and from ethnographies, but there is also another form of example: writings about travel. An intermediate form between ethnography and myth, these describe actual travels, but reveal through their presentation unconscious motivations and ideas about travel.

For all of these types of study material, we have a wide range of examples to choose from for our purposes. A great number of myths have travel as a central motif and travel writings have been a popular literary form for centuries (see Chapter 8 'Travel in Art and Literature'). Many ethnographies also have some form of travel at their core, perhaps not least because travel is a fundamental human behaviour seen across all cultures; and also because travel encompasses the many facets of humanity that form the subjects of anthropological study – for example beliefs, knowledge, habits, rituals, institutions, group and individual identity and material culture.

The central part of this chapter therefore contains a consideration of travel-related myths from the ancient world, the travel writings of medieval and early-modern travellers, and ethnographic accounts with travel at their heart: both those of 'traditional' societies and modern tourism-based travels. From the whole wide range of journey myths, travel writings and travel-related ethnographies only a tiny selection can be explored here. Those chosen represent a diverse range over time and place, and type of travel, although necessarily some practices have been omitted (for example commuting, migration or pilgrimage, which are covered in other chapters including Chapters 6, 7 and 12).

Specifically, this part includes discussion of *The Epic of Gilgamesh, The Odyssey*, the wanderings of the 14th-century Islamic pilgrim Ibn Battuta, the early 17th-century writings of Sir Thomas Palmer, travel within the Kula system in the Trobriand islands, the annual cycles of transhumant pastoralist societies in the Mediterranean, and some examples of more modern tourism. The overall intention is to blend practices of travel with ideas about travel in order to draw out, in the third part, insights and themes that will enable us to make some generalizations about why people travel.

Examples From Myth and Ethnography

The Epic of Gilgamesh

Many of the earliest mythologies in human society revolve around the importance of the epic journey as a form of enlightenment or self-revelation. The *Epic of Gilgamesh*, written in ancient Sumeria in the second millennium BCE, is perhaps one of the best examples, and is remarkable for its establishment of both the heroic and the spiritual dimensions of travel.

Gilgamesh was the half-legendary King of Uruk whose arrogance led the gods to create Enkidu, a wild man who was the equal of Gilgamesh in strength and who would teach him humility. According to the epic, Enkidu and Gilgamesh become firm friends, and travel to the Cedar Forest where they slay the demon Humbaba and the Bull of Heaven. For the latter act the gods punish Enkidu with death and Gilgamesh is forced to confront his own mortality. As a result, he sets out on an epic journey to find the secret of eternal life. This, he believes, is held by the seer Utnapishtim, a survivor of the Great Flood and the only man to have been given immortality. Eventually, Gilgamesh finds the seer, after an extraordinary journey across the Waters of Death and the Land of Night. Utnapishtim sets him a series of quests to achieve eternal life, including staying awake for six days and locating a magic plant. Unfortunately, Gilgamesh fails these challenges and, having lost the chance for immortality, returns to Uruk where he tells of his epic journey. The theme of home and homecoming looms strong in the *Epic*, with the knowledge gained through travel helping Gilgamesh to understand his own nature and origins more clearly. Homecoming at the end of the myth helps to provide a sense of resolution for the hero's many journeys.

The Odyssey

The Odyssey, Homer's epic poem recounting the homecoming of Odysseus from Troy to Ithaca and his beloved wife Penelope, is one of the best-known travel-related myths. The story of Odysseus's journey home (also his starting point of course) is full of incident and dangerous encounters, climaxing in his arrival at home dressed as a beggar. (Indeed, despite its fame as a tale primarily of travel and adventure two-thirds of the Odyssey's 24 books take place within or in the environs of his home in Ithaca — only eight being about the actual journeys themselves).

The central theme of *The Odyssey* concerns Odysseus's home and family themselves and the way that he deals with those who have been attempting to disturb its order by wooing Penelope in his absence. His killing of the suitors, his re-establishment in the eyes of the household of his true identity, and his recovery of the proper order of things in his house and home all speak of Odysseus's success in re-establishing the Homeric laws of hospitality from the disorder that would have come upon it if the suitors had been successful in their subversive intentions.

Odysseus's story has entered the European and global cultural blood stream by way not only of the epic itself but also of subsequent literature, classical painting, and at least one famous operatic libretto, Monteverdi's *The Return of Ulysses to his Homeland*. At the end of Monteverdi's opera,

Figure 9.2: Odyssey-themed tourist boat, Ithaca

In modern-day Ithaca tourists can enjoy a ride on an Oddyssey-themed boat, recalling Odysseus's return to his homeland.

Ulysses sings both of his long and difficult journey and, by contrast, of the safety and comforting nature of home: "After my long affliction, blessed consolation. Blessed harbour of peace, where I may yield myself to rest, forgetting all my woes."

Ibn Battuta

Ibn Battuta, the famous medieval Moroccan traveller, was born in Tangier in 1304. He initially set out on the Hajj, but his travels – from his birthplace to Mecca, the Black and Caspian Seas, India, China, and, finally, to sub-Saharan east and west Africa – took him to the centre and the edges of the Muslim world. On his return he dictated his remembered 'diary', the *Rihla*, which he entitled *A Gift to Those Who Contemplate the Wonders of Cities and the Marvels of Traveling*.

He spent nearly half his life away from his native Morocco, some of the time in parts, like the Turkish lands, in which he had no language with which to communicate. But, as David Waines (2010) observes, even in such places Ibn Battuta reports feelings of familiarity and of being made welcome:

> Wherever we stopped in this land, whether at hospice or private house, our neighbours ... came to ask after our needs. [On leaving] they bade us farewell as though they were our relatives and our own kin, and you would see the women weeping out of sorrow at our departure.

The theme of hospitality towards strangers is found throughout Ibn Battuta's descriptions: from the welcome offered in hospices, religious houses, and Christian monasteries, to the generosity of Yemeni merchants (known for their solicitous dispositions towards wayfarers and pilgrims), and protection afforded by authorities in remoter areas that kept the pilgrimage and trading trails safe.

There seems, in short, to be a sense that Ibn Battuta was made to feel at home throughout much of the vast area of the world in which he travelled. And, as far as our own interests here are concerned, we may readily agree that the pilgrim routes of the medieval Islamic world were powerfully expressive sites of mobility and cosmopolitanism.

Ibn Battuta was a learned and pious man. He worked for several years as a judge in Delhi and, apart from the law, was keenly interested in other intellectual, cultural, and aesthetic aspects of the people and cities he moved through. He reported how much he appreciated the designs and decorative aspects of religious buildings as well as the thinking and speaking of *imams* and priests.

We can count him as a traveller motivated not only to fulfil his Islamic obligation to complete the Hajj but also as a person who wanted to explore and know about how the world worked. And throughout, he was well disposed towards the people and communities he met on the way. His travel account suggests that he would have agreed with Ibn Khaldun that "travelling in search of knowledge is absolutely essential for the acquisition of useful learning and of perfection through meeting authoritative teachers and scholarly personalities" (Mackintosh-Smith, 2002).

Sir Thomas Palmer

The early-modern period saw an explosion of interest in travel as a result of the European voyages of discovery. This resulted in the development of taxonomies of travel: one of the most significant being the Elizabethan politician Sir Thomas Palmer's *An Essay of the Meanes how to make our travels into forraine countries the more profitable and honourable* (1606). Palmer viewed travel through a political lens, influenced by his own experiences, including being a member of the

Anglo-Dutch expedition that sacked the Spanish port city of Cadiz in 1596. Inspired by the attempts of the French philosopher Petrus Ramus to create a systemized table of human knowledge, Palmer's *Essay* included four extensive tables categorizing what he saw as the different forms of travel.

Palmer divided travellers into the categories of non-voluntary (those acting on behalf of the prince or state); involuntary (those who were banished or persecuted); and voluntary (which accords more with our idea of independent travellers today). In a reflection of his political culture, Palmer pressed the idea that it was noble for the traveller to serve the state. Those who acted as emissaries and ambassadors Palmer described as honourable, while those engaged in subversive activities as 'intelligencers' or spies Palmer classed as not honourable in the sense of being out of sight rather than contemptible. Indeed, Palmer recognized that spies needed to be 'persons of notable esteeme to support the policie of the Estate', and should possess qualities including 'speede and faithfulnesse'.

For the voluntary travellers, Palmer provided a range of guidance on where, when and how to travel. Something of the norms of Palmer's society can be found in his recommendation that travel should be restricted for law clerks (who might subvert the legal system), for women and for those of dubious religious affiliation (reflecting the anti-Catholic paranoia of Elizabethan and Jacobean England). The religious concerns of Protestant England are also evident in Palmer's recommendations on where to travel, in his attack on the malign effects of travel in Catholic Italy and Rome, which was the 'forge of every policie that setteth Princes at odds', and 'the seller of wickedness and heathenish impieties.'

The kula *of the Trobriand Islands*

An anthropological account of why people travel could not be complete without a mention of Malinowski's (1922) *Argonauts of the Western Pacific*, arguably the greatest ethnography of all time and with a title drawn from the mythical Greek story of Jason and the Argonauts.

Malinowski described society and culture in the Trobriand Islands, an archipelago of some 450 square kilometres and 18 or so islands east of the New Guinea mainland. He focused on the system of inter-island communication known as the *kula*. This involved people visiting one another, from one island to another, in canoes laden with ceremonial valuables – red shell necklaces (*soulava*) and white shell armbands (*mwali*) – as well as more practical trading items such as pigs, yams and salt. There were two features of the *kula* upon which Malinowski placed particular emphasis and which have been the subject of anthropological debate ever since. The first concerned the difference between the ceremonial and trade items. The former were always regarded as of greater value than the latter. Thus whenever a canoe landed at an island, its occupants would be hosted at a feast during which the elder of the group of guests would hand over the necklace or bracelet to the elder of the host's group *as a gift*. Trading between the two groups would then take place – but this activity was always thought to be less valued that the ceremonial gift itself. The second emphasis was upon the fact that the receiver of the gift(s) would be expected, before much time had elapsed, to make his own journey across the sea where he would, in turn, become guest and ceremonial giver to a host in another island. In this way the *kula* was a system that brought all the islands together in a perpetually circulating system of gift exchange.

Malinowski placed a lot of emphasis on the way that each *kula* journey was a collective effort. Thus prospective travellers would be recruited (by a distinguished elder) on kinship principles co-operatively to build and decorate the canoes to be used, to gather trading items to take with them, and collectively to appear as representatives of their island when meeting (and festively celebrating) with their chosen hosts.

Mediterranean shepherds

J. Campbell's (1974) study of the *Sarakatsani* describes life and work in a sheep-rearing society for whom biannual travel is built into the patterns of their social and economic life. They live in the mountainous region of north western Greece where the weather (extremely cold high up in the mountains in the winter, warmer on the coast; hot in summer on the coast and pleasantly cool in the mountains) necessitates small groups of brothers bringing sheep down to the coast in the winter for the sheep to raise their young. The sibling groups return back up to the mountains with their sheep in the summer for cheese making and social life among the wider community. This kind of nomadic lifestyle (known anthropologically as transhumance) was until relatively recently quite typical of the hills behind northern Mediterranean coasts and is comparable to the movements of Bedouin goat and sheep-herding communities along the southern coasts. In some senses it is a form of routine travel comparable to modern commuting, both being examples of travel 'for work'.

Like Malinowski, Campbell explored the social and cultural consequences of transhumance: extremely close bonding of male

Figure 9.3: Tourists riding horses on La Réunion island

The Indian Ocean island of La Réunion (French territory) is popular as an eco-tourism destination, which many visitors imagine as a natural paradise, exotic and removed from their more Northern homelands.

siblings working with and guarding their flocks in the coastal winter, balanced by social life of a more relaxed kind and within a wider community in the mountain summers. The latter periods are those when money comes in (from the selling of produce as well as the marketing of sheep themselves) and weddings and other festivals take place. Furthermore, patterns of transhumant movement up and down the Mediterranean slopes contributes to the linking together of pastoralists and settled agriculturalists living and working in towns, villages, orchards and terraces of the hills.

'Eco-tourism' in La Réunion

David Picard's (2011) study of the Indian Ocean island of La Réunion[2] starts off by observing the abundance of trees, including many camellias, and other floral features of this volcanic island. Being particularly interested in how the island is imagined by French visitors, tourists and observers, as well as by others from the Global North, Picard locates the island as belonging to a symbolic field in which 'natural' features of the world (flora and fauna for example) are positioned vis-à-vis 'scientific' features (products of engineering for example) in such a way that implies superiority of the latter over the former. 'Northern' minds, Picard argues, thrive on having a sense of control over nature. Put another way, historically France had real colonial power over the island. It no longer has this. What it does have, though, is a sense of itself, along with other 'Northern' and/or 'developed' countries, as a 'scientific' (implying modern, rational, democratic, and so on) state. This collective assumption is given additional legitimacy from its relation to an imagined 'natural' island. (Arguably Britain has a comparable relation with the islands of the Caribbean.)

Following his placing of the island in relation to French and other Northern visitors in this way, it is not surprising to read Picard's description of the considerable economic importance the island's government gives to the natural world and its recognition that its tourist market is founded upon ecologically 'friendly' tourism, an outcome of which has been the building of a prominent eco-museum. He also describes government involvement in what tourists and others perceive as 'environmentally friendly' tourism education and training, including the training of guides.

Romance in Cappadocia

Hazel Tucker's (2002) study of Goreme village in Cappadocia (Turkey) is set within romantic landscapes of moon-like rock cones. Her field research paints a portrait of village and region as a magnet for young, sometimes female, tourists attracted by the landscape and also the prospect of meeting young, often male, villagers. She describes how liaisons between the young hosts and guests cause anxieties among the families of the former. Elder family members worry that the youth of the village will be attracted not only by individual tourist women but by the wider seductions of life in the imagined heartlands of Western Europe that might beckon following a transformation of temporary relationships into more permanent ones.

Given the unique character of the landscape in and around Goreme it follows naturally enough that public institutions at local, national and international levels should have become engaged in environmentally protective policies in the region. Tucker herself addresses, inter alia, co-operative ventures between the Turkish government and UNESCO. Her ethnography thus combines close reading of family life, the changes in the social organization of the village as it becomes a part of the tourist domain, and the policy interventions of authorities concerned to conserve the region's natural features.

Figure 9.4: Goreme National Park, Turkey

Tourists admiring the curiously shaped rocks in Goreme's so-called 'Love Valley' (Cappadocia, Turkey). An ethnography of the village reveals the impacts that tourism has at family, village and national levels.

Fishing and national identity in the Slovenian Adriatic

Natasha Rogelja and Anna Spreizer (2017) preface their examination of tourism in the northern Adriatic with detailed descriptions of the sea and its maritime industries, including fishing. The authors examine the economics and politics of fishing and show how these involve engagement with many local, national and continental institutions – fishing boat owners, unions, tourists, as well as local, national and continental authorities. At the same time, they show how fishing enters visitors' imaginations in a specific and significant way. They describe how Slovenian visitors to the coast find themselves symbolically poised between two contrasting fish and the metaphorical associations these have with Slovenian identity. The Adriatic mullet is a fish that is always on the move, swimming across national maritime boundaries, and around the Mediterranean. By contrast, the sea bass is farmed (and thus contained) in Slovenian fishponds. They argue that it would be hard to find a clearer pair of allegories of Slovenian historic attachment to the former Yugoslavia (and wider world), on the one hand, contemporary independence and self-sufficiency, on the other.

The opening chapter of Rogelja and Spreitzer's ethnography of the Slovenian coast is influenced by Cohen (1973) and Selwyn (2011).

The former defines and offers an analysis of what he calls 'drifter tourists', by which he means tourists who 'drift' (with sharp eyes and a reasonable amount of imagination) around urban townscapes and rural landscapes looking out both consciously and unconsciously for cultural 'meanings' in the surroundings through which they move. The latter applies Cohen's insights to an actual case of a walk along the south eastern coast of England from the town of Hastings in Sussex to the promontory of Dungeness in Kent.

Insights and main themes

The ethnographic and mythic evidence presented so far has provided us with a rich seam of interwoven thematic threads that help us assemble a set of ideas about why people travel.

Hostility, danger, death – and immortality

A clear theme that arises in both of our ancient myths is that of danger and hostility encountered by travellers on their journeys. In their descriptions of demons, Waters of Death, harpies, Sirens, trickster kings, and others, both myths introduce and then emphasize the presence of different forms of hostility in the shape of actual and/or potential hostile beings waiting to do our heroic travellers down.

It is a fairly short step from hostility to the association between travel and danger. It cannot always have been plain sailing for our argonauts in the Trobriand archipelago, and the dangers inherent in herding sheep up and down the coastal mountains of the Mediterranean are clearly understood by the groups of sibling shepherds for whom kinship solidarity in the face of the tough realities of transhumance is a necessity. Palmer also touches on hostility and danger in his warnings against travelling to the 'wicked' Catholic states, reflecting the fears of his Protestant countrymen.

A logical companion of danger is of course death, ever present in the trials faced by our mythic heroes, and the relation between physical death and the potential to become immortal through reputation. The motivation for Gilgamesh's travels lies primarily in the problem of human mortality and his attempt to circumvent this. Setting out on his first expedition with Enkidu, Gilgamesh remarks on the fame he hopes to achieve: 'People's days are numbered, Whatever they attempt is a puff of air ... If I fall on the way, I'll establish my name: "Gilgamesh, who joined battle with fierce Humbaba" (they'll say).'[3] Travel and the sense of quest it entails (see Chapter 2 'Biological Perspectives

on Travel') thereby offers a means of overcoming mortality. This is
made even more central in Gilgamesh's travels to find Utnapishtim
and the secret of eternal life: a quest in which heroic adventures and
achievements are central. Indeed, the historian of travel Eric Leed
(1991: 28) has proposed that Gilgamesh ought to be considered the
first travel writing, reflecting through mythology the way in which
'circumvention of death, too, is at the root of travel literature, those
stories of journeys that seek to fix and perpetuate something as transient
and impermanent as human action and mobility'. We can see that
there may be something also in the *Epic of Gilgamesh* that reflects the
desire of the ancient Sumerians to achieve immortality for their own
culture (not just for the individual Gilgamesh). In the words of the
historian Brendan Nagle (2009: 16): 'This magnificent poem ... can
be considered a metaphor for Mesopotamia's own heroic struggle to
resist decay and leave a name for itself among the peoples of Earth.'

Hospitality

The theme of hospitality (juxtaposed as it sometimes is with its
cousin hostility) runs through many of the texts. The climax of
Odysseus's homecoming consisted of his re-establishment of the laws
of hospitality from the attempts by the suitors to subvert them, which
in turn re-established his own place as the fount of hospitality in his
rightful kingdom. For our Trobriand argonauts, travel is founded upon
common principles of hospitality. When our *kula* canoeists arrive at
their destination they are welcomed and feasted by their hosts, the
exchange of ceremonial armbands and/or necklaces confirming the
solidarity between hosts and guests. These are moments when gift
exchange and hospitality merge into powerful expressions of social
solidarity, neighbours solidifying their relationships as friends and
trading partners. Reciprocal hospitality is also the foundation of Ibn
Battuta's travels, which repeatedly highlight and exemplify practices
of hospitality across the Muslim world and beyond. Such an itinerary
as his would have been impossible were it not for a shared system of
hospitality throughout the areas in which he travelled.

Home

Related to hospitality, and often placed in contrast with the concepts
of danger and hostility, is the theme of home. It may at first sight
appear surprising that one of the ideas that binds many of our travel
texts together is the idea and reality of home. This is a theme that

seems not so much concerned with travelling itself but with the geographical, social and emotional place from which travellers start and finish their journeys. Yet ideas about leaving home and returning home are cornerstones of any explanation of why people travel. Thus, whether Ithaca or Uruk, the homes of our mythic heroes – and the act of homecoming – play central roles in both stories. Odysseus's travels are guided by the unfaltering desire to return home, thereby re-establishing order and propriety in his kingdom. Such order comes at the end of travels that he describes in some detail as full of danger and potential disorder. This seems common across ancient mythologies, from the Gilgamesh and Odysseus myths examined here, to others such as Jason and the Argonauts and the return of the Israelites in the Book of Exodus: travel offers the opportunity to better understand where one belongs.

We see this theme in our other examples too. We glimpse, with some intensity, the dual homes of the shepherds: small and tightly knit on the coast in the winter, flowering outwards larger social formations of home in the summer uplands. In a rather comparable way Ibn Battuta's home was undoubtedly Tunis but, equally certainly, was also the entire Muslim world. Home is an important undercurrent in the writings of Thomas Palmer, who is primarily concerned with the contribution travel can make to good governance at home. Enlightened, civilized government derives in part from a deep understanding of the life and work of others in the world. For the inhabitants of Goreme, it is the arrival of travellers from elsewhere that brings ideas of home into sharp relief. In short, travel, in both myth and practice, becomes the means and/or stimulation for the recognition and definition of home.

Identity: self, group and nation

A pre-occupation with home (homeland too) leads inevitably to the asking of fundamental questions about individual and collective identity – about, to put it simply, who we are.

Every traveller starts out on a journey carrying not only his/her luggage but also his/her own history and background: Gilgamesh set off as a king, Ibn Battuta set out as a devout Muslim and scholar, tourists to La Réunion set off as Northern European. And so on. Our starting point, therefore, needs to be the self of the traveller as shaped by his/her own society, culture, and history. We also need to bear in mind travellers are more than passive carriers of their background: every act of travel also takes part in the shaping of travellers' worlds. We may illustrate from our data.

Odysseus and Penelope appear as the archetypical, ideal, husband and wife and it is these roles and the relationship between them that lie at the beginning and end of the epic. Arguably, the central concern is with the struggle against all the odds – of a long and dangerous journey home, in the case of Odysseus, and the various tempting offers from the suitors, in Penelope's case – to conserve and thus reproduce their roles and obligations to each other as a married couple.

Thomas Palmer's ideas about, and ideals for, travellers are founded upon early-modern principles of using travel to benefit the country of the traveller. A key point of travel, as far as Palmer is concerned, is to observe others and their societies, to learn about what goes on elsewhere in the world for the good of their own societies. Palmer describes such activity as honourable and noble, showing how travel was considered an important route in cultivating the identity of a gentleman.

In modern popular travel and tourism literature, much has been made of the transformative effect of travel in enabling the traveller to 'find oneself' and 'shape your own story'. We see this sense of the personal reflected in our modern-day tourist ethnographic examples. Tucker's youthful travellers in Cappadocia construct narratives of their travels in which romantic love in romantic geographical settings plays a part in the shaping of their own personal worlds.

From a sense of individual identity we can move on to consider how travel is implicated in the formation of group identities in our examples, whether that be kin, class or national identity. For the *kula* canoeists, membership of a family group is an essential pre-requisite for travelling: kinship groups are responsible for producing the canoes. Coming together to build canoes is thus a case of reproducing and shaping kin groups. (We can think of familial rites of passage such as marriages and funerals in northern European society when families present themselves to guests in ways that express their values and dispositions.) For the Trobrianders, by sailing from one island to another, island-based kin groups travel with the explicit and/or implicit aim of reproducing – shaping and reshaping – wider collective identities in the archipelago itself, binding the islands together within a single system of repetitive gift exchange. This clearly plays a central part in the establishment of a shared sense among the islanders of common identity. The *kula* canoes thus tell us a story about people travelling in order to express, conserve and protect themselves and their societies.

In our example of tourism in La Réunion, we can see ideas about national and supranational identities, and how those group identities of travellers can be formulated in contrast to the perceived (and created) identities of the host country. Picard argues that government-assisted conservation of the island's coral reefs and natural resources may be compared to liturgical ritual that has as much to do with social control as with the reefs and plants themselves. His entire book is designed to place issues of self and other within a symbolic universe in which the islanders of La Réunion are rendered not just protectors of the island's flora and fauna but themselves as an integral part of that natural world. For observers from the wider ('Western' or 'Northern') world this global garden state is thus incorporated into a symbolic repertoire of nostalgic colonialism behind which global economic liberalism may operate, as it were, behind the garden fence. The attraction of travelling to La Réunion is partly linked to the sense this island, with its abundance of flora, gives of a global order in which the 'developed', scientific, Global North establishes its supremacy vis-à-vis the less developed, 'natural' South. Colonialism itself may have passed but it maintains a sense of itself in this garden state.

Rogelja and Spreitzer's tourists on the Slovenian coast are preoccupied with fish and their metaphorical capacities to reflect insights into Slovenian identity. We might even say that these tourists travel to their coastline in search of their puzzling and contradictory identity, in which national independence seems juxtaposed with regional solidarities (Yugoslavia, Austrian-Hungarian empire).

These paragraphs have sought to identify two features about travel and the selves of travellers: that travellers everywhere have always carried their cultural baggage with them, and that travelling itself contributes to the shaping of that baggage. The journeys that travellers make are both shaped by their identities and contribute to shaping them.

External drivers: cultural, economic and political

So far we have concentrated mainly on the selves of individual travellers and the reasons they may travel: to make relationships, to fulfil religious obligations, to experience types of collective solidarities, and so on. But we need, in order to complete or at least add to the picture, turn our attention to some of the institutions that play roles in determining reasons for travelling, and directions to go. Once more we can turn to our case studies.

Our collection of travel accounts all reveal travel as an integral part of the society and culture of the travellers' worlds. For the Trobrianders, the feasts and gift-giving festivities are dependent on the *kula* journeys. The Hajj is a mandatory religious duty for all Muslims physically able to make the pilgrimage. *The Odyssey* belongs to a mythic tradition in which travel routinely plays a determining role. Palmer's advice fitted into a world view of travel shaped by the cultural prominence of the Age of Discovery and the gathering of knowledge about the other for the benefit of economic and political advancement, and good government at home. Our Greek shepherds exemplify another aspect of travel and the motivation to travel. The shepherds' biannual movement up and down the mountain and city workers' twice-daily streaming over the bridges of the Thames are in fact quite comparable responses to the pragmatic demands of work. In this collection the role of such institutions as familial gatherings, religious leaders, narrators of myths, royal patrons and their governments all clearly play decisive roles in the shaping of travel.

In the contemporary world the links between everyday life and travel are also complex and varied, and it is impossible to address a question about why people travel without placing travellers in their more everyday settings of life and work at home. Contemporary travel has been shaped in several different yet interlocking ways by the slave trade and colonialism (as travel in pre-modern times was shaped by other trading routes). Thus, the global map of sea and air lanes has been strongly influenced by a global political economy (with its historic travel imperatives) shaped by the Western powers and by the wars initiated by or involving those powers. Nowhere is this more true than with regard to contemporary refugees, the highest number of those attempting to travel to Europe coming from Afghanistan, Libya, Iraq and Syria. Refugees (living, dying and dead) arriving on the shores of the Italian island of Lampedusa is a palimpsest of this colonial/post-colonial cartography of mobility. In terms of our cases, we can see this reflected in the flow of travellers from more economically developed nations to the 'tropical paradise' of La Réunion, or the 'romantic' natural wonderland of Goreme. In both cases, relevant authorities (La Réunion government, the Turkish government and UNESCO) play a role in supporting the sense of natural and universal value that La Réunion and Cappadocia are widely thought to have. In this globalized era we are also seeing shifts eastwards once more, with major trading and exchange hubs in the Far East and renewed attention to the old 'spice routes' showing again how human travel reflects and is shaped by global shifts in power and other external drivers.

Knowledge and beauty

A number of our cases also show that travel has always been underpinned by ideas and values that, while overlapping at several points with the politico-economic framing of the world discussed above, also have independent lives of their own. The quest for beauty – in nature, landscapes, urban spaces, art, human and animal forms, for example – has always been at the heart of the experience of travel. Is not the economy of London lifted by its museums, art galleries and music venues? And may we not conclude from this that the search for beauty – and, indeed the pleasure inherent in its discovery – is crucial to the understanding of why people travel?

Travellers to La Réunion and Goreme are in no small part seeking to see for themselves the renowned beauty of those places; and Ibn Battuta repeatedly recorded his sense of wonder at the beauty of the cities through which he passed, the title of his diary incorporating both. The essence of awareness of beauty is recognition. After all, the perception of beauty by a lover of his/her loved one implies a recognition of the other as an expression of being part of the same world and field of moral and aesthetic values. Put another way, self and other come together as one through mutual recognition of beauty. The same is true of the recognition of the beauty of a building or a city. Travellers in Ibn Battuta's mould find buildings and cities beautiful because they reflect and refract ideas and values that they feel they possess themselves. In part, Ibn Battuta travelled to recognize parts of himself in the 'wondrous' cities through which he passed.

Conclusions

Summary

Our nine examples, varied as they are across time and place, myth and ethnography, reveal a number of overlapping themes that we might weave together to help us answer our question: why do we travel? From our cases we see the elision between the material/physical, the biological, and the social that has underlain motivations to travel from the earliest days of human evolution (and which, in a variety of ways, carry through to the present). People have always travelled to seek the material means of life, as the Greek shepherds and Trobrianders show us in their travel for food and trade. But travel fulfils many more socio-cultural and psychological roles of key importance. Travel offers the opportunity to strengthen social bonds and identity through the giving and receipt of hospitality, and a way to explore and better understand our own home. The safety of home is placed in contrast to the dangers on the road (or sea), but the dangers of travel also provide the chance for immortality, as our mythic heroes show us. The search for and affirmation of identity is another major motivation for travel revealed by our examples, from Gilgamesh's desire for immortal fame to the negotiations of national identity projected onto the fish of the Slovenian coast.

Another fundamental motivation for travel is to know, and know about, the world. Knowledge gained through travel has, of course, been used in a multitude of ways: from the recognition and definition of politico-economic and socio-cultural boundaries to the pursuit of scientific understanding as well as spiritual/aesthetic/artistic fulfillment. And, as we have seen, the diplomatic function of travel, found so clearly in the *kula* as a means of promoting social solidarity and good neighbourliness, leads us inevitably to thinking about Palmer and the role of diplomacy in colonial projects and, beyond that, to the role of travel in the control of the world's resources. The motivations for travel are shaped not only by individuals' physical, social and emotional states, but by socio-cultural institutions from the family to the global.

Concluding comments

The renowned anthropologist, Claude Lévi-Strauss, wrote in 1955 of his travels and ethnographic work among tribes in the Brazilian rainforest, beginning his book with a somewhat surprising sentiment: 'I hate travelling and explorers.' Whatever his personal preferences for travel, this statement attests to the close association between travel and the discipline of anthropology. The classic image of an anthropologist is perhaps part intrepid explorer, part scholar, studying in detail the lives of peoples in distant lands. Even before the practice of travelling to undertake fieldwork emerged within anthropology, there were those who aimed to better understand 'mankind' by what they could learn of cultures outside their own through the writings of other travellers. And in more modern times, when the anthropologist's gaze has been increasingly directed towards home, travel still forms a core motif of many studies (the Anthropology of Travel, Tourism and Pilgrimage (ATTP) is an academic field which has emerged in the last two decades).

Why is travel so intimately tied with anthropology? And might an answer to this help us understand further an answer to our core question: why travel? Some (eg Myers, 2011) have described the practice of anthropology as 'making the strange familiar and the familiar strange'. We might argue that this statement also describes the underlying purpose – and a major outcome – of travel itself. When we travel we come to know about the world (making the strange familiar), and we also place ourselves in new situations so that we learn about ourselves (making the familiar strange). In other words, perhaps we may sum up in a single sentence what we have learnt from all the above: the reason people travel (from an anthropological point of view) is that they are driven to explore how they are shaped by the world and how the world is shaped by them.

Notes

[1] This chapter is dedicated to three-year-old Alan Kurdî , who drowned in the Mediterranean, on 2 September 2015. He was part of a refugee family fleeing war and looking forward to finding a new home in the West (the family was aiming for Canada). His death draws attention to the facts that our world is shaped by refugees and that millions of people (71 million in 2018 according to the UN) travel because they are forced to do so. As we move through our own investigations about why people travel we will keep Alan and his family in mind.

[2] The island is an overseas department of France.

[3] *Epic of Gilgamesh*, 19 [tablet 2: 186–94].

References

Campbell, J. (1974) *Honour, Family and Patronage: A Study of Institutions and Moral Values in a Greek Mountain Community*, New York: Oxford University Press.

Cohen, E. (1973) 'Nomads from affluence: notes on the phenomenon of drifter-tourism', *International Journal of Comparative Sociology*, 14(1–2): 89–103.

Dufour, R. (1977) 'Les mythes du week-end: Aliénation ou libération?' *The Tourist Review*, 32(3): 15–16.

Leed, E. J. (1991) *The Mind of the Traveler: From Gilgamesh to Global Tourism*, New York: Basic Books.

Levi-Strauss, C. (1973). *Tristes Tropiques,* London: Pan Books.

Mackintosh-Smith, T. (2002) *The Travels of Ibn Battuta*, London: Macmillan.

Malinowski, B. (1922) *Argonauts of the Western Pacific*, London: Routledge.

Monteverdi, C. (1928 (1637)) *The Return of Ulysses to His Homeland*, London: BBC

Myers, R. (2011) 'The familiar strange and the strange familiar in anthropology and beyond', *General Anthropology*, 18(2): 1–9.

Nagle, D. B. (2009) *The Ancient World: A Social and Cultural History*, New Jersey: Pearson.

Palmer, T. (1606) *An essay of the meanes how to make our travailes, into forraine countries, the more profitable and honourable*, London.

Picard, D. (2011) *Tourism, Magic and Modernity: Cultivating the Human Garden*, New York: Berghahn.

Rogelja, N. and Spreizer, A. (2017) *Fish on the Move: Fishing Between Borders and Discourses in the NE Adriatic*, New York: Springer.

Selwyn, T. (2011) 'Shifting Borders and Dangerous Liminalities: The case of Rye Bay', in H. Andrews and L. Roberts (eds) *Liminal Landscapes: Travel, Experience and Spaces In-Between*, London: Routledge.

Selwyn, T. (2018) 'Tourism, Travel, and Pilgrimage', in H. Callan (ed) *The International Encyclopedia of Anthropology*, Chichester: John Wiley.

Tucker, H. (2002) *Living with Tourism: Negotiating Identities in a Turkish Village*, London: Routledge.

Waines, D. (2010) *The Odyssey of Ibn Battuta: Uncommon Tales of a Medieval Adventurer*, Chicago, IL: University of Chicago Press.

10

Tourist Travel

Hazel Andrews

On 13 December 2012 a British woman alighted from an aeroplane in Madrid and was greeted ceremoniously as the one billionth international tourist of that year by the United Nations World Tourism Organization's (UNWTO) Secretary General. The tourist identified as the one billionth was occupying a symbolic role in the complexities of tourism statistics,[1] but this event highlights the sheer scale of this type of travel. In the years since then – at least up until the 2020 COVID-19 pandemic – the tourism industry has become one of the largest and fastest growing sectors in the global economy (although also one of the hardest hit by the pandemic). In 2018, tourism accounted for over 10 per cent of global GDP – one in ten jobs; and the 1.3 billion international tourists per year were dwarfed by the number of domestic tourists, which were estimated at around four billion per year.[2] Such numbers have been accompanied by enormous environmental and cultural impacts, both locally and globally.

How is it that tourism has grown to be such an integral part of contemporary life that such a huge figure has been reached? What are the roots of this form of travel? What motivates and what enables people to undertake such journeys? This chapter will address these questions, in order to offer perspectives on the book's central question 'why travel?' It will explore the history of tourist travel, and the development of different types of tourism, before pulling these strands together to look in more depth at the underlying motivations for holiday travel. The voluntary nature of most tourist travel enables us to gain valuable insights into travel motivations. From here the chapter will look forward, to examine prospects for the future given some of the

Figure 10.1: Sun, sea and sand on a crowded beach

Sun, sea and sand is to many of us the archetypal image of tourism, but tourism is becoming increasingly varied in terms of who participates, where they go and what they do there.

negative impacts of tourist development and the environmental limits and technological opportunities that we might face. Since tourism can result in both costs and benefits for the destinations and for the global environment, understanding tourists' expectations and motivations can help to ameliorate problems and to enhance the positives.

Who is a tourist?

To start, it is worth reflecting on the question 'who is a tourist?' We can begin with the idea of a tourist as a holidaymaker. We probably associate the idea of holidays with notions of pleasure and something that we undertake in non–work time. However, definitions of tourism are not as straightforward as we might think. Not all forms of travel that are counted as tourism necessarily involve leisure and pleasure or operate outside non–work time. For example, the business traveller, those engaged in volunteer work, and people visiting friends and relatives are all classified in many official statistics as tourists. According to the UNWTO: 'A visitor (domestic, inbound or outbound) is classified as a tourist (or overnight visitor), if his/her trip includes an overnight stay.'[3] This is a very broad definition, which could potentially include anyone who travels away from home regardless of the purpose of their trip and if they do not take up permanent residence.

Social anthropologist Valene Smith provides a narrower and potentially more useful definition that hints at why people might become tourists. For Smith, a tourist is a 'temporarily leisured person who voluntarily visits a place away from home for the purpose of experiencing a change' (1977: 2). The idea of change and difference is a common theme related to tourists' motivations, but as this chapter will demonstrate there may be many other reasons for tourist travel besides. What might be more useful to consider is a continuum of motives for travel, which include innate desire, business and all those who travel within the conventional understanding of what it is to be a tourist for leisure and pleasure purposes. This chapter is primarily concerned with the leisure traveller.[4]

It is also helpful to look briefly at *who* are tourists – are there patterns in terms of nationality, gender and age in who practises tourism? Although tourism is undoubtedly a global phenomenon, much of our understanding of what it is and the motivations behind it are based on tourism as practised by the Western world. Until recently, most tourists were from the more affluent countries of North America, western Europe, Australia and New Zealand. However, recent years have witnessed a huge growth in tourism numbers from elsewhere, particularly China, as wealth for the middle-classes increases and gives more people the ability to travel. China is now the most powerful outbound tourist market; in 2018 Chinese tourists made over 150 million international trips, spending over US$261 billion, which is more than twice the amount spent by the world's second largest outbound market, the US.[5]

In many cultures men have traditionally travelled more than women – at least in terms of travel with overnight stays. But modern tourism seems to buck this trend showing indications that women make up a greater number of leisure tourists. For example in South Korea, female tourist arrivals are higher than male, particularly among Asian visitors (60 per cent of whom are female).[6] Similarly, American women make tourist trips more often than their male counterparts, and they are more likely to travel solo and in single-sex friendship groups than men are.[7]

Tourism is an activity undertaken by young and old. The 'grey market' (retirement age or older) is a substantial part of the tourist industry, as many older people increasingly have the time, money and motivation to travel; and with an aging population in most affluent countries, the number of older tourists looks set to keep growing.[8] The picture of the 'typical tourist' is thus changing and broadening.

Despite its broad official definition, many people have negative associations with the term 'tourist' and would rather refer to themselves as a 'traveller'. The advent of so-called mass tourism following World War II has often received negative press. This is sometimes in terms of the ways in which tourists behave (witness the headlines in summer 2014 about the behaviour of tourists in Mallorca: 'Magaluf's summer of shame: the sex scandals that have rocked holiday resort'[9]). The unfavourable view of mass tourism is also based on the imagined lack of independence associated with a package tour (travel being done in the 'wrong way') coupled with the idea that the holiday is being undertaken for the 'wrong reasons'. Again, we can see that the motivations for travel are a key part of cultural understandings of what tourism is or should be. In order to understand why people can be judged for undertaking holidays for the 'wrong reasons' we need to consider the historical development of tourism, which allows us to see how technical, economic and social factors have interacted to form modern ideas and practices of tourism. A look at the history of tourism shows us that motivation alone does not lead to travel. For people to take part in tourism there are three key requirements that must all interact: ability, motivation and mobility.

Historical development of tourism

If we look to the distant past, we find evidence of early forms of travel for pleasure by the ancient Greeks and Egyptians. 'Seeing the sights' was a motivation for leisure travellers at least as far back as the 4th century BCE, with Hellenic writers listing the Seven Wonders of the World as 'must sees' (literally *themata* 'things to be seen'). In the 2nd century AD, the Greek traveller Pausanias is attributed with writing ten guidebooks for a Roman audience detailing sights of interest in Greece – the sorts of things that we might see on a tourist itinerary today. Other reasons for leisure travel in antiquity include the attendance of festivals and viewing or participating in events. For example, people travelled for the Olympic Games (first recorded in 776 BCE) and the Roman Colosseum was an attraction for the masses. This may be regarded as a forerunner of what we now call sports or events tourism. Leisure was important in these ancient societies but given the strongly hierarchical social structure the practice of leisure was the preserve of the elite. As empires expanded so did trade links which encouraged people to travel for business and trade. In the Ancient World people also travelled for religious purposes, including pilgrimages to the Oracle at Delphi. Such trips, although not necessarily for leisure or pleasure, would, if they involved an overnight stay, be classed as a form of tourism under the UNWTO definition.

The expansion of the Roman empire saw development of facilities to support the ability, mobility and motivations for pleasure travel. The roads for trade and troops gave greater ease of movement across Europe, the accumulation of wealth by the upper classes gave increased opportunities to purchase leisure activities, and second home ownership to escape the heat of Rome was common. Along the road network *mansios* – early hotels – were constructed and, as well as travelling for military and trade purposes, people travelled to spas for the waters. With the collapse of the Roman empire, travel patterns and attitudes changed. People still journeyed for trade and religious purposes but increased danger and expense meant pleasure trips were limited.

Excursions for purposes other than trade or religion had a resurgence in Europe with the Grand Tour: a tour of the great sights of Europe, which was seen throughout the 18th century as essential to completing the education of a young English gentleman. In her work on the origins of sightseeing Judith Adler (1989), however, noted that the 16th and 17th century origins of the Grand Tour were not initially to see but to listen and learn the art of oratory for use in court life. Underpinning such activity is the idea of education: that motivations for travel are based on learning from and about another culture. This also demonstrates that the notion of the holiday to see the sights is linked to deep seated socio-cultural ideas about which of our senses is the most important. In Enlightenment Europe seeing becomes pre-eminent because it is regarded as more scientific, detached and truthful. We may be familiar with adages such as 'seeing is believing' and 'eyewitness'.

It is this sort of attitude – travel for education – which has led to the maligning of some present-day tourism activity, for example, by those tourists who show no apparent interest in the culture of the destination but rather seek out that which is familiar to them. At the same time, some holiday practices focus on the body rather than the mind; for example, sunbathing, drinking, eating too much, or sexual activity. Again, these 'bodily' motivations are not always widely appreciated as virtuous reasons for travel. Regardless, such pursuits are enormously popular and form one of the main motivations for much leisure travel, a factor often exploited by destinations in their marketing. Some destinations may focus on 'wholesome' bodily practices: spas, yoga retreats, relaxation in the sun or within natural surroundings. On the other hand, destinations like Las Vegas are often promoted with an emphasis on opportunities to 'misbehave' – for drinking, gambling or sexual activity.

We can see similar 'bodily' motivations in historical travel too, not least in the 17th and 18th centuries with the rise of a form of health tourism. In Europe it became popular for wealthy elites to travel to coastal regions for the believed health benefits of being immersed in sea water and breathing in the coastal air, or to places where natural spa waters were thought to have healing effects. One of the best examples of this is the patronage of the Prince Regent (later George IV) of Brighton on the south coast of the UK.

These early tourists had the financial ability to be mobile and the motivations in terms of education, pleasure and medicine to embark on the journeys. It was, however, industrialization that led to the opening of travel to more people. As wages increased people had greater disposable incomes to spend on leisure activities. The technological developments associated with industrialization gave rise to faster and bigger transport networks, particularly railways, allowing more people to travel. What we see, therefore, with the industrial revolution is the spread of the ability, mobility and motivations to travel for pleasure.

No examination of the development of tourism would be complete without reference to Thomas Cook. Cook organized the first package tour in 1841; it ran for 12 miles between Leicester and Loughborough and cost one shilling for the return rail fare (around £3.40 in today's money, so affordable to many). By 1868 the company professed to having organized trips for two million people. The success of Thomas Cook was not just down to advances in technology – the speedy and convenient mass travel enabled by rail networks – but also stemmed from the recognition that a rested workforce is a healthier workforce. For example, the 1871 Bank Holiday Act in the UK gave workers more 'free time' by guaranteeing time away from work, during which they could undertake short journeys for leisure purposes.

In the first half of the 20th century conflict in Europe and economic depression impeded travel for pleasure; but economic improvements in the post-war period, full employment, holiday pay and higher disposable incomes increased people's ability to holiday. Mobility was also increased with the rise in private car ownership, and the advent, in the 1950s, of civilian passenger air flights. The decade that followed saw an increase in travel companies offering package holidays abroad – most notably to Italy and Spain. The combination of more money and continuing technical advances made tourism – and particularly overseas tourism – increasingly possible, leading to the advent of mass tourism, with sun, sea and sand as the main motivating factors.

An ever-expanding array of niche tourism products

As the ability to travel for tourism purposes has developed and involved increasing numbers of people, the reasons for travel have also expanded. There is a growing array of activities and holiday types that people can engage in, for example, fishing holidays, yoga retreats, cooking breaks and adventure tourism. People can go on weekend breaks, city breaks, winter holidays for skiing or 'summer sun', as long-haul destinations have come within reach for a larger number of people. In addition, tourists are not necessarily restricted to one destination, for example, going on a cruise (sea, river or fjord) has become a popular form of holiday.

This ever-increasing variety of activities and destinations have come to be labelled as 'niche tourism products', not just because they relate to a specific activity but also because they differ from mass tourism products.

Cruise holidays, which were once considered a niche product, have experienced such a growth in tourist numbers that they have in

Figure 10.2: Cruise ship *Carnival Victory*

Cruises are increasing in popularity and large ocean cruisers now act as a tourist destination in their own right.

recent years become all-inclusive, floating mass tourist destinations in their own right. An estimated 22 million passengers were carried on ocean cruises in 2015 and the industry expects to grow by 3 per cent per year.[10] This tourism is controversial in terms of costs to the natural environment, and the lack of spending at the designated ports of call – outside of, for example, souvenir shopping – given that the tourists are entirely catered for on-board. This expansion seems set to continue even considering the 2020 global COVID-19 pandemic and high-profile media reporting of cruise ships as 'ideal incubators of infectious diseases'.[11] Despite this scenario, bookings for cruises in 2021 show an increase.[12]

So-called 'dark tourism' refers to destinations and attractions associated with human death, disasters and the macabre. The term came into usage during the 1990s and can refer to such places as the Hiroshima Peace Park, the war graves in Europe, Auschwitz, Ground Zero in New York, the Cu Chi tunnels of the Vietnam war, Elima Castle in Gambia (a prison of the slave trade), as well as military museums and the historical re-enactments of battles. As with other forms of tourism, we can find the antecedents much earlier. Indeed, the Crusade period of the 11th century AD saw visitors to the Holy Land to see the place of Christ's crucifixion; and the Colosseum of Rome was on the Grand Tour itinerary due to its association with death. The reasons behind this type of travel vary: education, to pay homage, morbid curiosity, spiritual and religious purposes, validation, thrill-seeking, or simply as a matter of convenience. Like many tourist attractions, dark tourism sights are not necessarily the main purpose or focus of holiday activity, but the tourist is coincidentally in the same place, and/or the site is featured on the itinerary for visits.

The centrality of any attraction or activity as a motivating force is an issue in other forms of tourism, especially those relating to arts and heritage. In other words institutions such as art galleries and museums can be integral to the decision to travel for some visitors (for example to visit a specific exhibition), while for others they are incidental – an interesting attraction but not the main reason for their journey. For example, many island tours of Mallorca include the composer Chopin's house in Valldemossa and are taken up by many of the island's charter tourists who are primarily holidaying for sun, sea and sand.

Health and medical tourism have emerged as growth areas. Going away for health reasons is not new (as the historical popularity of seaside resorts and spa towns demonstrates), but in more recent times travel for health or medical reasons has developed alongside advances in medicine, the affordability of treatment, and the availability of certain procedures and medicines. Therefore, travelling overseas for cosmetic surgery, transplant operations (often illegal) and routine operations is increasingly an underlying motivation for travel. In 2014 the *New York Times* reported: 'Seizing an opportunity to tap the steady and ubiquitous flow of China's newly rich who are traveling overseas, South Korea's government is promoting the country as a place to shop, eat, stay – and perhaps get a nip and a tuck.'[13] Perhaps a more recent trend in relation to pleasure travel is for marriage. Doubtless in antiquity people also undertook trips for their weddings, although the motivations for the union were more likely to be political than they are today. Now it is not uncommon to hear of people going on holiday to get married or for 'stag/hen parties'. There are numerous packages to choose from, to destinations that include, for example, Bali, the Caribbean, and Moominland in Finland, which is particularly popular with Japanese couples.

Looking back at this brief survey of the historical development of tourism or tourist-like practices we see that, in order for tourism to take place, people need the ability in terms of time and money, the means by which to be mobile (transport), and the desire to travel. Evidently people were, in the past, interested in seeing the sights, being educated and 'getting away from it all' even if it was not labelled as tourism or holiday making. What is also evident is that, since these early beginnings, the reasons for travel have developed with an increasing number of niche products, the activities of which form the basis for the motivation for the trip. However, we need to exercise caution since activities are not necessarily the underlying travel motivation. Consider, for example, the fact that, in some cases, a golfing holiday is a 'cover' for the conduct of extra-marital relationships (Andrews, 2011).

Why people go on holiday

For many, holiday travel is now such a fixture of social life that the answer to the question why people go on holiday might appear to be obvious, with ready answers being: 'for the weather', 'to relax', 'to see something different', 'to get away from it all' or 'to learn something'.

In academic terms, the reasons given for going on holiday have been categorized into 'push' and 'pull' factors. Push factors relate to individual needs: for example, escape, entertainment, education, relaxation, play, time with friends or family, meeting others, sexual opportunity, prestige, self and wish fulfilment, and shopping. To some extent the tourism industry also works to create push factors by marketing to generate a demand. Once the desire to travel has been stimulated, the destination the tourist chooses will have the pull features to satisfy that desire. For example, shopping is one of the most universal of touristic practices, being both a main motivating factor for a trip as well as an incidental part of the holiday. The Dubai Shopping Festival which, since 1996, takes place at the start of every year, sells items ranging from luxury goods, including cars, gold and diamonds, to crafts and food from market stalls. Clearly the purpose is to attract those who wish to shop, and according to some sources the 2015 festival attracted 56 million visitors from around the world.[14]

The motivations for popular travel are shared across cultures. To a Western audience, holidaying for fun and to de-stress are familiar concepts. Research has shown similar underlying motivators for Indian holidaymakers: novelty seeking, stress busting/fun, and education. Similarly, Chinese tourists also exhibit desires to view something different, experience excitement, and engage with education, rest and relaxation, as well as add to their prestige and ego-enhancement. In Japan, domestic tourism activities have involved visits to hot spring resorts for the purposes of relaxation, quiet and escape from the hustle and bustle of city life. Similar motivations have also been identified among Mexican domestic tourists who leave the crowded and noisy cities for weekends at the beach.

Despite these similarities across broad cultural groups, likes/dislikes and needs will vary between individuals and social groups. The requirements of the holiday for a traditional nuclear family is most likely different from that of the 18–30 singleton, or those in the so-called 'grey market'. Other factors, such as gender, sexuality, class and ethnic background may all have a bearing on holiday-taking decision processes and underlying motivations. For example, the holiday-taking motivations of people with different ethnic backgrounds and cultural histories within Britain can vary. For many in the UK-based African-Caribbean and Asian communities, using holidays to visit relatives overseas, or to explore ethnic heritage, can be more important than holidaying for sun and sand.

At the same time places that were once part of various European empires form sites of fascination or drivers for touristic activity for those without family in the destination. This link has at times led to tourism being categorized as a form of neo-imperialism in which the tourists come from the core areas of power to visit the less developed (former colonies) and financially poor peripheries where the 'natural resources' of good weather, fine beaches and 'exotic peoples' form part of the attractions used to appeal to tourists.

The idea of the core–periphery relationship can also be applied in Western Europe where the development of tourism activity has increasingly been to places that were on the margins and economically poor, for example, resorts in the Mediterranean. Although many such destinations have undoubtedly benefitted from tourism income and may not be now categorized as 'poor', there are no safeguards against a return to the metaphorical periphery, as exemplified by the economic situation in Greece. Although around half of global tourism is still between richer nations, this core–periphery relationship is a telling and increasingly prominent factor in global tourism, especially since the tourism sector in 'emerging economy' destinations is showing faster growth than that in advanced economies.[15] We can also see this core–periphery relationship reflected in much domestic tourism, where people from the industrial heartlands often travel to the poorer, less developed regions for holidays.

Another issue that influences peoples' type of holiday choices is the degree of independence they want to exercise over the organization and conduct of their vacation. Some will prefer as much independence as possible – the backpacker, explorer and adventurer for example – while others prefer to travel in the knowledge that everything has been organized for them and they have a point of reference in the form of a guide or tour operator representative in the destination. These preferences may in part be dictated by what the tourist is seeking from their holiday – adventure and challenge versus rest and relaxation perhaps – but are often dependent on the individual's personality and previous experiences, as well as factors like age, class and gender. There has been much research on the psychology of travel choices, which indicates that perceptions of risk and risk aversion, which are key factors in decisions about travel destination and type of holiday, vary depending on individual personality and experience, socio-economic and cultural background.

The reasons for travel cited above often relate to the activity that tourists engage in but activities do not explain everything and other approaches to understanding tourists' motivations have emerged from the academic literature. One is the suggestion that because the modern person feels alienated, they need to go elsewhere to recapture a sense of structure and belonging. Associated with this search are concepts of wholeness, authenticity and meaning in life, which are always located in places and cultures other than one's own. Although a complex and much debated term, 'authenticity' has largely been taken to mean 'the truth' or 'real'. For example, the holiday can be thought of as an opportunity to discover one's 'true-self', or, in seeing how 'the other' lives, something real or truthful about another culture or humanity in general. The usefulness of authenticity in understanding tourists' motivations has received a lot of attention in the academic literature not least in terms of how and by whom authenticity should be defined. Nevertheless, authenticity remains a feature of many tourism organizations' marketing; for example Thomson Holidays (now TUI) describes the Greek island of Thassos as 'Authentic Greece'.[16]

During the Roman empire, second home ownership in the hills above Rome developed for the purpose of escaping the oppressive summer heat. Similarly, a feature of the British colonial era, particularly in India, was the development of hill stations in high-altitude locations, which also served – in part – the same purpose. Being able to 'escape' to the hills was a sign of wealth, luxury and power. The idea of luxury in relation to holidaying in hill stations still holds resonance today with specialist tour operators appealing to potential customers both at home and overseas for holidays and honeymoons based on the spectacular, unspoilt scenery, seclusion, amenable climate, and the romance and glamour of a bygone era. For example, Kodaikanal Tourism[17] is advertised thus:

> Wish to run away from the scorching heat and enjoy nature at its best? Rush to the kaleidoscopic land of Kodaikanal …. The hill resort offers some of the most breathtakingly beautiful spots … experience the colonial India at the Kodai Club …. The 114-acres of Golf Links form the other colonial legacy that will sweep you off your feet with its undulating green velvet carpet.

In this advert we can identify all sorts of holiday motivations other than authenticity. Escapism is clearly one, but also opportunities to play, perhaps be educated by experiencing the colonial setting (and seeing other attractions listed in the brochure) and, as the company's website images suggest, seeing the 'exotic' other in the form of local people.

The issue of searching for authenticity in tourism is an attractive one but it does not translate to all forms of holiday. For example, Las Vegas has replicas of the Eiffel Tower, Egyptian pyramids and the Statue of Liberty, and people delight in the fun and hyper-reality of the place. Elsewhere in the world replica monuments are built – for example the construction of Angkor Wat in India – with the idea of making a Hindu temple accessible to greater numbers of Hindus than the real one in Cambodia by reducing the need to travel as far. Replicas of the Eiffel Tower also exist in two Chinese cities and a theme park in the city of Chongqing contains copies of Mount Rushmore, the New York skyline, and the pyramids. Other manufactured destinations elsewhere in the world include the Tropical Islands resort 50 kilometres south of Berlin, which contains a rain forest, sandy beaches and a tropical village.

In such destinations tourists can easily see the sights and have an experience even if the attractions are not the real thing. Sightseeing comes up time and again as a reason for travel both throughout history and across cultures. However, we need to be careful not to over-privilege sight to the detriment of the other senses: for example, feeling hot and sweaty, getting sunburnt, tasting different foods, hearing different sounds and smelling new odours. The practice of tourism includes the use of the whole body.

Sightseeing can go some way to explaining what some tourists might do when on holiday, but it is not necessarily a satisfactory explanation of motivation for travel — one could ask why people feel the need to sightsee. One idea is that we are looking for something different, which in turn helps us to reflect on who we are. All people try to make sense of the world around them and their role within it. One way to achieve this is through a relationship with ideas of an 'other'. We can say who we are in opposition to who we are not. Holidaying in places where there is a marked cultural difference from our own heightens our awareness of our sense of cultural self-identity compared to the cultural identity of a different group of people.

The opportunity to engage with or see other cultures as part of the holiday can lead to clashes in culture. The behaviour of tourists can lead to discontent among local people and authorities, as well as earning the embarrassment and disapproval of the tourists' home nation. For example, high profile complaints about the behaviour of Chinese tourists (including the act of a teenager graffitiing his name on an Ancient Egyptian temple) led the Chinese government to issue guidance for its citizens on how to 'behave properly' while abroad.[18] Similarly, the behaviour of British tourists is often reported to cause upset and, according to *The Guardian*, 'Brits regularly top surveys of the nationality that locals least want to see propping up their bars.'[19]

The freedom associated with going on holiday — removing oneself from the familiar constraints of our day-to-day lives and social expectations — can lead us into a position where we feel we can do what we want. For some, this is based on the thinking that what happens on holiday stays on holiday. However, with increased social media, and the fact that many people travel with their friends and family, the reality is that what happens abroad travels home. This may be simply in the memories we hold of our time away or in some cases living with the consequences of our activities. For example, high incidents of sexually transmitted diseases have been found in Australian men returning from holidaying in Thailand, during which time they engaged in sexual activity with local prostitutes.

In thinking about self and identity as a motivating force for travel we can also consider the idea that travel increases social standing and enhances the ego. Thus the stories that some tourists tell about their trips, the knowledge accumulated, or the types of experiences they have had, can be used to portray an image of the traveller (to themselves and to others) as knowledgeable, having survived unusual experiences; in short of being 'well-travelled'. This idea has a long standing in studies of tourism (for example Dann, 1977) and might be seen as playing a role in diverse activities: from the 18th-century Grand Tour to the more contemporary desire to get a tan or be seen to have visited the most prestigious ski resort. For some tourists the journey itself may provide an opportunity for social status and ego enhancement, whether that be through a feeling of exclusivity and luxury while sitting in first class, or an arduous and risky journey 'off the beaten track', which in itself bestows a sense of exclusivity and difference from the crowd.

The idea of travel to enhance the ego has been linked with environmental concerns, as well as the increased recognition that tourism can bring problems for the host destination. Following the Rio Earth Summit in 1992 and the development of Agenda 21 – the UN action plan for sustainable development – it became fashionable for some to travel with ethical issues in mind and we see the development of tourism products to appeal to these concerns; for example, pro-poor tourism, green tourism, volunteer tourism. However, tourists engaged with these activities have sometimes received criticism that their true motivation is not the underlying ethical issues but how such travel enhances their own social standing and sense of self. In addition, the tourism industry has been criticized for simply creating another set of products for market gain without any real concern for the physical and socio-cultural environments in which tourism takes place. This is not to say, however, there are not real issues resulting from the practice of tourism including the exploitation of local people and degradation of nature. Much important work is undertaken by voluntary organizations to address such problems, and many people travel with genuine concern for such issues.

Travelling to build a sense of self is not confined to those with ethical concerns. The idea that travel broadens the mind is common across many cultures throughout history and seems to be backed up by some scientific evidence (see Chapter 2 'Biological Perspectives on Travel', Chapter 3 'Travel and the Mind' and Chapter 7 'Religious and Spiritual

Figure 10.3: A traveller sits alone on a cliff

The idea of travelling in order to 'find oneself' has gained a huge amount of popularity in recent years, to the point that many now ridicule the idea. Nevertheless, it is a concept with old roots among philosophers and religious thinkers.

Travel'). Despite this, there are contrasting views that travel may limit the imagination. The English writer Samuel Johnson (1709–84) argued: '[T]he use of travelling is to regulate imagination by reality, and instead of thinking how things may be, to see them as they are.'

While some travel may be undertaken to broaden the mind, this motive is not so useful in understanding why many holidaymakers seek familiarity in the destination and want to minimize certain aspects of difference from home. Many tourist resorts enable visitors to eat foods from their home culture and enjoy familiar activities without engaging with local culture or language differences: the popularity of fish and chip shops in Ibiza may be familiar to British readers. According to a recent study by ATOL (the Air Travel Organizer's Licence), a third of Britons who travel abroad return to the same place each year, often eating in the same restaurants and doing the same activities each time. Those who opt for familiarity may be seeking rest and relaxation more than the thrill of novelty or the desire to learn something; and psychological and social factors may influence this choice too. Even those seeking the 'exotic' may also unconsciously be wanting to learn something about home.

The prominence of photos (and, before that, travel paintings, sketches and journals) within the tourist experience may also be linked to the idea of one's identity. Photography forms a record of the holiday for the tourist's own personal recollections – relating to a sense of self, or ego enhancement – and for displaying to others – relating to social status. Holiday photos form a disproportionately large part of many people's personal photo library and thus a prominent part of their self-crafted story of self. For many tourists photography is a major activity within the holiday itself, and to some extent a motivating factor for travel. As Susan Sontag wrote in her book *On Photography* (1979), 'travel becomes a strategy for accumulating photographs'. This trend has increased in the last decade as technological changes have made the creation and sharing of photos easy and widely accessible. The rise in the popularity of 'selfies' is often attributed to the desire for ego enhancement and social status: the selfie-taker frames how they and their setting appear, poses, deletes and filters as desired. Some observers criticize this practice of viewing and capturing things through a lens as missing out on the 'real' experience but perhaps this criticism overlooks the many and varied underlying motivations of travel. It also ignores that the desire to share travel images with others may have motives beyond social signalling, including a wish to share experiences with loved ones who could not be there, or to inspire or educate.

Figure 10.4: Tourists view the *Mona Lisa* in the Louvre, Paris

Over-crowding at popular tourist destinations, and a preoccupation with capturing experiences on camera: two criticisms that commentators have levelled at modern tourism as detracting from an 'authentic' experience. But such criticism may overlook some of the varied motivations for undertaking tourist travel.

The role of the journey, as opposed to what tourists do at their destination, is also important. Is the journey merely an inconvenience that must be borne, or does the very act of physically travelling fulfil some travel motivations? The answer may be different for each traveller and each trip that they make. For some, the journey itself may form a major part of the holiday: for example those on cruises or long train journeys, or the small but increasing number of 'slow travellers' who eschew air travel in favour of more 'human-paced' travel in which change and distance can be more fully appreciated. But even for those who seek to be cocooned within a comfortable, fast vehicle, such as those air passengers who rarely glimpse out of the window as they traverse the globe, the journey may still play an important role. It can form a rite of passage, or a demarcation zone, enabling the traveller to leave behind normal life and fully enter the experience of being a tourist.

Conclusion

We have discovered that people around the world have been travelling for pleasure for thousands of years, and that despite the way in which tourism has developed into an array of specialist products, the underlying motivations for our travels are often the same as those in antiquity; and that they can also be found across cultures. What has changed is the sheer number of people on the move.

Given that we can find parallels between contemporary tourism and trips in antiquity, this suggests that there are some intrinsic reasons for travelling. These can perhaps be understood as an innate wish to engender some form of change. Such change might be educational, perhaps to learn about another culture or language; or physical, such as getting a tan, having a rest, or breathing mountain air. Or the change desired might be psychological, for example the wish to find one's 'true self'; or social, such as the hope to improve one's social standing with tales of luxury or adventure. Whatever the desired change, what is evident is the idea that this change cannot be brought about by staying put.

As touristic practice, this journeying is only possible for those who have the ability, mobility and motivation to allow travel to be enacted. As the factors that influence ability and mobility change, we might expect to see the development of new tourism products; for example, with increased technological advances space travel is becoming a reality and will open up more opportunities for escapism, sightseeing, education, and so on.[20] Technology may also feature in decreasing the demand for travel. For example, the online, virtual world *Second Life* has many virtual tourism environments, and rapid advances in virtual reality technology already enable 'armchair travel'. Whether such forms of artificial travel will replace the real physical movement of people or satisfy their motivations for travel is yet to be fully tested.

Due to the global COVID-19 pandemic, the testing of virtual travel may come sooner than expected. With many of the main tourist-generating markets under lockdown, tourism is one of the hardest hit economic sectors as the restrictions on travel lead to holiday cancellations and no bookings. What the ramifications will be for tourism are unknown. A key factor will be the economic situation at both the level of the household and on national and global scales. However, the tourism sector has weathered many storms: the oil crisis of 1974–75, the attack on the World Trade Center in 2001 and the resulting conflicts in the Middle East, and terror attacks in numerous destinations, eg Bali 2005 and Tunisia 2015 – after which *where* people choose to travel changes rather than *if* they choose to travel at all. And, as we have noted in relation to cruise tourism, COVID-19 has not halted bookings for future trips.

Whether the reasons for tourist travel will change remains to be seen. One of the propellants for the early development of leisure travel was the desire to see for oneself. This cannot be easily replaced – regardless of how sophisticated virtual worlds become, they will remain just that: virtual. In addition, motivations such as the desire to see friends and relatives, experience different weather and engage in sporting activities, are likely to continue to prompt people to go on holiday. And, to take another lesson from history: the end of the Napoleonic wars in 1815 also ended a 20-year closure of continental Europe to many Britons. Once travel became easier people headed abroad in greater numbers than ever before (Buzard, 1993). COVID-19 might prove to be the cause of a new growth in tourism activity fuelled by the lifting of restrictions on the apparent innate need to be physically mobile in some form.

Notes
[1] www2.unwto.org/
[2] According to statistics from the UNWTO and the World Travel and Tourism Council (WTTC) www.wttc.org/about/media-centre/press-releases/press-releases/2019/travel-tourism-continues-strong-growth-above-global-gdp/ and www.wttc.org/research/economic-research/economic-impact-analysis/
[3] IRTS 2008, 2.13 https://www.unwto.org/glossary-tourism-terms
[4] Research from the European Union shows that of the 1.2 billion 'tourist trips' (ie trips with an overnight stay) made by EU residents in 2013, nearly half were

for holidays, leisure and recreation – which is what we might more colloquially consider to be tourism. A third of the trips were to visit relatives and friends, and nearly 12 per cent were for professional purposes. Most of these trips were fairly short, mostly under three nights in length. Three out of four trips were within the tourist's own country of residence, indicating that even within the EU, with the ease of travelling between countries, most tourism is still domestic.

5   www.telegraph.co.uk/travel/comment/rise-of-the-chinese-tourist/

6   http://kto.visitkorea.or.kr/eng/tourismStatics/keyFacts/KoreaMonthlyStatistics/eng/inout/inout.kto

7   http://gutsytraveler.com/women-travel-statistics-women-travel-trends/ and www.usatoday.com/story/travel/2013/04/25/vacation-travel-study/2110505/. US women also study abroad more than men do: www.washingtonpost.com/news/answer-sheet/wp/2015/10/09/why-do-more-u-s-women-study-abroad-than-men/

8   Within Europe, the over-55s make up around a third of all tourists but although this is a substantial portion of the market, it is actually slightly less than their proportion of the total population. The 55–65 age group participates in tourism at a similar rate to other age groups and makes up 15 per cent of tourists, whereas the over 65s are the most populous age group but they travel relatively less than younger groups. See: http://ec.europa.eu/eurostat/statistics-explained/index.php/File:Share_of_the_EU_population_participating_in_tourism,_by_age_groups,_EU-28(%C2%B9),_2013.png

9   www.mirror.co.uk/news/world-news/magalufs-summer-shame-sex-scandals-4151973

10 According to Cruise Lines International Association (CLIA).

11 www.theguardian.com/commentisfree/2020/apr/14/cruise-ships-coronavirus-passengers-future

12 https://nypost.com/2020/04/01/cruise-bookings-are-on-the-rise-for-2021-despite-coronavirus/; www.seatrade-cruise.com/news/singapore-positions-support-cruise-tourism-revival?fbclid=IwAR3SUh2Hemo0rf_QTaNteikDBphtTlxUuBOisYdZ_La85lO1OSdM6v9vn3s; https://qz.com/1830415/despite-coronavirus-outbreaks-cruise-bookings-are-up-for-2021/

13 www.nytimes.com/2014/12/24/business/international/plastic-surgery-tourism-brings-chinese-to-south-korea.html?_r=0

14 www.go-gulf.ae/blog/retail-spending-dubai/

15 According to UNWTO *Tourism Highlights 2017 Edition*, international tourist arrivals in 2016 were 55 per cent in advanced economies and 45 per cent in emerging economies.

16 www.thomson.co.uk/destinations/europe/greece/thassos/holidays-thassos.html

17 www.destinationsindia.com/hill-resorts-in-india/kodaikanal.html

18 www.xinhuanet.com/english/2019-01/28/c_137781742.htm

19 www.theguardian.com/travel/shortcuts/2017/jan/17/from-barcelona-to-malia-how-brits-on-holiday-have-made-themselves-unwelcome

20 www.wired.co.uk/article/spacex-blue-origin-space-tourism

References

Andrews, H. (2011) *The British on Holiday: Nation, Identity and Consumption,* Bristol: Channel View.

Buzard, J. (1993) *The Beaten Track: European Tourism, Literature, and the Ways to 'Culture' 1800–1918*, Oxford: Clarendon Press.

Dann, G. M. S. (1977) 'Anomie, ego-enhancement, and tourism', *Annals of Tourism Research*, 4(4): 184–94.

Smith, V. (1977) *Hosts and Guests*, Philadelphia: University of Pennsylvania Press.

Sontag, S. (1979) *On Photography*, Harmondsworth: Penguin.

11

Travel as Exploration: Science, the Unknown and Personal Discovery

Emily Thomas

Introduction

Exploration is often understood as discovery: travelling to places, or acquiring knowledge, that is new to us. Historian Paul Fussell (1980) conceives exploration this way, distinguishing exploration from other kinds of travel by the way explorers seek out 'the undiscovered', moving 'towards the formless and the unknown'. For Fussell, exploration is a heroic, athletic, paramilitary activity. He conjures up images of buccaneering explorers, travelling across seas and continents to reach distant lands: Christopher Columbus; Francis Drake; Scott of the Antarctic. Others conceive exploration more broadly. For example, historian William Goetzmann argues that exploration is 'something more' than adventure or discovery. He describes exploration as a kind of purposeful seeking, and argues it is the process of seeking that matters – for discoveries can be produced by accident (1966: xi).

  This chapter considers human exploration, and what it can tell us about the motivations underlying human travel. The first part briefly describes the history of exploration, focusing on the European 'Age of Discovery'. It asks why people explored, and explains the increasing role that science came to play, driven by the work of philosopher Francis Bacon. The second part looks at possibilities for explorative travel today. It argues grand journeys of discovery are still feasible, especially

205

Figure 11.1: *Columbus taking possession of the new country* **(1893)**

The explorer Christopher Columbus landing in the Caribbean. This picture, by Gergio Deluci, is from a 19th-century textbook.

in the shape of undersea or space travel. Further, personal journeys of exploration are available to all of us – there are always more places to see, more world to understand.

A very brief history of human exploration

Humans have been exploring for a very long time. Over the course of our history as a species, we have settled on continents all over the planet (see Chapter 2 'Biological Perspectives on Travel'). Historian Felipe Fernández-Armesto argues that the chronicle of our species has two major stories to tell. The first is one of 'divergence'. This occupies most of our pre-history, extending from the emergence of *Homo sapiens* around 300,000 years ago to the past few thousand years. During this period early human cultures formed, grew more disparate and dissimilar, migrating across continents. The second story is one of 'convergence'. This occupies the most recent 10,000 years and tells how humankind has gradually reconnected, starting to come together globally (2006: 1–4). Both stories are tales of exploration, but this chapter will focus on the second.

Written records from antiquity provide insights into the purposes and experiences of early explorers. Some of the earliest accounts come from voyages of exploration commissioned by the ancient Egyptian pharaohs. These often had a commercial motive: finding new trading routes or natural resources. One prominent Egyptian explorer was Harkhuf, a nobleman dispatched by the pharaoh around 2300 BCE, to seek the mystical African kingdom of Yam. Harkhuf's testimony, recorded on his tomb at Aswan, reveals how he returned from this expedition with '300 donkeys, laden with incense, ebony, heknu, ivory, panthers … and every good product'. Given the opportunities for disaster on such expeditions, it is little wonder that Harkhuf described himself as 'more excellent and vigilant' than any traveller who had previously ventured to discover Yam (Goedicke, 1981).

Commerce continued to motivate explorative travel in the ancient and medieval worlds. In the second century BCE, Chinese Emperor Wu of Han was especially active among ancient leaders in sponsoring expeditions to find new trade routes and alliances. At his request, diplomat Zhang Qian undertook several missions to discover more about the lands west and south of China. This resulted in the development of trade missions and the eventual establishment of what is now known as the 'Silk Road'. For seafaring peoples such as the Vikings, voyages of exploration were also motivated by the desire to find new lands to settle. Through such missions, Iceland was discovered and settled in 860 CE, and Greenland settled in 982 CE by Erik Thorvaldsson. His son, Leif Erikson, continued the family tradition of exploration, venturing even further west and founding the settlement of Vinland (probably in Newfoundland). By the medieval period, improvements in shipbuilding had permitted the expansion of trading routes even farther. Merchant explorers such as the Venetian Marco Polo and the Chinese Wang Dayuan in the 13th and 14th centuries made extraordinary journeys to the boundaries of their known worlds, returning to their rulers with fabulous tales of strange customs, goods and products.

The European Age of Discovery

The 'Age of Discovery' is a slice of European history, running from the 15th to the 17th century. It was an extension of the wider thirst for commercial knowledge and international trade that began flowering in the middle ages. By the 1400s, progress in shipbuilding and navigation techniques made long oceanic voyages more feasible. At the same time, European rulers were becoming increasingly competitive in their search for new trading routes to Asia and Africa. They were particularly interested in sea routes that bypassed overland routes from ports in the eastern Mediterranean, over which the Republic of Venice and Ottoman Empire held monopolies.

Portuguese, French, Spanish, Dutch and British sailors led the charge. Within a few decades, this environment of competitive exploration resulted in discoveries of lands and civilizations previously unknown to Europeans. The Portuguese monarchy sponsored sailors to find a maritime route to India around the coast of Africa; Vasco da Gama achieved this in 1498. Prior to this, the Italian mariner Christopher Columbus, having had his proposal rejected by the Portuguese king, was sponsored by the Spanish monarchs Ferdinand and Isabella to find a western trade route to India. Columbus's encounter with the Caribbean in 1492 sparked a plethora of further expeditions, inspired by tales he heard from indigenous peoples about lands laden with gold and spices. In the space of a few years, Columbus made further discoveries in central and northern South America. Meanwhile, on behalf of the English King Henry VII, John Cabot landed in Newfoundland and North America. Acting for the Portugeuese king, Pedro Alvares Cabral sailed further south west than intended and landed in Brazil. The search for a western trade route to east Asia culminated in the voyage of Portuguese sailor Ferdinand Magellan. Sponsored by the Spanish King Charles I, Magellan left Seville in 1519 with a fleet of five ships, on what was expected to be a two-year voyage. Magellan was killed after reaching the Philippines, but one ship returned in 1522, having completed the first recorded circumnavigation of the globe. Along the way, its sailors became the first Europeans to visit Patagonia, Guam, the Philippines; and sail (what are now known as) the Magellan Straits across the southern tip of South America.

Expeditions were also launched to discover new trade routes across the Arctic. In 1550s London, the Company of Merchant Adventurers to New Lands was founded, and sponsored an expedition by Sir Hugh Willoughby to find a north east trade route to China. Willoughby reached as far as Novaya Zemlya in the Russian Arctic. A few years later, Sir Martin Frobisher explored the northern coasts of the Canadian Arctic, vainly attempting to find the elusive north west passage to Asia. Around the same time, Sir Francis Drake completed the second circumnavigation of the earth – although this Crown-commissioned expedition was aimed less at new trading routes, and more at piracy against Spanish vessels in the Pacific. Nonetheless, these new routes resulted in successful trade. In 1704, one writer lists the products flooding into Europe:

> Gums, Drugs, Spices, Silks and Cottons, precious Stones, Sulphur, Gold, Saltpeter, Rice, Tea, *China* Ware, Coffee, *Japan* Varnish'd Works, all sorts of Dyes, of Cordials, and Perfumes, Pearls, Ivory, Ostrich-Feathers, Parrots, Monkeys, and an endless number of Ncessaries, Conveniences, Curiousities, and other Comforts and Supports of Human Life. (Anon, 1704: lxxiii)

Despite their rewards, these early modern trans-oceanic voyages were phenomenally risky. Ever present dangers included shipwreck, lethal diseases such as scurvy, and dehydration. There were mutinies: both Magellan and Drake executed fellow sailors for rebelling against their authority. There was also the possibility of conflict with unknown peoples. These mariners painted exploration as a predominantly male, swashbuckling activity. Yet many of these sailors did not return home. What could motivate their risk-taking?

The principal reasons were economic. The financial gains from securing control over new international trade routes drove European monarchs, and later merchant trading companies, to invest in the huge expense of such voyages. If successful, the explorers themselves stood to gain vast wealth, fame, and high status. For example, Columbus negotiated a contract with the Spanish crown that allowed him ten per cent of any revenues from the lands he found. Frobisher petitioned Queen Elizabeth for five per cent of all profits from any new routes he opened. The anarchic nature of early modern exploration also meant that riches were freely available from piracy and looting, the proceeds from which were sometimes shared among the crew. The prospect of troves of bullion in newly discovered lands encouraged further journeys of exploration and conquest. This drove the conquistador Francisco de Orellana, who sought the 'Land of Cinnamon' in the South American jungle, and became the first European to sail the length of the Amazon.

As travel increased, conquest and exploration required and enabled improvements in cartographical knowledge. By the 17th century, the shape of the world's continents were roughly outlined. Consider this world map (Figure 11.2), published in 1570, derived from plates made by the Flemish cartographer Gerardus Mercator.

The rough shapes of the Americas, Africa and Asia are all present. Of the continents, only Antarctica and Australia are missing, both blanketed under the legend *Terra Australis Incognita* (unknown southern land).

Figure 11.2: *Typus orbis terrarum* **by Ortelius (1570)**

A map of the world from a book of maps published by Ortelius in 1570, based on a map by Gerard Mercator, outlining the 'known' continents of the period.

Slowly, the possibilities offered by travel were recognized by intellectuals. The English philosopher Francis Bacon saw, further than anyone, the potential *scientific* uses of travel. Explaining how requires a bit of background.

Natural philosophy and Francis Bacon

In the 17th century, the discipline that we label 'science' did not exist as a distinct kind of enquiry. The closest thing was 'natural philosophy'. At its broadest, philosophy is the study of reality and our relationships with it. Philosophy has always included many different kinds of enquiries, such as ethics. Historically, philosophy also included 'natural philosophy', enquiries into the physical nature of our world that we would now consider scientific. Although natural philosophy covers biology, chemistry, physics and geology, it also covers topics that we would not now consider scientific, such as God's workings in nature.

During this period, philosophical and scientific enquiry were entwined. Descartes' pioneering theory of ocean tides was grounded in his philosophical understanding of matter. Newton tied his groundbreaking account of gravity and the heavenly motions with his understanding of God. Nonetheless, the natural sciences were beginning to emerge as distinct disciplines from philosophy and theology. In part, this was due to fresh emphasis on 'experimentalism'.

The material or physical world is the world that surrounds us, the world of tables and human beings, birds and hills, rocks and stars. Traditionally, the material world was investigated using logical principles or *a priori* reasoning. In contrast, an 'experimentalist' would gather data about the world through observation and experiment. Experimentalists include well-known figures such as Newton, and lesser-known figures such as William Gilbert (who, among other things, developed the word 'electricity'). However, preeminent among them is Francis Bacon.

Bacon enjoyed a tumultuous political career, and wrote on many subjects: the nature of religion, ethics, law, and society. He even produced a utopian novel. However, he devoted the last years of his life to detailing his vision of natural philosophy. He argued the medieval approach to science was foolish, comparing it to the way spiders spin webs out of themselves. In place of this traditional approach, Bacon argued for experimentalism. He compares experimentalists to bumblebees. They collect the products of nature, 'flowers of garden and field', and transform them into the honey of real knowledge (1964: 97).

Bacon gradually developed a new philosophy of science, arguing that information about the world should be collected through observation and experiment. Scientists could use that information to create axioms, which would be tested through further observation and experiment, ultimately leading to more general axioms.

Bacon set out this scientific method in his 1620 *The Great Instauration (Instauratio Magna)*. Bacon planned that humankind should create nothing less than a complete *historia naturalis*: natural history, or history of nature. The archaic word 'instauration' literally means renewal or restoration, implying that Bacon is looking to renew the sciences. He described the work involved as 'royal': it cannot be executed without great labour and expense, and requires many people to help (1900: 144). Consider the knowledge within the Natural History Museums in London or Washington. They hold information on everything from volcanoes to dinosaurs, yet this is only a fraction of the total Bacon envisaged. Just a few of the things Bacon requested information on included histories of the heavens, the seas, the history of flames 'and things ignited', fish, mountains and fog. These myriad enquiries could not be made wholly in laboratories or observatories. They required people to venture out into the world and bring back information about it.

Figure 11.3: Frontispiece from Sir Francis Bacon's *The Great Instauration* (1620)

The frontispiece to Bacon's book depicts ships sailing beyond the pillars of the known world in order to expand human knowledge. For Bacon, exploration and knowledge were entwined.

This is why travel, and oral or written testimonies of travel, were central to Bacon's enterprise. This is emphasized in the original frontispiece illustration of *The Great Instauration,* which depicts one ship sailing away into a boundless ocean, and another returning, riding low in the water with wealth. The ships sit between the Pillars of Hercules, the rocks flanking the Strait of Gibraltar. In Graeco-Roman mythology, Hercules, the adventurous son of the God Jupiter, travelled as far as these pillars, and they came to represent the limits of the known world. The pillars were inscribed 'nothing more beyond' (*nec plus ultra*), a warning that ships should sail no further.

In Bacon's frontispiece, the ships are sailing to and from seas *beyond* the pillars, symbolizing his view that we should expand the limits of our knowledge. Just as Columbus went beyond Europe, philosophers should go beyond medieval knowledge. Later illustrations of the pillars sometimes changed the inscription to 'go farther still' (*plus ultra*), echoing the motto of Charles V, Holy Roman Emperor in the early 16th century, who often sponsored conquistadores' explorations in the Americas. Beneath the ships, a line reads, 'Many shall go to and fro, and knowledge shall increase', a line borrowed from a Biblical prophecy (Daniel 12:1–4). For Bacon, science and travel were deeply linked through divine prophesy (McKnight, 2006; Thomas, 2020).

Although Bacon aimed to show that scientific curiosity would contribute to the glorification of God, not everyone agreed. Some worried that scientific curiosity might transgress the limits God imposed on humankind. Worldly curiosity was sometimes associated with vanity, pride, and disobedience (Hayden, 2012: 16–17). When Adam in Milton's *Paradise Lost* expresses curiosity about the motions of the heavenly bodies, the angel Raphael replies: 'Think only what concerns thee and thy being; Dream not of other worlds' (Milton, 2005: 8.2.72–178). Despite its critics, Bacon's new philosophy of science would have a huge impact on exploration.

Science and the Age of Discovery

In 1606, Sir Thomas 'the Travailer' Palmer produced a taxonomy of travellers. It includes ambassadors, spies, soldiers, exiles and private traders. It does *not* include natural philosophers. But that soon changed. After Bacon's death, a group of British natural philosophers established the Royal Society. It aimed to further Bacon's vision of developing a complete natural history. Like Bacon, members of the Royal Society were deeply concerned with gathering data about far-flung lands. They met regularly and discussed the latest travel narratives, as well as 'curiosities' brought back by travellers, such as animal bones or plant seeds.

In addition, the Royal Society began publishing calls for information. Robert Boyle, the founding father of chemistry, authored one such request, titled *General Heads for a Natural History of a Countrey,*

Great or Small (1665). It asked for details on longitude and latitude, temperature, meteors and the 'Store, Bigness, Goodness, Seasons, Haunts, Pecularities of any kind' of local fish.

The view that travel could be a form of data collection was taking shape. Later sets of instructions to travellers followed similar patterns. For example, Edward Leigh's 1671 'diatribe' on travel provides a long list of things to observe while surveying a country, including its latitude, climate, the 'goodness or barrenness of the Ground', 'the populousness of the people, its commodities, herbs, beasts, birds, fishes, and insects' (1671: 7–9).

All of this led to a new kind of explorer: the natural philosopher. Two of the earliest travelling scientists were the friends and colleagues John Ray and Francis Willoughby. They travelled to the west coast of England to study seabirds, toured Europe collecting animals and plants, and published natural histories of plants and birds based on their findings.

Expeditions began to include natural philosophers among their crew. Louis-Antoine de Bougainville's 1767–68 voyage took a botanist, an astronomer and a naturalist. (Unbeknown to Bougainville, the naturalist's assistant was Jeanne Baret, an exploration-minded woman who disguised herself as a man.) On his first circumnavigation of the globe, Cook outdid Bougainville by taking an astronomer, a botanist, and *two* naturalists (Leed, 1991: 194). At the start of the 19th century, Alexander von Humboldt followed in this tradition, taking the botanist Aimé Bonpland on his voyages to the Americas. Almost 300 plants and more than 100 animals are named after Humboldt, and more places are named after him than any other person: the state of Nevada was almost called Humboldt, and an area on the moon is called Mare Humboldtianum.[1]

Many other kinds of travellers also contributed to the Royal Society's project, including navy captains, colonial governors, ambassadors and merchants (their salaries helpfully paid by other sources) (Carey, 1997). For example, in 1664 the Royal Society fellow Henry Oldenburg wrote to John Winthrop the Younger, a governor of the Connecticut Colony, asking for information on cosmography, astronomy, navigation, mines, tides and the making of salt. His request produced a rattlesnake, some Indian corn, butternuts, various kinds of fish, and a hummingbird. All were exhibited at a Royal Society meeting.

Bacon's natural philosophy project was blossoming. Its successes led to immense public interest, and people became fascinated as never before with travel books, maps, atlases, geography, geology and botany. Many works ran through multiple editions and reprints, including Duval's

1662 *A Geographical Dictionary*, Meriton's 1671 *Geographical Description of the World*, and Bohun's 1688 *A Geographical Dictionary* (Hayden, 2012; Swann, 2001). The mapmaker John Sellers built a business out of printing atlases, coasting pilots, charts, navigation handbooks, and almanacs (Worms, 2008).

In 1704, the Churchill brothers published *A Collection of Voyages and Travels*, bringing together a variety of new (or newly translated) travelogues which covered places such as Chile, Japan, Greenland and the Congo. The travelogues are prefaced by an *Account of the Progress of Navigation*, part of which details the advantages of travel:

> Astronomy has receiv'd the Addition of many Constellations never seen before. Natural and Moral History is embellished with the most beneficial Increase of so many thousands of Plants it had never before received, so many Drugs and Spices, such variety of Beasts, Birds and Fishes, such varieties in Minerals, Mountains and Waters, such unaccountable diversity of Climates and Men. (Anon, 1704)

The Age of Discovery was literally expanding European knowledge. As von Humboldt (cited in Vogel, 1999: 6) put it, this period 'doubled the works of the Creation'. The discovery of Australia, New Zealand and the South Sea Islands brought around one third of the Earth's surface into the 'known world'. Once James Cook's 18th-century voyages had laid to rest the long-held belief in the existence of a vast land mass in the southern hemisphere (*Terra Australis Incognita*), there remained no new continents to be discovered.

Exploration during the long 19th century

Once the Age of Discovery passed in the mid-1700s, the outlines of the continents had been largely sketched – even if their interiors were not yet filled in. European trading posts and settlements had been established in many parts of the world. Yet the connection between exploration and science persisted, especially within British travel history. The following few examples hint at the many characters who ventured forth from British soil in search of new knowledge during the long 19th century.

In 1831, Charles Darwin boarded the *Beagle*. He embarked on a voyage that would last over four years, sailing around the coast of South America, the Falkland Islands, Tahiti, New Zealand and Australia.

The Admiralty had commissioned the *Beagle* with the primary purpose of conducting hydrographic surveys, to improve navigational information for the navy and commerce. The collection of natural history knowledge and specimens was also deemed important, hence the inclusion of Darwin as a gentleman naturalist on board. Darwin's work on the *Beagle* would eventually contribute to his groundbreaking theory of evolution by natural selection. Darwin himself noted the benefits of travel to scientific endeavour, stating 'nothing can be more improving to a young naturalist, than a journey in distant countries' (Darwin, 2008: 507–8). In his autobiography, Darwin claimed that he owed to that voyage the first real education of his mind: 'I worked on true Baconian principles, and without any theory collected facts on a wholesale scale' (Darwin, 1958: 119).

In the mid-19th century, the English scientist Francis Galton undertook a difficult journey into (what is now known as) Namibia, partly to map it. His cartographic efforts were rewarded by medals from the British and French Geographical Societies, and by having a genus of southern African plant named after him: *Galtonia*. In 1855 he published *The Art of Travel,* a handbook of practical advice for travellers needing to 'rough it' in 'wild countries'. A flavour of Galton's explorations are conveyed by its chapter titles, which include 'Rafts and Boats', 'Shooting, hints on' and 'Savages, Management of'.

In the 1890s, Mary Kingsley explored uncharted parts of west Africa. Upon the death of her parents, Kingsley was freed from domestic responsibilities, and she became one of the few female explorers of her time. She wrote that her motive for travelling 'was study ... of native ideas and practices in religion and law' (Kingsley, 1901). She contributed to European understanding of African cultures; became the first European to climb Mount Cameroon; and collected fish, insects and reptiles for the British Museum of Natural History. Some of these were new to science and later named after her, including the fish species *Brycinus kingsleyae* and the *Ctenopoma kingsleyae*.

Kingsley's 1897 *Travels in West Africa* describes an African forest goddess, who teaches the solitary wayfarer what herbs are good for eating and curing disease. She laments:

> I often wish I knew this lady, for the grim, grand African forests are like a great library, in which, so far, I can do little more than look at the pictures, although I am now busily learning the alphabet of their language, so that I may someday read what these pictures mean. (Kingsley, 2003: 512)

Perhaps this description echoes Kingsley's first explorations in her father's library, where as a child she is said to have educated herself, discovering travel and science. Kingsley died in her late 30s, working as a nurse in South Africa during the Boer War.

The early 20th century saw the 'Race for the Poles': explorers aimed to win renown for themselves and their country by being *first* at the Arctic and Antarctic poles. Along the way, they would obtain cartographic and scientific information. In 1910, the race for the Antarctic pole gripped the public imagination, and two parties started off. One was led by the Norwegian explorer Roald Amundsen. The other, larger party was led by the British explorer Robert Falcon Scott. Scott's expedition included geologists, biologists and physicists. Many histories claim that Amundsen was 'only' interested in reaching the pole, whereas Scott was equally interested in Antarctic research. More charitably, Amundsen was prepared to postpone scientific work in favour of winning the race to the pole (Fernández-Armesto, 2006: 1–4). In British histories especially, Scott's scientific aims are discussed with approval – the search for knowledge seen as more commendable than personal or national glory alone.

Figure 11.4: Scott and his men at the South Pole

This photograph, of Scott's team at Amundsen's base at the South Pole, was taken not long before their deaths on the return journey (1912).

Scott's team certainly suffered considerable hardships in the pursuit of science. To illustrate, one of the British scientific aims was to further understanding of the evolutionary links between reptiles and birds, by studying Emperor Penguin embryos. These penguins are native to Antarctica, and are the largest living penguin species. They breed during the Antarctic winter, trekking tens of miles over the ice to breeding colonies. In July 1911, three men left the team's base camp: Edward Wilson, Apsley Cherry-Garrard and 'Birdie' Bowers. They trekked across the Ross Ice Shelf to the only known Emperor Penguin breeding colony. Their journey took five weeks in almost continual darkness, in temperatures that would freeze mercury. Cherry-Garrard describes its 'horror':

> [I]t would be so easy to die .... The trouble is to go on .... It was the darkness that did it. I don't believe minus seventy temperatures would be bad in daylight, not comparatively bad, when you could see where you were going, where you were stepping, where the sledge straps were. (1937: 258–9)

Despite immense difficulties, they succeeded in obtaining three eggs – later returned to Britain for study.

The following Antarctic summer, the race for the South Pole really began. Amundsen reached it first, in late 1911. In early 1912, Scott and four companions also reached it, only to die on the return journey from starvation and cold. In one of his last letters, Scott wrote: 'I may not have proved a great explorer, but we have done the greatest march ever made and come very near to great success' (2005: 416). Despite this tragedy, Scott's expedition was hailed a scientific triumph. After his death, the geographer and explorer Clements Robert Markham wrote that 'the principal aim of this great man ... was the advancement of knowledge', and Scott's scientific results were 'extensive and important' (2005: 4). This view is still held today.[2]

We should not forget that all these 19th-century journeys – and many others – were pushed through not just by intrepid explorers, but by large teams of people and animals. Historians have recently started to uncover the hidden role of local guides and workers, including many women, in 19th-century European expeditions. Through this research, historian Felix Driver argues that the story of exploration 'becomes a genuinely human story, less about the exceptional qualities of eccentric individuals, more about working relationships and intersecting lives'.[3] In the middle of extreme difficulty, many explorers have found it is their team that gets them through, physically and emotionally. Spanish mountaineer Edurne Pasaban argued that you succeed at such things by having 'good people' around you: a team who 'support' and 'love' you.[4]

What motivates exploration?

We have seen that large-scale drivers such as the economics, politics and science of nations have motivated and funded many expeditions. Yet these expeditions could not have taken place without the explorers and their teams, who often undertook great hardships. What lies behind their exploratory urge?

For some there has been the lure of wealth and power, fame and glory: discovering riches in far off lands or being the first to navigate a new sea route. The thrill of adventure, of overcoming challenges, has also motivated people to leave behind the routine and restrictions of home. When explorers push themselves to their physical and psychological limits, to discover the unknown world, they also often wish to discover more about themselves. They want to know their limits, and push beyond. 'We find out more about ourselves in adversity than in comfort', says adventure travel writer Andrew Mazibrada.[5]

But not all explorers seek adrenalin. 'I think we often confuse thrill-seeking with exploration', says deep-sea cave diver Kenny Broad, a *National Geographic* 'Explorer of the Year'. He explains that many explorers undertaking high risk activities are 'meticulous' risk managers: 'It's about keeping your adrenaline down ... you don't want to be overcome with the emotions.'[6]

Some find thrill in encountering the unknown, gaining new knowledge. From 17th-century natural philosophers working to Baconian principles, to 21st-century oceanographers exploring the deep sea, countless explorers have been motivated by the thirst for knowledge. This is often accompanied by a desire to benefit others through their discoveries. High-altitude archaeologist Constanza Ceruti explains that although fear is constant, they try to leave it behind, because 'we are so aware that the archaeology work is important ... you are helping to preserve this heritage for future generations.'[7]

When asked what keeps him going through difficult challenges, the renowned explorer Sir Ranulph Fiennes offers a personal motivation: 'I often conjured up the image of my father, my grandfather and long lines of Fiennes watching my flagging efforts, and I pressed on because I didn't want to let them down.'[8]

Is exploration still possible today?

You might think that the polar regions were the last unexplored places on Earth, so Scott and Amundsen's achievements marked the end of human exploration. In this vein, travel writer Malcolm Jones (2011) claimed: 'There remain almost no undiscovered corners on the planet'. However, I argue explorative travel is still possible. Here are just a few 21st-century stories of exploration.

In 2009, one of the world's largest underground caves was explored in Vietnam. Son Doong was found to contain an underground forest, complete with species unknown to science.[9] The same year, the mountains lying under the two-mile thick Antarctic ice sheet were mapped for the first time. To examine the buried mountains, the team flew aeroplanes fitted with radar, magnetic and gravity sensors over the ice. The measurements allowed them to 'see' the rock beneath, and found mountains higher than the Alps.[10]

Our planet contains as many as a hundred peoples who have not had significant contact with wider modern society,[11] mostly living in the

Figure 11.5: Climbers ascending Manaslu summit

A queue of mountain climbers on Manaslu, Himalayas, whose peak is over 8,000m high – the 'death zone'. Images of over-crowding on these mountains, particularly Everest, have prompted some to wonder 'Is exploration possible anymore?'

dense forests of the Amazon and New Guinea. Although indigenous rights organizations warn against making contact with these peoples, in 2014 first contact was made with another tribe living in the Amazon.[12] In 2016, a photographer accidentally flew over an additional as-yet-uncontacted tribe, and took some stunning photographs.[13]

Some of these discoveries are discoveries for *all* humans. In the future, most exploration stories will be of this kind, because we will be venturing into places that are not currently habitable for humans. There may be many more caves under the earth, some of which do not have passages leading to the surface. We have explored very little of the Earth's seas: according to the US National Oceanic and Atmospheric Administration, 'more than eighty percent of this vast, underwater realm remains unmapped, unobserved, and unexplored'.[14] This lack of knowledge was highlighted in the search for Malaysian Airlines Flight 370, which disappeared mid-flight in March 2014; its wreckage has not been recovered, despite extensive searches. Oceanic exploration will improve our knowledge of the sea floor, weather systems and environmental change. It will almost certainly uncover more creatures new to science.[15]

Finally, looking up, we have explored only a fraction of outer space. Humans have long been fascinated with celestial bodies. Some of our earliest surviving stories are about interplanetary travel, described by one literary theorist as the 'ur' (earliest or original) form of science fiction (Roberts, 2006: vii). Some seeds of modern space travel were planted during the Age of Discovery. In the early 17th century, Galileo used his telescope to study the moon, and found mountains there. In 1665, the natural philosopher Robert Hooke gleefully wrote:

> By the means of *Telescopes*, there is nothing so *far distant* but may be represented to our view; and by the help of *Microscopes*, there is nothing so *small*, as to escape our inquiry; hence there is a new visible World discovered to the understanding. By this means the Heavens are open'd, and a vast number of new Stars.

John Seller's 1700 *Atlas Caelestis*, atlas of the heavens, dwells on the moon. He notes that, like our own planet, it is composed of solid and liquid parts, which is why many astronomers have conceived the moon 'as it were another Earth' (1700: 12).

In the 20th century, humans took this fascination further, sending robots, animals and humans into space. In 1969 we set foot on the moon. As so often in stories of exploration, the search for new

Figure 11.6a: Map of the moon from Seller's *Atlas Caelestis* (1700)

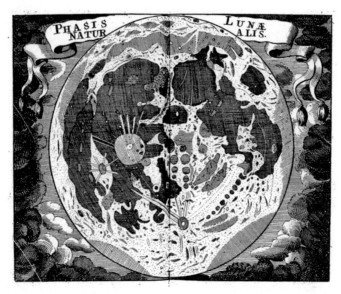

Figure 11.6b: Astronaut on the moon, Apollo 15 mission (1971)

Improvements in telescope technology allowed humans to map the moon, an early example being Seller's atlas from 1700. Humans first visited the moon 269 years later. James Irwin can be seen here saluting the US flag during the Apollo 15 mission.

knowledge went hand-in-hand with political and economic concerns. The 'Space Race' of the Cold War was inspired, fuelled and funded by the rivalry of two political superpowers, driven by their ambitions for economic and political dominance.

We cannot yet explore the whole heavens, but we are trying. *Voyager 1*, one of NASA's unmanned spacecraft, has travelled further than any other man-made object. Launched in 1977, it has since left our solar system. *Voyager 1* is now travelling through interstellar space, and will drift close to a star in the constellation of Camelopardalis in around 40,000 years (unfortunately, it will stop transmitting information over the next decade or so).[16] In 2016, humans launched a satellite into orbit around Jupiter, and a programme was announced that will build nano-spaceships with the aim of reaching the star system nearest to us.[17] In 2017, Vice President Mike Pence stated that the US is 'at the dawn of a new era of space exploration'. Pence is a key supporter of establishing a US military space force.[18] He has called for a return to the moon, and 'American boots on the face of Mars'.[19] In addition to US efforts, a number of national space agencies and private companies are now actively working on sending crewed missions to Mars. This includes billionaire Elon Musk's company SpaceX, which aims to create a Martian colony.[20]

Although some question the benefits of investing time and resources in space travel, outer space has captured the human imagination for centuries, and shows no signs of waning. Space programmes have also led to unexpected scientific discoveries with widespread commercial and humanitarian uses, such as mobile phones, surgical technologies, and the memory foam mattress. The political, military and economic ambitions of governments and companies, combined perhaps with the personal desires of key figures for glory or thrill, are driving a new era of space travel. The urge to journey beyond our world, to discover more great unknowns, looks set to continue the story of human exploration well into the future.

More personal journeys of exploration

The introduction to this chapter explained that exploration is usually understood as travelling to places, or acquiring knowledge, that is new to *us*. Who is 'us'?

'Us' might mean all humans. In this sense, exploring Mars will be new to us. But the 'us' can also be more specific. For Viking explorers, the 'us' are the Vikings. For Chinese explorers, the 'us' are the Chinese. Exploration is often only considered from the viewpoint of the explorer, who defines what is unknown and what remains to be discovered. For early modern European explorers, discoveries reshaped their understanding of the world. As historian Anthony Pagden explains: 'A new world of European moral and social understanding had begun with the discovery of the New World of America' (1993: 111). But at the same time, the indigenous peoples who were subjected, often in a very damaging way, to the consequences of such 'discoveries' also had their worldviews transformed. Europeans labelled America the 'new world', but it was not new – America and its peoples were already there. The only newness lay in peoples' fresh understanding of the world.

The meaning of 'us' can change across time, as well as geography. Take the 'discovery' of lost cities. The great temple complex of Borobudur in Indonesia was rediscovered in the early 19th century. In the same period, Mayan ruins were found in the Mexican jungles – including Chichen Itza. In the early 20th century, archeologists discovered the tomb of Tutankhamun in Egypt and the 'lost' Incan city of Machu Picchu in Peru. In 2016, archeologists discovered an enormous Mayan tomb in Belize.[21] Many ruins are likely still out there, and all will be new to 'us', 21st-century humans.

'Us' can also be personal. Just as the voyages of Columbus and Humboldt counted as exploration because they were exploring places new to European knowledge, we can each explore places that are new to *us* personally. As Goetzmann (1966) perceptively observed, the process of seeking is integral to exploration, and curiosity drives our own voyages of discovery (see Chapter 2 'Biological Perspectives on Travel' on human curiosity). That feeling of discovery, of newness, of expanding horizons, is open to us all. We just have to go somewhere we have not been before. The Swiss adventurer and travel writer Ella Maillart recognized this:

> Travel can also be the spirit of adventure somewhat tamed for those who are no Frobishers ready to find new straits, but who would desire to do something they are a bit afraid of – you can feel as brave as Columbus starting for the Unknown the first time you decide to enter a Chinese lane full of boys laughing at you, when you risk climbing down into a Tibetan pub for a meal smelling of rotten meat, or simply when addressing a witty taxi-driver in Paris. (1950: 114–26)

I argue the difference between a 'Club Med' trip to France, and a traveller's journey across China, does not lie in the distance, but in how much of the place we visit is new to us. The travel writer Paul Theroux touches on this when he describes the phenomenon of 'Travelling-to-China-or-Peru-Without-Leaving-America', where travellers surround themselves in a Western cocoon. He writes:

> I am calling attention to the phenomenon because it is so far from the traditional notion of travel as going away .... The interest in travel today, which is passionate, arises out of the fact that there is a form of travel prevalent that is now very easy – people want to find an antidote for the immobility that mass tourism has produced; people want to believe that somewhere, somehow, it is still very dangerous, bizarre, anxiety-making and exotic to travel, that one can still make discoveries in a glorious solitary way. (1985: 134–5)

Theroux argues this urge to leave the Western cocoon drives people to ride by donkey across Ethiopia, or sail slowly down the Ganges.

It is becoming ever easier to travel without *exploring*: to travel without coming into contact with the unknown. Yet exploring is still possible for each of us. We do not have to travel under the sea, or ride rockets to Mars, to make discoveries. We just need to challenge ourselves to encounter the unfamiliar, to step into the unknown. Ride mules through the Horn of Africa, or stick our thumbs out by the side of a road in Uttar Pradesh.

Notes

[1] www.independent.co.uk/news/people/profiles/alexander-von-humboldt-the-eccentric-explorer-was-the-most-famous-man-in-the-world-after-napoleon-a6703346.html
[2] www.bbc.co.uk/news/science-environment-16530953
[3] www.theguardian.com/education/2009/dec/08/nineteenth-century-explorers-local-guides
[4] https://floratheexplorer.com/ranulph-fiennes-an-explorers-motivation/
[5] www.sidetracked.com/why-explore/
[6] www.npr.org/2011/09/20/140637118/explorers-push-the-limits-despite-the-risks?t=1566341984665
[7] www.npr.org/2011/09/20/140637118/explorers-push-the-limits-despite-the-risks?t=1566341984665
[8] www.telegraph.co.uk/women/mother-tongue/familyhistory/6359868/Ranulph-Fiennes-the-chilling-and-thrilling-truth-about-my-family.html

9   You can even visit it virtually. See http://news.nationalgeographic.com/2015/
    05/150520-infinity-cave-son-doong-vietnam-virtual-tour-photography-
    conservation/
10 www.theguardian.com/environment/2009/feb/24/antarctica-mountains
11 www.survivalinternational.org/tribes/uncontacted-brazil
12 www.theguardian.com/world/2014/aug/01/amazon-tribe-makes-first-contact-
    with-outside-world
13 www.theguardian.com/world/2016/dec/22/photographer-shows-first-
    images-of-uncontacted-amazon-tribe
14 https://oceanservice.noaa.gov/facts/exploration.html
15 www.scientificamerican.com/article/just-how-little-do-we-know-about-the-
    ocean-floor/
16 https://voyager.jpl.nasa.gov/mission/interstellar.html
17 https://breakthroughinitiatives.org/News/4
18 www.washingtonpost.com/opinions/mike-pence-its-time-for-congress-to-
    establish-the-space-force/2019/03/01/50820a58-3c4e-11e9-a06c-3ec8ed509d15_
    story.html?noredirect=on
19 www.scientificamerican.com/article/pence-calls-for-ldquo-new-era-of-space-
    exploration-rdquo-at-nasa/
20 www.theguardian.com/science/2018/nov/19/space-how-far-have-we-gone-
    and-where-are-we-going
21 www.theguardian.com/science/2016/aug/06/maya-snake-dynasty-
    tomb-belize-ruins

References

Anon, cited in A. Churchill (ed) (1704) *A Collection of Voyages and Travels, Vol I*, London, p lxxiii.

Bacon, F. (1900) *The Works of Francis Bacon, Vol VIII*, Boston, MA: Houghton Mifflin. p144.

Bacon, F. (1964) *The Philosophy of Francis Bacon*. Edited by B. Farrington. Chicago, IL: University of Chicago Press.

Boyle, R. (1665–66) *Philosophical Transactions* 1: 186–9.

Carey, D. (1997) 'Compiling nature's history: travellers and travel narratives in the early Royal Society', *Annals of Science*, 54: 269–92.

Cherry-Garrard, A. (1937) *The Worst Journey in the World*, London: Penguin.

Darwin, C. (2008) *The Voyage of the Beagle*, New York: Cosimo Classics.

Darwin, C. (1958) *The Autobiography of Charles Darwin 1809–1882*. Edited by N. Barlow. London: Collins.

Fernández-Armesto, F. (2006) *Pathfinders: A Global History of Exploration*, Oxford: Oxford University Press.

Fussell, P. (1980) *Abroad: British Literary Travelling Between the Wars*, New York: Oxford University Press.

Goedicke, H. (1981) 'Harkhuf's travels', *Journal of Near Eastern Studies*, 40 (1): 1–20.

Goetzmann, W. (1966) *Exploration and Empire: The Explorer and the Scientist in the Winning of the American West,* New York: Alfred A. Knopf, p xi.

Hayden, J. (2012) 'Intersections and Cross-Fertilization', in J. Hayden (ed) *Travel Narratives, the New Science, and Literary Discourse 1569–1750,* London: Routledge.

Hooke, R. (1665) *Micrographia,* London.

Jones, M. (2011) 'Paul Theroux and the Death of Travel Writing', *The Daily Beast* (June 05, 2011): https://www.thedailybeast.com/paul-theroux-and-the-death-of-travel-writing

Kingsley, M. (1901) *West African Studies* (Second, expanded ed), London: Macmillan.

Kingsley, M. (2003) *Travels in West Africa,* Mineola, NY: Dover Publications, Inc.

Leigh, E. (1671) *Three Diatribes or Discourses,* London.

Leed, E. J. (1991) *The Mind of the Traveller,* New York: Basic Books.

McKnight, S. A. (2006) *The Religious Foundations of Francis Bacon's Thought,* Columbia: University of Missouri Press.

Maillart, E. (1950) 'My Philosophy of Travel', in M. A. Michael (ed) *Traveller's Quest: Original Contributions Towards a Philosophy of Travel,* London: William Hodge, pp 114–26.

Markham, C. R. (2005) 'Preface', in R. F. Scott *Journal: Captain Scott's Last Expedition,* Oxford: Oxford University Press.

Milton, J. (2005) *Paradise Lost.* Edited by D. S. Kastan. Indianapolis, IN: Hackett Publishing.

Pagden, A. (1993) *European Encounters with the New World,* New Haven, CT: Yale University Press.

Palmer, T. (1606) *An essay of the meanes how to make our trauailes, into forraine countries, the more profitable and honourable,* London.

Roberts, A. (2006) *The History of Science Fiction,* London: Palgrave Macmillan.

Scott, R. F. (2005) *Journal: Captain Scott's Last Expedition,* Oxford: Oxford University Press.

Seller, J. (1700). *Atlas Caelestis,* London.

Swann, M. (2001). *Curiosities and Texts: Culture of Collecting in Early Modern England,* Philadelphia: University of Pennsylvania Press.

Theroux, P. (1985) *Sunrise with Seamonsters: Travels and Discoveries 1964–1984,* London: Penguin, pp 134–5.

Thomas, E. (2020) *The Meaning of Travel: Philosophers Abroad,* Oxford: Oxford University Press.

Vogel, U. (1999) 'The Sceptical Enlightenment: Philosopher Travellers Look Back at Europe', in N. Geras and R. Wokler (eds) *Enlightenment and Modernity*, New York: Palgrave Macmillan.

Worms, L. (2008). 'Seller, John (*bap.* 1632, *d.* 1697)', *Oxford Dictionary of National Biography.* www.oxforddnb.com/view/article/25058

PART III

Limits and New Horizons

12

Technology and Travel

Glenn Lyons

Introduction

Travel in its *material* sense is about transcending distance: about getting from A to B. Since the advent of the first dugout canoes many thousands of years ago, and probably long before, technology has been with us to help us reach our destinations. We live now in a world in which travel is almost inconceivable without some form of technology: from the highly coordinated system of thousands of jet aircraft traversing the globe every day, to the use of a smartphone to guide (or at least accompany) us around unfamiliar streets.

Transport-related technologies have had a profound effect on human travel. Broadly speaking, transport technology has accompanied and supported society's travel through three key aspects in the evolution of our transport systems. The first of these has been creating the assets for physical movement – the vehicles and infrastructure for transcending distance. The second aspect has been managing these assets to ensure they are as efficient as possible in providing a throughput of movement of people – signalling technologies or apps providing real-time travel information, for example. The third aspect has become how to manage the appetite for travel itself such that the assets can sensibly accommodate the demands placed upon them – for example computing technology that enables dynamic pricing to help airlines manage demand.

However, such an overview of technology's contribution to travel is only the tip of the iceberg. This depiction of technology represents only one category of technology that might be labelled 'transport

Figure 12.1a: Horse and cart transport in Tibet

Figure 12.1b: Futuristic drone flying over a city (CGI)

From horse and carriage to autonomous drones – technology has had profound and complex impacts on human travel. Both 'old' and new technologies will continue to shape our travel behaviours in future.

technology'. Alongside this are two other categories: 'substitution technology' and 'non-transport technology'. To understand the significance of these categories (which will be clarified in a moment) one needs to step back from the narrow functional thinking associated with technology helping people get from one location to another. Travel inherently stems from people's need or desire for access. As human beings our existence depends upon being able to reach other people, goods, services and opportunities. This ability to reach has been seen as central to social and, especially, economic wellbeing. It has been seen as synonymous with travel. However, access is more than travel from A to B, as the two further categories of technology reveal.

Substitution technology reflects a category of technology that has enabled us to reach things without needing to travel to them. From humble beginnings such as the sending of smoke signals as a substitute for face-to-face exchange of information, we are now in a world in which substitution technology enables us to be physically remote from people, goods, services and opportunities and yet connect to them. In effect, information makes the journey across the telecommunications infrastructure as an alternative to individuals making the journey across the transport infrastructure. The significance of such technology has been catapulted to the fore in 2020 in the face of the COVID-19 pandemic.

Non-transport technology is a category vast in scope and the most challenging in terms of its relationship with travel because the consequences for travel are indirect and in many respects can be unintentional and unanticipated. Non-transport technology is that which is designed to address aspects of human existence remote from the direct goal of transcending distance. For example, technology to prolong the storage of food. Packaging and refrigeration have made it possible to keep food for longer. Perhaps unintentionally, this reduced the need to travel so frequently to obtain food. What was unanticipated is that food storage technology would make warehousing and supermarkets a possibility by joining forces with the car and its flexibility to transcend distance and carry goods. This has affected consumption behaviour to the detriment of 'local shops' such that greater dependency on motorized mobility has been created.

Recognizing the great diversity of technology and its bearing on travel, this chapter sets out to examine the different relationships technology has with travel — especially in the digital age. Humans and human systems are complex and not (or may not always appear) rational, and technology and human travel are entwined in sometimes unpredictable ways. It is therefore important to take a 'socio-technical approach' to our understanding: account needs to be taken of how people engage with the technological possibilities and what consequences may arise. As Sarah Sharples, Professor of Human Factors, has explained: '[T]here are many factors that influence our individual and collective attitudes to technology including past experiences, emotional attachments, productivity needs, cultural expectations and social pressures. All of these aspects need to be appreciated if we are going to engineer transport systems that will serve people well.'[1]

It is also useful here to distinguish between the idea of 'invention' and 'innovation'. An invention may be seen as a novel technological development that makes it *possible* to do old things in new ways, or to do new things. Invention only translates into innovation if the technological developments bring about *actual* effects in society through the nature and extent of take-up of the invention. It is these actual effects and their causes that are of key importance for understanding the relations of technology and travel.

With these complex relations in mind, the chapter will turn to consider where we might be heading, and how we might better shape that future. It will consider emerging technologies and the potential for the resurgence of existing technologies, as well as examining the role of policy-making in innovation and technological regimes. We are at a remarkable point in time where humanity faces the existential threat of a climate emergency while needing to deal with the immediate shock to the global system from COVID-19. Understanding the role of myriad technologies in shaping our future has perhaps never been so vital.

Socio-technical relationships of travel

Historical trends indicate that when technology offers the possibility of more efficient, quicker, safer, and more comfortable travel across greater distances, humans tend to take up these opportunities and travel more (where they can afford to do so). As described in previous chapters, improved ships and navigation technologies enabled increased exploration and trade; the advent of trains, steamships and jet air travel led to increases in leisure travel and the development of mass tourism; and trains, metro systems, buses and cars have all increased the distances and numbers of people commuting by motorized means to work, impacting the development of suburbs and cities. Despite this clear trend towards increased travel overall, it is remarkable that at the day-to-day level the amount of *time* we spend travelling does not show the same trend. Indeed, there is international evidence to show that at the aggregate level in any country the average amount of time spent travelling per person per day remains rather constant over time at around one hour (see Chapter 5 'The Economics of Travel'). What can of course change is how this hour per day becomes manifest in terms of the distance covered and the means of travel used. In general the more 'advanced' societies have become, the more resource-intensive the consumption of one hour of travel per day has become, and the further distance is travelled, increasing our geographical scope of access.

Clearly then, technological developments impact on our travel behaviour by changing the quantity and quality of our travel, but, as we will now explore, relations between technology and travel can be surprising and hard to predict.

Increased efficiency of transport technologies

A great many technologies have helped to increase the operational efficiency of travel, usually with the aim of enabling people to get where they are going more quickly and cheaply and, now, increasingly, to reduce the environmental impact of that travel (see Chapter 14 'Travel's Place in the Environment'). Alongside these are information technologies that support the traveller in their use of the transport system. Travel information services can alert individuals to their travel options, they can enable individuals to make optimal choices about how to travel and they can assist individuals in executing successfully their travel. Such services are becoming increasingly intuitive, usable and useful to travellers as they evolve. Satellite navigation systems in cars (and in the palms of pedestrians' hands), for example, are now commonplace.

However, this says little about the socio-technical perspective on the technology–travel relationship. If we look at how people actually engage with these technologies in reality, we see that increases in operational efficiency do not produce straightforward impacts on travel.

Mr Spock v Homer Simpson: non-rational responses

In relation to travel information services, developers can have a tendency to anticipate their (level of) use through assuming a 'Mr Spock' model of end users. Mr Spock (the Vulcan in *Star Trek*) is entirely logical and would wish to be in possession of all the facts about his options in order to make a decision that minimizes the 'cost' of travel. He would have an inherent appetite for using information services. In practice, many end users could more readily align with a 'Homer Simpson' model – travel for Homer would be no big deal so long as he can get where he needs to go in reasonable time and with reasonable ease; there are many other things apart from optimizing his travel to occupy his mind (in Homer's case, Duff beer, donuts, and sleep). People's travel can be heavily conditioned by habit and prior experience; by familiarity and (sufficient) predictability such that they have limited appetite for information that may enable them to rethink their travel unless prompted to do so by conditions of uncertainty or anxiety over the consequences of a journey destination not being reached on time. Thus individual travellers may have a limited interest (as opposed to a total disinterest) in operational efficiency of travel.

Emotional attachment to transport technologies can also create 'non-rational' travel choices. Car owners are often emotionally invested in their vehicles and in the act of driving itself, which may represent to them independence and freedom, resulting in a preference for driving even when other modes may be cheaper, quicker or healthier. Despite the development of more fuel-efficient cars, which are often smaller and well suited to city-driving and parking, in recent years it is larger, less-efficient SUVs that are showing a big growth in popularity, perhaps in part due to feelings about size and status rather than purely rational choices over cost or efficiency.

Induced demand

Improvements in operational efficiency, and in the physical capacity of a transport system, can make it easier for people to get from A to B, and might therefore be expected to improve the efficiency of a system overall, or reduce congestion in that system. But, it has been found that in many situations, if technology makes it easier or cheaper, there may be more appetite for travel that will result in more travel (and need for yet further operational efficiency). This is known as 'induced demand' or more broadly as Jevons Paradox.[2] This has plagued the attempt of roadbuilding to 'solve' congestion.

Substitution technology

In the face of what might appear too much travel in society, it has been compelling for some time to be able to offer substitutes for travel through technological innovation. Substitution technologies, which allow us to communicate and reach things at a distance, have been with us since the time of smoke signals and, in the digital age, the possibilities are vast – and the resilience they offer in times when physical travel is limited, such as during the COVID-19 pandemic, is now highly significant for society. But do we find that these substitution technologies substitute for and therefore reduce overall travel? In fact, the impact is often not so straightforward (even putting aside the imponderables arising from COVID-19) (Mokhtarian, 2009).

Direct substitution

Much of our interaction in society is about information exchange, whether in relation to work, shopping or leisure activities. Indeed, taken to the limit, beyond the maintenance of, and sustenance for, our bodies and our need to reproduce, our existence is about sensory input – information – from sight, hearing, taste, smell and touch. Whether virtual reality could directly substitute for some of these sensory experiences is a possibility of much relevance to the future of travel (see Chapter 14 'Travel's Place in the Environment'). Shopping for and purchasing of goods has rapidly evolved from high streets, superstores and shopping malls to now include e-shopping in a way that is redefining the retail sector. There has also been particular interest in how technology might substitute for travel in the course of work – both the prospect of avoiding daily commuting (and the peak periods of traffic and congestions it creates) and avoiding business trips to participate in meetings.

Thanks to technology, substitution for work-related travel is now *possible* for a growing share of the population. The question is, to what extent is substitution innovation diffusing into work and business practices? Teleworking or homeworking is a substitution practice for which some commentators had high hopes. Yet the 'rush hour' still seems alive and well in cities across the world (or had been until the arrival of COVID-19). At the same time there has been evidence of growth in the number of people who work from home – especially on an occasional basis. According to the Office of National Statistics, in 2015 4.2 million people in the UK worked from home for at least some part of the working week, and the trend is increasing. Homeworking, at least on a part-time basis, seems then to be replacing some work-related travel. Peak travel numbers are still increasing but not as fast as the population increases; and with improvements in digital connectivity we may yet see much wider uptake of remote-working practices, resulting in reduced commuting. It is perhaps remarkable to note that, according to the National Travel Survey, over the 20-year period since the mid-1990s, the average number of commute trips per person per year in England has gone down by nearly a fifth. Perhaps an acceleration of this trend will be one of the consequences of COVID-19.

Technological substitutes for meetings (between two individuals or many individuals) have grown in availability, maturity and affordability. Multi-way teleconference calls are now relatively easy. Skype has brought videoconferencing to the masses and tablet computers and smart phones are increasing the portability of where and when one can 'meet' with others without a need for physical co-presence. Despite these improvements, business travel has shown steady growth. Yet at a national level, the National Travel Survey shows average business trips per person per year down by over a quarter in England in 2017 compared to the mid-1990s.

Functional thinking would suggest the take-up of substitution technology would be rapid and considerable – if the purpose of meeting is to exchange information then why would one invest time in travel when substitution is available to achieve such exchange? There are of course a number of answers that functional thinking can obscure. Consider the motivations for an individual attending a business meeting (especially one that may be abroad and involve an overnight stay): (1) there is a business norm of meetings and attendance – it is expected; (2) there is a need to acquire or impart information; (3) there is a need to be able to exert influence over decision-making; (4) there is a feeling or need to be seen to be present at the meeting in terms of status or recognition; (5) attendance is an opportunity for networking and serendipitous encounter; (6) attendance holds prospect for some sociability outside of the business of the meeting; (7) attendance is an opportunity for a welcome break from the office (or perhaps home) environment; and (8) attendance allows the experience of new places and cultures. Intriguingly, some of these motivations can also be turned around into reasons for not wishing to physically attend a meeting – for instance being away from the office or from family at home would be resented. Reflecting on such a list of considerations highlights why technology innovation is understood to 'diffuse' into society – people need to evolve their social and business practices concurrently with absorbing technological developments into them. Thus for some, and perhaps a growing proportion of people, some substitution has come to be part of their working lives as technologies have matured and practices and norms have changed. It should also be remembered that diffusion of innovation does not always happen at a steady rate, and may appear slow at times but gather momentum and then seem sudden (time will tell whether the global response of self-isolation to

COVID-19 will bring about significant and sustained change in this regard). The experience afforded by technology of communicating at a distance will likely also continue to be enhanced.

Latent and generated demand

As has been mentioned earlier, through technology making it easier to travel there can be the unintended consequence of more travel taking place, ie technology can ultimately increase a need or desire for travel. A similar consequence can derive from substitution technology. The notion of substitution is founded upon virtual mobility replacing (some) physical travel for a given set of activities in which an individual engages. However, this may presuppose that the set of activities does not change as a consequence of the use of substitution technologies themselves. For example, in a household with limited car ownership there may be latent demand for car use from other household members besides those who rely on the limited car ownership for work-related travel. If a car becomes available at home because of homeworking, it may be used for new motorized trips – thus more or alternative travel has been generated by the initial substitution of travel.

Technology in the form of the Internet is enabling unprecedented exchange of information including peer-to-peer sharing and spreading of news and advice through social media. This can highlight to people activities, or destinations for activities, that they were not previously aware of as well as providing guidance on how to get there. This may ultimately generate a demand or desire for more activity engagement and therefore more travel.

According to geographer John Adams, historic trends for telecommunications (ie substitution technologies) and travel 'have correlated strongly and positively, and today the most physically mobile societies are also the heaviest users of all forms of telecommunications' (Adams, 2000). These trends suggest that the release of latent demand, or generation of new demand, may have a very important role to play in travel behaviour patterns, particularly in an increasingly digital and connected world.

Some latent demand could be socially important to unlock. In the UK alone around 11 million people have some form of disability, but travel surveys show that on average they make far fewer and shorter trips than those with no disabilities. Improved assistive technologies and more accessible transport options could therefore potentially make a large difference to the lives of individuals and to the travel patterns of the country.[3]

Redistributing travel

A significant feature of the digital age – for better or worse – appears to be that the spatial and temporal constraints associated with our activities and thus where we need to be and when are becoming less stringent. In times gone by it was much more common to be expected to be at your employer's premises between a set start and finish time in order to undertake work. To undertake shopping and purchasing required one or more retail outlets to be visited between opening and closing times. Co-ordinating social or business exchanges required an agreed specific 'where' and 'when' to be clearly established in advance to ensure successful rendezvous.

This has now changed and has had impacts on our patterns of when and where we travel. Consider the case of paid employment. For a growing number of knowledge workers there is the possibility of working from home for one or more days a week. This reflects substitution of travel because of greater flexibility of location. However, recent insights have emerged into part-day homeworking, which appears to be more commonplace than occasional whole-day homeworking and which introduces within-day spatial and temporal flexibility to work. Part-day homeworking involves a number of forms, but two in particular are splitting the working day in two and working either from home for the earlier or latter part of the day as an accompaniment to working in the traditional 'workplace'. Both forms have the potential to displace when the morning and/or evening commute takes place. The latter appears the most prevalent form of part-day homeworking. Reasoning includes the opportunity to address afternoon childcare responsibilities before returning to the activity of work later in the evening; it also reflects the appeal of countering the afternoon 'productivity dip' following lunch by using the dip time for commuting home with the resulting change of scene helping to energize a new bout of work activity at home. Travel has thus not been substituted by homeworking technologies so much as redistributed to different times of day.

There has been recent talk of the 'death of the mall' as large out-of-town precincts fall out of favour in the face of online shopping and a resurgence of interest in city centre retail and leisure. Here it appears that substitution and redistribution may be working in tandem. People are able to browse for and purchase 'routine' goods online rather than at the 'all under one roof' malls. Novelty shopping and the social appeal of shopping can then be better fulfilled in the setting of urban centres thus redirecting the physical travel associated with shopping.

In relation to social encounter, mobile technology has meant that rendezvous can be a less precise and more adaptive proposition. It seems the days of 'so we will all meet at 7.30pm in the *Queen's Arms*' may be numbered. Groups of friends can declare they are going to be 'in town' on a given evening between some broad time parameters; as the evening in question progresses and individuals arrive into town updates on location and intent are exchanged and points of rendezvous emerge with the associated (local) travel consequences.

Enriching travel

For many years in the transport planning profession it has been convenient to treat travel as a derived demand – a means to an end arising from the need or desire to participate in activities. What followed was a clear interpretation that travel was distinct from activities. Allied to this has been a presumption that less time for travel and consequently more time for activities is a good thing. If travel can be speeded up, any cost involved will be offset by the (economic value of) time saved. The advent of mobile technologies has been shining a new light on this. It is now strongly apparent that travel time is also activity time – in other words we are multitasking when we travel – undertaking the activity of travel while also engaging in other things that may (depending upon the means and the mode of travel, and upon the travelling environment itself) include: sleeping/snoozing; reading for leisure; working/studying; talking to other travellers; window gazing/people watching; listening to music or watching video; making phone calls or texting; checking emails; Internet browsing; accessing social networking sites; playing games; eating or drinking; or simply indulging in inner reflection.

Mobile technologies have moved from the paperback novel and handwritten diary of the Victorian era to smartphones, laptops and tablet computers. People use technologies on the move to enrich their experience of time. For some, travel time is very much seen as an important gift to themselves – 'me time' to do with as they please away from the expectations of others (Jain and Lyons, 2008). It is also seen as transition time to go 'backstage' and adjust from one life role at the journey origin to another at the destination (eg from breakfast table parent to committee meeting chair). Technology on the move is not, however, necessarily positive as a given. Travel has an inherent appeal for some as an 'interspace' in which they are not reachable by others or by expectations of others. Technology can remove this protected space or 'infect' it by rendering you able to be reached and expected to respond.

Figure 12.2: Rail passengers working on digital devices

Travel time or activity time? Mobile technologies are reshaping the travel experience.

Intriguing questions arise regarding society's notional travel time budget of one hour per person per day. If travel time is being used for activity time, does this count as part of the budget? For example, previous national time use survey insights included revealing that the average person in Britain watched television for 1–2 hours per day. If such viewing can be transferred into the travel environment might that mean that this could compensate for longer journeys and thus foster more travel? Travel time use supported by technology can also have association with substitution and redistribution effects. For example, it is now conceivable to be able to do one's grocery shopping online while travelling home on the train from work. This could remove the need for an evening trip to the supermarket or remove the need to do the online shopping in the evening at home and instead enable one to travel out somewhere for an evening drink.

There are signs that this relationship between supposed 'substitution' technology and travel is intensifying. For instance there has been a marked increase in the prevalence of mobile technologies among rail travellers in Britain during the first two decades of this millennium with an increase recorded in the proportion of rail travellers indicating that their time on the train is considered very worthwhile.

Technology can indirectly affect travel

The complexity of the relations between technology and travel becomes even more apparent when one recognizes the category of technologies above referred to as 'non-transport' technologies and also the time lags between cause and effect and the fact that effects can also often be indirect.

An example of a time-lagged effect is the way in which homeworking technologies are indirectly changing the demand for connectivity between cities. Since the ability to homework reduces the weekly total distance travelled for commuting it can offer an individual the 'affordance' of being able to live further away from a (new) employer's premises when they are faced with a relocation opportunity. This may not necessarily be in the form of the once assumed contribution of teleworking to urban sprawl but could facilitate a growing tendency to live in one city and work in another. Perhaps this will constitute part of the market for high speed rail in Britain – further enabled by the way in which technologies can help travellers make worthwhile use of their journey time.

An example of indirect effects of non-transport and non-substitution technologies could also emerge in relation to an ageing society and the use of 'assistive technologies' (ie technologies intended to help assist individuals live as independently as possible and for longer). There is uncertainty over the future availability, capability, take-up and consequences of such technologies, but it is clear that with a growing proportion of older people in society, where and how they choose to live will have substantial consequences for patterns and amounts of travel. These consequences will relate not only to the older people themselves but also those other people with whom they interact and receive support from.

Analysts of how technology and travel interact would dearly love for there to be observable, isolated and tangible cause–effect relationships. Unfortunately, as we have seen, it has become ever more apparent that the reality is not nearly so straightforward and increasingly less so. We turn now to consider the future and how our knowledge of these complex relations can help us in better shaping travel for people and the planet.

Future – limits and frontiers

It is clear that we face a future of environmental limits – we cannot continue to satisfy our seemingly innate desire for travel in the current resource-intensive and polluting way. Technologies have transformed

Figure 12.3: Hyperloop-style transport system (CGI)

The Hyperloop, using magnetic levitation and vacuum tubes, could achieve very high speeds and some say it may revolutionize inter-city transportation.

the way we travel and the impact that travel has on the world; what then are the future technological prospects for transforming human travel? There are multiple developments in terms of transport technologies across 'technology readiness levels'. These concern new forms of transport mode and different forms of propulsion and control. Some commentators talk of society being on the cusp of a transport revolution; others emphasize the heightened scope for hype in an ever more digitally connected world of social media. Indeed it might be suggested that it is more than a coincidence that one of Elon Musk's areas of interest and investment is called the 'Hyperloop' (see Figure 12.3 and later text).

'New frontiers': emerging technologies

The invention of the combustion engine changed the landscape of human travel, enabling the development of trains, cars, planes and motorized boats. Now that the need for urgent reductions in greenhouse gas emissions is more widely recognized, alternative, low carbon power sources for these vehicles is the focus of much research and development (as discussed in Chapter 14 'Travel's Place in the Environment'). Hybrid-fuel and electric vehicles, as well as greatly improving fuel efficiencies of internal combustion engine vehicles, represent prospects for greater energy efficiency of travel consumption as well as an ability to reduce harmful emissions at the point of use. Another technology now emerging is that of the autonomous vehicle – with the capability of conveying its passenger(s) from A to B without the need for a human driver. This offers up many prospects should widespread adoption ensue. At the limit, if all vehicles were autonomous, there could be significant reduction in, or total removal of collisions; there could be more energy-efficient driving of the vehicles with reduced emissions; and there could be smaller 'safe driving' headways between vehicles thus allowing the transport system to achieve more throughput of vehicles with lower delays. However, such touted benefits over-simplify the myriad of plausible consequences of a 'driverless future' with potential for rebound effects and unintended outcomes casting doubt over proponents' claims that automation offers a brighter future environmentally or otherwise (Lyons, 2020a). Irrespective of the advent of autonomous driving, technologies are supporting improvements to traffic management through the ability to monitor and control flows of vehicles (and people) to improve operational efficiency of the system (though not without the potential to induce more demand).

Electrically powered cars are already on our roads, and advances are being made in battery technologies to allow greater storage capacity and quicker charging (and with significantly falling battery costs). Infrastructure for charging points and an increase in renewably generated electricity are of course needed too. Hydrogen-fuelled cars are also in operation and, although it seems likely electric cars will be more popular in the near-term, hydrogen may find greater uptake in fleets of vehicles like heavy goods vehicles, buses and taxis and there is considerable investment in hydrogen fuel globally. Removal of 'tailpipe' emissions could play an important role in enabling us to maintain some aspects of our current travel systems and behaviours with a reduced climate impact, although the resources required for batteries and renewable electricity generation are also limited. The danger here would be to suppose that behaviour change is not also needed – particularly if decarbonization of transport and hence the overall economy is to happen at the rate that scientists now point to as necessary to help avoid climate breakdown. The mantra that becomes ever lounder is that 'business as usual is no longer an option' – yet relying on technology alone to decarbonize transport could imply greening business as usual will be enough.

There are other mechanical transport technologies in development that may more fundamentally change how we travel and in turn change the shape of society itself. Hyperloop (as already touched upon above) is one such technology: a magnetically levitated train or pod travelling in a vacuum tunnel, capable of reaching speeds faster than jet aircraft. It is a technological prospect that provokes mixed reactions. Given the timescale needed to prove technology readiness and in turn secure investment in adoption at scale, it seems unlikely in any case that this technology is going to play a part – for good or ill – in decarbonizing transport within the next 20–30 years – the critical window of remaining opportunity in relation to climate change.

In addition to advances in mechanical technologies, the future of mobility looks likely to be shaped by improvements in digital technologies and internet connectivity. 'Mobility as a Service' (MaaS) has emerged in recent years as a new term reflecting the prospect of consumers being able to access multiple modes of transport through a single platform (on their smartphones) for planning, booking and payment. This could potentially combine with developments in driverless technology to redefine the position of the car in society from a mode associated with private ownership for individual use to one that is fleet operated and shared, leading to higher vehicle occupancies. MaaS represents a possibility to offer a strongly evolved mobility system beyond the private car (Lyons et al, 2019) and indeed beyond the car in terms of alternative modes both established and emerging (the latter including shared bikes, e-bikes and e-scooters). Once again, however, the nature, extent and pace of change beyond the hype remains unclear.

'Old frontiers: existing technologies'

It is important that in looking forward we do not get distracted only by the hi-tech, or big infrastructure projects but consider also how existing technologies will be used. 'Too often the agenda for discussing the past, present and future of technology is set by the promoters of new technologies', claims historian David Edgerton. Instead he argues for accounts of technology and society that consider technology in use. In such accounts, he says, 'technologies do not only appear, they also disappear and reappear, and mix and match across the centuries.' In relation to travel this is hugely important. Today in the UK, over a quarter of journeys are made on foot (in terms of trip numbers not mileage) and, as Edgerton points out: 'Since the late 1960s many more bicycles were produced globally each year than cars' (Edgerton, 2019: xxii). Walking may indeed be undergoing a renaissance, encouraged by pedestrian navigation technology in the palms of people's hands (Lyons, 2020b) and by a wave of interest in FitBits (and other step-counters) that raise the importance of daily exercise in people's consciousness.[4] Any future of human travel must take into account the needs of pedestrians and cyclists as much as the driverless pod. It is relevant also that, although we have the capability to power vehicles electrically without fossil fuels, these methods still require the production and maintenance of resource-intensive technologies such as the rare metals in batteries and PV cells, and concrete and steel in wind turbines. Renewable-fueled electrification will not be a panacea. Indeed, some argue that a further revival of 'low tech', human-powered modes of transport are necessary for a healthier and more flourishing human society. In 1973, economist E. F. Schumacher promoted the idea of 'appropriate technology': that which is small-scale, decentralized, labour-intensive, energy-efficient, environmentally sound, locally autonomous and people-centred, such as bicycles, and animal-powered transport. In the following year, philosopher Ivan Illich argued that 'High speed is the critical factor which makes transportation socially destructive.' In more recent times too, commentators have noted the negative impacts of high speed travel and hypermobility. Author Rebecca Solnit writes that high speed travel can remove us from a close relationship with the earth, a view echoed by many who promote 'slow travel' (Solnit, 2003). And geographer John Adams (2000) contends that continuing our trend towards ever increasing hypermobility could have very negative social and environmental impacts and that instead we need to be 'fostering the local at the expense of the remote, and foregoing some of the benefits of mobility to protect and enhance what we value in nature and our relations with friends and neighbours.' (Adams, 2001).

A focus on 'appropriate technologies' is relevant from a global perspective too, and prompts us to remember that access to many technologies is unequal and looks set to remain so for many years to come. We may view ourselves as living in an age of air travel – and certainly the number of flights taken pre-COVID-19 (even in the face of a new trend of 'flight shame' seen in Sweden in particular – the home of Greta Thunberg), and the resulting impact on the environment and economy has been substantial – but over 80 per cent of the world's population has never flown. It may be that currently-in-use, less glamorous technologies are the key to meeting many of our mobility needs without contributing hugely to climate change. People and governments in cities across the world are coming to recognize the benefits of cycling and are enacting policies to promote it. And charities and entrepreneurs have set up projects to enable cycling in lower income countries, particularly by investing in technologies to help build and maintain bikes locally from locally-sourced materials (including bamboo). The future, as always, will be shaped both by the new technologies we choose to pursue as well as how we deploy the older ones.

Automobilities to multimobilities: technological regime change

Change is taking place in society on a continual basis socially, economically, technologically and environmentally. This change tends to be rather slow and can be imperceptible. Change can appear incidental rather than fundamental – especially when one is in the midst of an incumbent regime – an established way of the world as we know it. We have been in the automobility regime for some decades – a world (at least in those countries with high levels of car ownership) defined by the dominance of the car both functionally and symbolically. There are many people with professionally vested interests in this regime enduring. However, history shows us that regimes do not last forever and that over time niche developments can build in significance until they become a force for change that ultimately brings about a transition from what will be the old regime to a new one. Regime transitions are not events – they are processes; and they can take several decades to unfold. For instance the socio-technical transition from sailing ships to steamships took some 60 years. Nevertheless, although behavioural change at a systemic level is usually a slow process, under certain circumstances, such as extreme disruption (as epitomized by the COVID-19 pandemic), people are capable of adapting to change quickly.[5] We may be looking at further extreme disruption in a number of contexts in the coming century due to environmental and technological changes.

Uncertainty in recent times has been looming large for policy-making in relation to transport. This became apparent when attention was drawn to so-called 'peak car'. In the early part of this millennium, and beginning before the global economic downturn of the 2000s, we saw a flattening off and in some cases a decline in how much car use was taking place – set against an historic pattern of almost uninterrupted growth. It has been suggested that there are three plausible futures ahead of us for travel (Lyons and Goodwin, 2014): one in which we will see car traffic growth resume if and when economic activity increases (and there were some signs of this before the 2020 pandemic); another in which (at least on a per person basis) we will see no further growth as saturation has been reached; and a third in which car use will be on a path of decline. This comes right back to the heart of the question 'why travel?' Many argue that economic drivers are principally responsible for the amount of travel. However, there is a growing sense that other social and technological drivers may also be coming into play in a way that may be bringing about structural change to our societal system.

My hypothesis is that we are, perhaps, a third of the way through the main transition period from the automobility regime into a new regime – which I refer to as the multimobilities regime (Lyons, 2015). The transition period reflects the collision and merging of the motor age and the digital age. There are compelling signs of gradual but powerfully cumulative effects of how technological innovation is permeating into our everyday lives and social practices and bringing about influence over important life stage and lifestyle decisions. If access, social participation and enriched experience are taken to be key goals determining why we travel then it seems physical travel is no longer the only means of realizing these goals. Virtual mobility has an increasingly strong presence and is deeply intertwined with physical travel and especially motorized travel. The balance of power is shifting. Earlier in this chapter, I considered the ongoing evolution in transport technologies. However, evolution in substitution technologies and non-transport technologies could be even more significant for travel.

As the transition continues we will see a stronger presence of multimobilities in society. This could be characterized by a strong trend of urban growth (if not urbanization) accompanied by less appetite for driving licence acquisition and vehicle ownership. Digital connectivity could marry up with greater proximity and thus greater inclination towards walking, cycling and shared transport within urban environments (once the anxiety of proximity to others brought about by COVID-19 has subsided). Allied to this could be a growth in demand for rail travel to connect people between urban centres. Distinctions between physical and virtual may well blur and individuals could move seamlessly and flexibly between physical and virtual interaction and may favour physical forms of mobility that lend themselves to digital engagement while on the move and that provide attractive environments through which to experience travel. In this new regime the car could still have its place and be far from functionally insignificant – whether autonomously driven and electrically powered or not – but it may become a background technology in society rather than occupy the foreground as it has done in recent decades.

Conclusion: policy-making for technology and travel in transition

There has been interest for some time, at least among academics, in the implications developments in technology have for the shaping of our transport system, the demands placed upon it and the implications for policy-making by governments. However, this has been far from matched by interest from policy makers and politicians. There are a number of possible reasons for this including the absence of robust, conclusive insights into technology's effects on travel. There is also a tendency for constrained thinking, which focuses on transport technologies and 'technological fixes' for more easily agreeable goals (eg policies that focus on technological fixes to increase energy efficiency rather than thinking more broadly). These two factors result in policy-making that tends to be inactive or reactive at best. A proactive response would require a political appetite to influence and shape the consequences of technology for travel by employing forms of direct or indirect market intervention.

It is now asserted that, faced with an increasingly complex world, it is becoming increasingly difficult to produce forecasts of future travel demand that have credibility. Combined with the lack of certainty over the impacts and disruptions of climate change and the complexity of interactions between technology and travel, there is a need instead to embrace uncertainty. Uncertainty can be turned from its negative connotation into a positive one by relabelling it 'opportunity'. Rather than trying to anticipate the future and respond to it, there should be greater confidence in the capacity for policy-making to help shape the type of future we want. In other words, not 'predict and provide' but 'decide and provide'.[6] Grasping this opportunity calls for policy makers to turn their attention to this book's question of 'why travel?'. Given the environmental crises that we face, and the myriad technological developments now possible, the need to do so has never been so urgent.

Notes

[1] Sarah Sharples, speech given at ITC Annual Lecture, 2016.

[2] https://en.wikipedia.org/wiki/Jevons_paradox

[3] https://assets.publishing.service.gov.uk/government/uploads/system/uploads/attachment_data/file/ 533345/disability-and-travel-factsheet.pdf

[4] https://www.linkedin.com/posts/glenn-lyons_walking-pedestrians-futuremobility-activity-6578556549696937984--9jb

[5] Sarah Sharples, speech given at ITC Annual Lecture, 2016.

[6] Future Uncertainty Toolkit: Understanding and Responding to an Evolving Society (FUTURES): see www.mottmac.com/futures

References

Adams, J. (2000) 'The Social Implications of Hypermobility', in *Proceedings from the Ottawa Workshop*, Paris: OECD.

Adams, J. (2001) 'The Social Consequences of Hypermobility', *RSA Lecture*, 21 November 2001, text available at: http://john-adams.co.uk/wp-content/uploads/2006/hypermobilityforRSA.pdf

Edgerton, D. (2019) *The Shock of the Old*, London: Profile Books

Ilich, I. (1974) *Energy and Equity*, London: Marion Boyars Publishing.

Jain, J. and Lyons, G. (2008) 'The gift of travel time', *Journal of Transport Geography*, 16, 81–9.

Lyons, G. (2015) 'Transport's digital age transition', *Journal of Transport and Land Use*, 8(2), 1–19.

Lyons, G. (2020a). *Driverless Cars – A Great Opportunity for Society? Final Report of the Driverless Cars Emulsion Initiative*, Bristol: University of the West of England and Mott MacDonald. https://uwe-repository.worktribe.com/output/5859439

Lyons, G. (2020b) 'Walking as a Service – does it have legs?' *Transportation Research A: Policy and Practice*, 137, 271–84, https://doi.org/10.1016/j.tra.2020.05.015

Lyons, G. and Goodwin, P. (2014) *Grow, Peak or Plateau – the Outlook for Car Travel*, Report of a roundtable meeting in London supported by the New Zealand Ministry of Transport, 20 May.

Lyons, G., Hammond, P. and Mackay, K. (2019) 'The importance of user perspective in the evolution of MaaS', *Transportation Research A: Policy and Practice*, 121 (Special Issue on developments in Mobility as a Service (MaaS) and intelligent mobility), 22–36.

Mokhtarian, P. L. (2009) 'If telecommunication is such a good substitute for travel, why does congestion continue to get worse?' *Transportation Letters*, 1, 1–17.

Schumacher, E. F. (1973) *Small Is Beautiful. A Study of Economics As If People Mattered*, London: Blond & Briggs.

Solnit, R. (2003) *Motion Studies: Time, Space and Eadweard Muybridge*, London: Bloomsbury.

13

Placemaking and Travel: The City Is Where the People Choose to Go

Deborah Saunt and Tom Greenall

Introduction

People love to be on the move. They need to be on the move to prosper and survive, and to feel connected. Yet the streets and public spaces of a city have a far greater role to play than simply providing the means to access one's destination. So, what role does a *sense of place* have in determining how and, crucially, why people travel? The space in between buildings – the roadway and pavements, and the more formal spaces of a city that are designed for congregation – are a critical aspect of the urban environment called 'the public realm': the common ground that brings everyone together. It is the most fundamental of territories that should welcome and accommodate everyone, in all weathers, day or night, and yet be robust and safe enough to stand up to the colossal pressures placed upon it. It is where culture is nurtured, friendships are made, and the city flourishes by virtue of the exchanges it fosters. But how can we design complementary transport infrastructure and public space when there are seemingly so many competing constraints? Indeed, as we write, the immediate future of the public realm is changing due to the unforeseen and unprecedented impact of a global pandemic and the social distancing required to combat its spread.

This chapter will explore such questions, examining how travel, place and human connectivity are intimately related, from physical, cultural and psychological perspectives. In this chapter, we will draw on the experience and evidence that we have gathered as directors of London-based architecture, urban design and research studio, DSDHA, through both practice and academia. Our work is informed by a deep and rigorous understanding of a place – its history, its people, its morphology and its natural attributes. As such, this chapter focuses on our experience of London, but with wider lessons drawn from around the world that are applicable more generally.

The chapter will first look back, to see where we have come from; making a brief survey of historical relations between human settlements and travel, which will take us from the siting of the first villages to the layout and development of modern cities. We then turn to psychological and behavioural insights about how our ways of travel can impact upon our experiences of the places we live and move through. Looking at issues as diverse as mental maps, the impacts of the automobile and the resurgence of cycling, we will see the importance of aesthetic and psychological experience of travel and place. The chapter closes by offering lessons on how we can build better for our travel needs in future by responding to the diverse characteristics of each place and adopting a human-centred approach rather than a one-size-fits-all solution. It is essential, we argue, that we plan for the 'long now' (Brand, 1999), fully considering the needs of the future in order to make good places and good journeys for all.

How we reached here: the history of placemaking and travel

Where cities started

Settlements generally occur where paths cross and people can meet. Here, exchange takes place, and public spaces emerge as a setting for collective gathering and sharing. These spaces are influenced by environmental as well as social factors; each is different as a result of the particular constraints and opportunities afforded by natural features such as topography and orientation. However, the aspects that always persist are the routes and connections that serve them. Nascent settlements invariably establish themselves at such intersections – the places where paths cross, water runs nearby, natural resources are abundant, protection or defence is aided by landscape features, or even at places of natural beauty. The convergence of these elements leads

Figure 13.1: Mapping the journeys of 100 people in central London

100 Conversations: Mapping of the journeys of 100 people interviewed as part of DSDHA's West End public realm project for the London Borough of Camden. The different colours denote the nature of the interviewee – resident, worker, student, or visitor.

to the establishment of places that are destinations in themselves such as ports or major religious sites.

Exchange (of goods, services, ideas) lies at the heart of why most cities share common evolutionary traits or growth patterns, which are often less the result of any 'grand design' for a formal city arrangement, and more because of the innate human instinct to congregate, share and trade. Bringing people together with resources, ideas and power is at the heart of why cities exist.

Where this coincidence of movement and people has occurred, invariably there has been a propensity for public spaces to be created to facilitate the gathering of people for meetings, events and exchanges to happen. This effective 'placemaking' at the heart of a community has meant that public space persists as the simplest and most successful device for allowing cities to flourish. While over time this form of gathering also began to take place undercover and then in buildings, which were limited in their scale and durability due to technological advances, the importance of public space has continued to be an essential component in creating and sustaining civic society.

Routes + place; never the same journey twice

Routes have always been carved across landscapes, coping with natural migrations and shifts in population. These have been predicated on finding the path of least resistance, discovered through persistent trial and error to minimize effort and maximize the distance covered without exhaustion. Look at the desire lines that people leave in the snow or across a field; laid before you is evidence of the human instinct to expend the least effort to cross the greatest distance in the shortest amount of time.

Migratory paths became the desire lines between settlements, across differing topographies, so that every journey is essentially specific to its place, responding to the twists and turns of the ground beneath one's feet. The nuances of place literally shape and form a route, cradle it or even sever it (think of a valley at once encouraging movement along its length but by virtue of the hills or mountains that define it, also hindering journeys laterally).

Social significance was gradually ascribed to the landscape and with it came belief systems and culture, so much so that routes are imbued with meaning, like the Songlines (Daley, 2016) of indigenous Australians who navigate great distances by singing the songs in the appropriate sequence, or the principles of *feng shui* that has long informed the organization and orientation of Chinese cities.

Walking, then riding, and later driving rudimentary vehicles, made land passage possible but not free from difficulty. Water has always been the key means of transport between more remote destinations irrespective of land-bound constraints, giving rise to such coastal communities as those along the Amalfi coast. Communities here have prospered where proximity to water offers abundant food while the Lattari mountains historically provided natural fortification against attack. The Euphrates has nurtured the beginnings of civilizations on its banks, and Iceland's first population was distributed strategically in fragile settlements that clung to the coast. Travel by sea, river and across lakes acknowledged the benefits of movement by water, giving rise to the ambitious construction of man-made, long-distance canals, aqueducts and great seaports. These first 'motorways' allowed the exchange of goods and people to take place more easily, partnered with the strong desire for personal and state profit, formalizing commerce as a key driver of city development.

The first towns

Look at historic maps and you will see how settlements grow where routes cross, and the available means of transport coincide. In the pre-industrial city, the migratory paths of wild animals were superseded by the paths taken by farmers herding livestock to market, known as drovers' roads. Take the plan of any city built before the railways, and there you will be able to trace the influence of food. The first measured survey of London, John Ogilby's *Large and Accurate Map of the City of London* of 1676, shows just how closely the city mirrored the landscape that fed it. London's sheep and cattle, many from Scotland, Wales and Ireland, approached from the north and the west, streaming down country lanes to Newgate, where the city's livestock market was held before moving to Smithfield. The surviving street names – Cheapside, Poultry and Cornhill – attest to the fact that this was once London's central food market.

Urbanization and economic development are closely related phenomena. Exploiting the intersection of routes by both land and water, Venice epitomizes the extreme (and in many respects irrational) risks that the mercantile elite were willing to take to overcome natural obstacles in pursuit of profit. Situated on 118 small islands, the city is seasonally flooded by the Adriatic, but it is also this unlikely logic that provided the foundations for Venice's unique character and sense of place.

The morphology of the city is fundamentally driven by the mode of transport of the day. In cities across the world, street widths, and consequently building plots, were dictated by the amount of space needed to move. Historic Arabic city planning principles took the height of a person on the back of a camel as the minimum height for building overhangs or covered routes, and the narrow streets of the medieval city often mimicked the dimensions of a cart's narrow axel, with sharp turns reflecting their short wheelbase. Likewise, the towns and cities of modernity are characterized by their ring roads and numerous roundabouts, designed to accommodate the faster speeds and large turning circles of the motor vehicle.

From travelling to commuting

Transport technology's impact on the morphology of the city extends beyond the immediate metrics of the street. In 1994, Italian physicist Cesare Marchetti, described an idea that has come to be known as the 'Marchetti constant'. In general, he declared, people have always been willing to commute for about half an hour from their homes each day (Marchetti, 1994).[1] This principle has profound implications for urban life and for the spatial organization of the city. The value of land is governed by its accessibility – the reasonable speed of transport to reach it. Even if there is a vast amount of land available, that land has little value unless transport infrastructure makes it quickly accessible to the urban centre. This means that the physical size of cities is a function of the speed of the transportation technologies that are available. As speed increases, cities can expand.

Until the industrial revolution, people principally moved around cities on foot or by horse-drawn carts and carriages. With services concentrated in the centre of cities, the radius of development from the heart of the city was limited to roughly one mile – the approximate distance a person can walk in 30 minutes. Most cities from the ancients to the industrial revolution did not grow much bigger than a two-mile diameter. Ancient Rome packed as many as a million people into an area only a little more than this. Medieval Paris stretched about two miles from the Bastille to the Louvre; Vienna's Innere Stadt measures only one mile in diameter, and the historic City of London is nicknamed the 'Square Mile' for a reason. Beijing's walls enclosed an inner city about three miles in diameter, which into the 20th century still made up most of the developed area.

It was not until 1830, when British civil engineer, George Stephenson, opened one of the world's first railways between Manchester and Liverpool, that the upper limit for the area of a functioning city could be challenged. The London and Greenwich railway opened soon after in 1836, and new lines quickly began radiating out of central London. The arrival of the railways meant that people could now move at an unprecedented rate: ten miles or more in half an hour. But instead of gradually extending the city outwards as you might expect, the railways instead created villages around their stations (the slow acceleration of steam trains meant they could not stop frequently, so new development could not be continuous along the track).

It was the development of the tram that allowed the suburban boom, which so drastically redefined the boundaries of the city. In practice, the tram could cover about four miles in a half hour – much slower than the railways carrying executives to their semi-rural estates, but much quicker than the horse-drawn carriage and pedestrian. Suddenly the city itself was no longer limited to a few square miles, and developable areas grew exponentially. Based on the Marchetti constant, a 30-minute walkable commute would allow a two-mile diameter, which covered over three square miles; whereas a tram could cover an eight-mile diameter or 50 square miles (English, 2019).

But London – the world's largest city for most of the 19th century – needed a faster means of transportation still. With the poor clustered in extreme density and squalor near their places of employment in the city centre and dockyards, and the middle class spread into the suburbs, London had become a more low-rise and less dense city than its European neighbours. The problem it suffered was getting from the various train terminals at speed to jobs in London's business district. It was not feasible to build elevated viaducts through some of the world's most valuable real estate. Charles Pearson promoted an ingenious solution: go underground. The first London Underground line opened in 1863, using steam trains – the forerunner to the Tube we know today.

The shape of cities today

The average one-way commute time today remains about 26 minutes (English, 2019). The endurance of the Marchetti constant has proven that the average speed of our transportation technologies does more than anything to shape the physical structure of our cities.

In the development of the contemporary city, acknowledgement of this is increasingly formalized: its layout, organization and, increasingly, its density are governed (at least in terms of planning policy) on the capacity and spatial requirements of the available forms of mobility. In London, a measure of the Public Transport Accessibility Levels (PTAL) of a given location is the determining factor in decision-making regarding the density of new development. The arrival of Crossrail – with its 200-metre long trains carrying up to 1,500 passengers – will increase the PTAL ratings of both central London locations and suburban regions, facilitating the continued expansion of the city, both upwards and outwards.

The introduction of smart technologies into both transport systems and the urban fabric more broadly promises to increase capacity further. 'Intelligent' parking systems will increase the efficiency of available spaces, while the long-anticipated arrival of autonomous vehicles will force a reconsideration of several long-held principles of highway design. These contemporary transport requirements are likely to be charmingly compromised by the competing interests of heritage and conservation; fibre optic cables laid along the same routes trodden by cattle. It is these compromises that will generate new cultures, unique identities and provide opportunities for alternative forms of placemaking.

The mentality of place and travel: psychological and behavioural insights

Mental maps and movement

The way we move through a city is shaped by our own unique sense of personal geography – or mental map – as well as our abilities in spatial navigation (Lynch, 1960).[2] These routes are constantly refined in our minds, and our assessment of the preferred route can depend on a number of factors. Time of day is one such factor: for example, people sometimes travel a different way to and from work to avoid traffic congestion or take a back street when a main shopping street becomes busier later in the day. Or, more recently, they take a route with fewer interactions to maintain social distancing.

Weather, too, plays a role; so much so that architecture adjusts to maintain comfortable walking routes, like Bologna's covered arcades protecting people from sunshine and rain, and creating a great environment for doing business under shelter. In contrast, there are other global examples where segregated under- or above-ground walking routes linking one building to the next create huge protected networks, but little sense of place, for example Montreal's subterranean mall network or Hong Kong's elevated pedestrian routes – the longest outdoor escalator system in the world – that covers 800 metres in distance and traverses over 135 metres from top to bottom (Frampton et al, 2012).

Negative impacts of transport interchanges/stations

Travel has always had negative impacts. Open to attack, vulnerable to accidents, exposed to nature, polluting and noisy, journeys are not without hazards. Communal, public transport is seen as the last resort for those with no alternative during public health crises.

In cities, the buildings near to transport infrastructure usually turn their backs to keep anti-social aspects at bay; the view from the train is most typically of the 'back of house' of cities – back gardens, sidings and industrial areas. Therefore, the lack of active frontage makes travel feel less safe, reinforces its impact as a boundary condition, and fosters the sense that major transport infrastructure is relegated to peripheral and less desirable locations. Similarly, London's Park Lane, despite being next to a royal park and in a wealthy neighbourhood, was notorious for highwaymen and had no front doors along its route, only garden walls. Even today it is bounded by a huge roadway without many redeeming features.

These conditions strongly affect our perceptions when arriving in a city. Why are the areas around a railway station typically poor quality? Is it just the noise and pollution? Or the effect of transport logistics demanding space on the ground for supporting activities and causing pedestrian movement and public space to be pushed out so that it does not feel comfortable to spend time there? Or even the diurnal ebb and flow of commuters making the condition around stations feel unpredictable and, therefore, unsafe?

The root of many of the problems is the decision-making framework used in the selection of sites for transport infrastructure. Usually on the edge of the urban settlement, railways were located here to minimize impact on the existing city and because of the relatively cheap and more easily developable land. Consequently, these places became characterized by severance, local travel was made less easy, and human life was placed secondary to infrastructure, which rarely had a human scale. As a result, people chose to live or work elsewhere, values dropped, and the area falls on harder times. But, as cities have densified, and pressures for land have intensified, the design and placement of new transport infrastructure has to be more rigorously considered to ensure that it promotes activity, fosters community, creates new jobs and employment space, and – importantly – prioritizes connection and permeability rather than severance. The city no longer has enough space for a back-of-house.

Mobility – the way forward

In *The Speed Handbook: Velocity, Pleasure, Modernism* (2009), Enda Duffy historicizes the sensations and pleasures of speed during the modernist period. Since then the automobile has conquered space at the expense of pedestrian areas and public space. Moreover, the incessant rise of car ownership and car culture has altered both human perception and the experience of everyday life in the urban environment.

In response to this phenomenon, which afflicts many cities worldwide, urbanists such as Alison Smithson, Venturi/Scott Brown/Izenour and Lynch/Myer/Appleyard started to carry out experiments aimed at raising the awareness of the impact of motorization. Their aim was to put the subject back into the centre of the analysis and shift the perspective on transport infrastructure from a mere problem of engineering to one of art and architecture.

In *The View from the Road,* Lynch, Myer and Appleyard describe the experience of driving as a type of musical notation: 'a sequence played to the eyes of a captive, somewhat fearful, but partially inattentive audience, whose vision is filtered and directed forward'. They point out that 'vision, rather than sound or smell, is the principal sense. Touch is a secondary contributor to the experience, via the response of the car to hands and feet' (Appleyard, 1964). In line with these observations, Venturi, Scott Brown and Izenour suggest, in their seminal book, *Learning from Las Vegas,* that the speed enabled by the automobile, by distorting a driver's perception of space, has called for a hybrid form of architecture/landscape that prioritizes visual communication over other spatial qualities (Venturi et al, 1977). Applying these ideas to a wider scale, Alison Smithson's *AS in DS* (1983) – a diary of a passenger's eye on English roads in the 1970s – marks the beginning of a new sensibility to the car's impact on urban planning.

Today, while we strive to reprogram our car-centric environments to make space for other road users, it seems urgent to revisit these experiments and adapt them to the experience of cycling and walking. Only in this way can we develop a deeper awareness of our urban space and mould it to successfully accommodate other means of transport and mitigate the current tensions. Furthermore, new road-users have started to compete for their space in the city. Cyclists are dramatically changing the experience of moving through London. As more and more of them whizz past the lines of cars, it is clear that on short trips through the inner city they are now faster than any other means of transportation as transport infrastructure comes under increasing pressure.

However, beyond its documented logistical, health, environmental and social benefits, cycling can cause significant conflict on our roads. In accommodating this mode of transport, the approach has been to replicate 20th-century models and scar our city with a mesh of flyovers, segregated pedestrian and cycle paths. This ruins the urban setting while fuelling tensions between different road users. This is particularly evident at the junctions, where cyclists cross paths with other modes of transport. It is here that the modernist narratives of 'speed', 'segregation' and 'efficiency' – as the imprint of last century's process of motorization – still resonate and cause the most issues for the integration of different users. Due to its lack of flexibility, all this expensive infrastructure also risks becoming obsolete. The future introduction of autonomous vehicles will alter the way users navigate and share the public realm.

In metropolitan areas, as we travel more and for longer, the journey is an increasingly significant part of our experience of the city. However, the human experience of moving from one place to another is largely overlooked when it comes to urban planning. What if we could make our transport infrastructure work harder by programming it to not just accommodate movement but also to incorporate places to work, shop, relax and access (or even produce) culture? It is very hard to do this. You need to understand the user groups, their habits, and the existing conditions on the ground by evaluating the city 'as found', via fieldwork, mapping, and conversations with those who frequent these locations. But the benefits of incorporating multiple uses are numerous, essential even, to ensure the city remains diverse and inclusive and provides the necessary spaces for all forms of work and life to coexist.

As recipients of the 2016 Research Fellowship in the Built Environment – awarded by the Royal Commission for the Exhibition of 1851 – DSDHA has investigated the nature of London's urban mobility, taking into account the often overlooked aesthetic and psychological experience of moving through a city. We have devised a human-centred methodology for the design of places in the historic centre, which integrate cycling and walking journeys with other established and upcoming modes of transport, rather than segregating them. Taking into account a number of parameters, including the impact of panoramic views on different users' speed and modality of travel, this methodology seeks to improve the quality of our public spaces, mitigate the current tensions, and make cycling and walking in London a more pleasurable and accessible mode of transport: one open to people of different ages and abilities. In the following sections we reflect on some of the lessons learnt – lessons which are applicable to many places that face similar challenges to those experienced in London.

Better urbanism: how can we build places that better reflect our travel needs?

Critiquing the past to ensure we don't repeat our mistakes

London is a unique place, a crowded mega-city with a resilient, organic and wonderfully informal street and road pattern at its core. Its centre, unlike other European or American cities, has not been carved up with too many 19th-century boulevards and 20th-century highways, yet the automobile has still been at the top of the 'food chain' since the last century, greatly impacting the mode and speed at which Londoners have engaged with the city.

> During the past decades heavy attacks have been made on the space available in the city by the great number of cars and the amount of traffic, which has increased proportionately. On account of this situation the size of pedestrian areas have been reduced. The car has rolled into the city like an assassin; by now most city-dwellers – either in their role of pedestrian or car-driver – have lost the ability to observe changes in the use of space in the city caused by the presence of the car. But the car remains a dream come true. (Otto Das 'Because the Car Has Come to Stay', in A. Smithson's, *AS in DS*, 1983, p 4)

In 1963 the Ministry of Transport published the influential report *Traffic in Towns*, by the architect, civil engineer and planner Professor Sir Colin Buchanan. It proposed a range of solutions for dealing with the effect of the car on the urban environment, the most notable of which were segregation, and pedestrianization, which were implemented over the following decade. This separation of road users had detrimental impacts on towns and cities, devastating previously vibrant centres and increasing vehicle speed to a level that was intimidating and hazardous to pedestrians and cyclists. The fight back against this dominance of the car began over 45 years ago, with the campaigns against, and abandonment of, the segregated 'Ringway' proposals. In the early 1980s the Greater London Council, under Ken Livingstone, set up a specialist cycling unit to promote the introduction of cycling infrastructure. In the late 1980s/early 1990s the London Assessment Studies concluded that major road schemes should not be pursued, and that better use should be made of the existing road network. This led to the 'Red Routes' and the construction of new underground rail capacity. In the mid to late 1990s, reflecting a desire for a better urban environment (such as promoted in the city studies led by Lord Rogers), there was increasing momentum for streetscape improvements, eg The Strand, and Regent Street. Dutch notions of 'shared space' or 'simplified streetscapes' began to influence urban designers and traffic engineers. An early UK example was the improvement of Kensington High Street, where guard-railing and unnecessary street furniture was removed, kerb-lines realigned and pedestrian crossings made more direct, creating a much improved and less cluttered street scene.

Yet, by the 2000s, due to an unprecedented population surge (an increase of nearly two million inhabitants since the early 1990s), London was often gridlocked and polluted. The city was (and still is) under severe pressure to use its physical space wisely and sustainably, without destroying its quality and history. At this point a combination of more incisive policies (for instance, dramatically increasing bus and underground funding, and in 2003 introducing the central London congestion charging zone) and infrastructural changes were implemented, all with the aim to rebalance traffic towards alternative means of transport to the car – from the highly sophisticated and expensive Crossrail, to the more 'ordinary' issue of making it easier and more pleasurable to walk and cycle within the dense historic core. Technologies like trains and bicycles – which in the 19th century, before the advent of cars, were symbols of progress and modernity – have thus been re-evaluated and given more space within a less car-centric urban landscape.

London, however, is not like Amsterdam or Copenhagen, small cities with more ordered, compact and coherent layouts. Its sheer scale results in longer commutes, 'journeys' rather, through radically different urban conditions, across the city's 32 boroughs, plus the City of London – each with its own political, administrative and physical identity – and through a street pattern that changes moment by moment, straight to winding, leafy to truck-thronged, wide to narrow. By refuting the Modernist claim that a single solution is suitable for all situations and adopting a more human-centred approach to design, might we better reflect the diverse characteristics and behaviours of different locations to create public spaces that are more inclusive of local populations?

Solving the segregated city

'Every journey matters', according to the slogan of Transport for London, the local government body responsible for Greater London's transport system. And it does – not only from the perspective of the person on the move, but also in terms of the experience of those places through which transport infrastructure passes.

We can start by valuing the whole journey beyond the traditional lens, which assesses only its economic benefit and see it instead as a continuous experience for the traveller themselves. This would give visibility to aspects of the journey that are currently undervalued or not recognized at all, including them in the cost–benefit equation – such as the health, wellbeing, social impact and environmental consequences.

Making sure that the human experience and quality of public space is considered as a core component of the journey is key, especially if the journey is multimodal – as most are – as travellers have to move between modes, from plane to train to bicycle, or continuing a journey by foot from a bus stop.

Would better quality space encourage more people to take journeys by public transport rather than by private car? What benefits to wellbeing as well as cost, time and convenience can it offer? Is it important to have a place to pause or wait, meet and feel safe with other people of all ages and backgrounds? Does offering a great destination that feels like it is part of the city and that also allows for an easy transfer at the end of a railway line, rather than a purely functional, placeless interchange, which is isolating and isolated as a piece of infrastructure, encourage people to use the train? Can we create cohesion and connectivity, as well as encourage active travel by linking good public spaces (such as a green route) with better sight lines? That could offer people a more enjoyable path and draw them away from a congested or polluted street. Can a flexible, temporary solution to a transport infrastructure and its associated public space be tested before huge, fixed investments

Figure 13.2: The Bambouseraie at Broadgate Plaza, London

DSDHA's transformation of an underused and windswept thoroughfare built above the railway lines of London's Liverpool Street Station into an immersive, tranquil environment that is equipped with USB charging points in the island seating modules to promote outdoor working.

are made? And can drastic yet temporary changes as a response to a pandemic be quickly implemented and then reversed?

To address these questions, we need to fundamentally shift our perspective away from the notion of construction projects being finished *products* and instead think of projects as existing over time and monitoring their *performance* as an outcome not just a capital cost.

After Modernism – a shift in priority

Cities have become segregated by infrastructures, where mobility, and its social and economic advantages, come at a price. But is it inevitable that this success be coupled with negative consequences, such as pockets of inequality, pollution and unhappiness? This does not have to be the case if places are prioritized in tandem with travel.

Over time, the way cities have evolved has been recast by 20th-century Modernist principles of an 'international style' that did not take regional specificity into consideration. Following the principle that free movement is a public good, the same variety of road types have been used indiscriminately from Brazil to Birmingham, Detroit to Dhakka, typically following a model where work and home are located in separate zones of the city, and the infrastructure for private transport dominates the space in between. This urban uniformity leads to the loss of a sense of place in our newer cities where places designed around people, which are perceived for their more 'organic' quality, get squeezed out of the development equation. While older cities continue to appeal as destinations because they have great places and unique identities, they can be perceived as failing to offer the model for growth, convenience and the integration of 'smart' technologies that new cities offer. This is a conundrum that vexes urban designers the world over.

We are at a critical point for any city-maker or nation-builder, where the nature of human movement has to be re-evaluated through several lenses: who has priority – humankind or the machine, community versus individual, economy versus health, global climate change versus personal freedom to travel and a right to roam at a local scale?

We find it hard to capture the lessons from history while embracing the future. The lack of continuity in city-building knowledge that used to be handed down generation to generation is inevitable, given the disruption that progress and globalization has delivered. Is it possible to build on the qualities of human-focused, organically developed cities throughout the world while addressing contemporary demands for connectivity and efficiency? Can we forge new ways of making cities where people *want* to be, rather than just spaces where people *have* to be? With the rise in remote working (somewhat enforced by current circumstances), what can cities and journeys offer beyond places of work and commuting?

Placemaking design philosophy – what makes a good place?

Delivering good urban design that better reflects our travel needs is like holding several conversations simultaneously. It takes concentration and consideration, empathy and vision, and above all collaboration. City-makers and designers must have these skills in order to make good public space in an existing or emerging urban context. Trial and error has shaped historic spaces, so adapting the city 'as found', or starting from scratch, demands a compression and distillation of knowledge to design good public spaces that encourage active travel as well as making a great place in which to be.

Of course, this is hard to do and is doubly difficult given the range of interested parties involved – planners, urban designers, highways and transport engineers, politicians, local authority officials, landowners, amenity and community groups, residents and temporary populations like daily workers or students. And given this complexity, it is a challenge to enable this process to be more widely understood by the general public too. To create a great foundation for our cities, encouraging and enabling people to understand what decisions help shape their local area should be at the heart of any school curriculum because with good city-making comes good governance, healthy communities and meaningful engagement.

Scales of infrastructure and local/global networks

Starting with heavy infrastructure is critical as it will often have impacts beyond the original intentions of those responsible for their design. The hidden phenomena of one new path of movement inadvertently cutting off another small route is a case in point of the need to identify those who win and those who lose as a result of transport infrastructure projects. Uniting regions is hugely positive for national benefit, yet it will inevitably disrupt local, less 'valued' routes. A new strategic railway line such as High Speed 2 (HS2) unites major cities but also severs thousands of smaller, minor local routes that provide vital connections between communities. As these are statistically insignificant individually, the cumulative impact of their severance goes unrecognized, yet the effect can be devastating.

Figure 13.3: Masterplan for Central Somers Town, London

Somers Town in the London Borough of Camden is an area that has suffered as a result of its severance from neighbouring areas by the imposition of the major London stations, Euston and St Pancras. Since 2014, DSDHA has been working with the local authority and the local residents to develop a landscape-led masterplan for Central Somers Town that will see the creation of new affordable housing, a primary school, a community building and play facilities, as well as a new park.

At an urban scale the same dislocation can happen. Looking at maps of where social deprivation occurs in cities, one can clearly trace where the Victorian expansion of railways, and earlier 18th- and 19th-century canals, cut off and thus created poorer areas. Today, this means that lives are still negatively affected daily by past decisions and, over time, life opportunities in that area drop. A daily walk to school for children and their families becomes unnecessarily burdensome if they are forced to use a diverted path or an uninviting footbridge as their only means of access to public services and amenities. Consequently, investment falls, businesses fail and ultimately health declines. So, ensuring that the small-scale journey is safeguarded in the design of nationally significant infrastructure must be a future priority.

Bespoke yet standardized components when planning infrastructure

The acontextual or placeless appearance of poorly designed transport infrastructure is exacerbated when it is constructed from a standard kit of parts. This approach might be a cheaper and more expedient solution in the short term but also it is invariably less flexible and less responsive to local needs.

Budgets for transport projects are typically based on short timeframes and evaluated within specific criteria. However, the cost-benefit ratio needs to be understood against the long-term consequences that poor design can lead to. Railway underpasses, for example, are chosen from a catalogue of standard Department for Transport approved specifications to address a functional requirement. This provides a ready-made solution that can be imported into any context, reinforcing a one-size-fits-all culture. When underpasses all look and feel the same, the person who is forced to use them becomes dehumanized, compounding the sense of personal anonymity. Alternatively, by adopting a more responsive design approach, using local materials where possible, a sense of place can be nurtured.

Infrastructure for the 'long now': towards time-based urbanism

As a system, transport straddles the pressures of individuals' and society's immediate needs and inequities on the one side with desires for long-term positive outcomes and sustainability on the other.

For many cities, this might translate into reconciling immediate with longer-term goals, such as ensuring that those most vulnerable (eg children, disabled people and the elderly) have access to affordable transportation while replanning the city to accommodate autonomous vehicles. Yet even when transport stakeholders see the value of addressing both time horizons, it can be incredibly difficult to imagine and pursue true transformation.

As Stewart Brand describes in *The Clock of the Long Now: Time and Responsibility* (1999), after the Apollo programme began returning colour photographs of the Earth from space, the Earth's problems lived in a new context, 'the big here', and took on new dimensions, stakeholders and rationales. Having planet-scale perspective on atmospheric health, ocean health and climate stability made national approaches obsolete. What might a similar context shift for transport infrastructure be? When considering transport infrastructure as a long-term proposition, what might the 'long now' in public space look like? What forces and dynamics might shape it? How can we reconcile the 'immediate now' global crisis of COVID-19 or the next pandemic with the long-term global crisis of climate change? How might we cultivate a 'long now' mindset in order to reframe pressing urban challenges in ways that reveal purposeful approaches and thoughtfully scaled solutions?

At a planetary scale, understanding future environmental conditions is important for creating better places for travel. Is it going to be hotter, cooler, dryer or wetter? Is it wise to even invest here when mitigation may only be staving off inevitable changes?

Given the climate crisis we are facing, it is critical to look at this across scales of time when designing new infrastructure. What are the likely climate impacts here, and what is the most robust, flexible response? Is a fixed, traditional solution even feasible? Building less, better might be the best policy to embrace, which is what New York City discovered after the impact of Hurricane Sandy left traditional rail and road transport unusable. The few river ferries the city owned had proved invaluable to moving people safely. This has spurred future investment in transport into watercraft as light infrastructure as opposed to heavy solutions, and now the ferry service has been hugely expanded to popular success, with ecological benefits too. Should other cities do the same and embrace an approach where distributed infrastructure like this also spreads benefits across a broader territory, with lower costs, as well as creating user-delight along the way as river fronts regenerate and communities are reinvigorated?

The continuity of change – what have we learnt?

The one constant in transportation technology from the mid-19th to the mid-20th century was change. New modes repeatedly extended the boundaries of cities and changed the way we lived. But that was a relative anomaly over the course of human history. Since then, not too much has changed. A person can navigate London almost perfectly with a 50-year-old map.

This has had real consequences. In sprawling metropolises like London, that are growing in population, highways quickly become overcrowded; expanding them is costly and ultimately ineffective. The speed of moving through the city (above ground at least) is slowing inexorably as congestion increases and people are accepting longer commuter times and travelling greater distances for work. The cost of new rail infrastructure – like Crossrail and HS2 – is prohibitively expensive and faces formidable ideological opposition. And the vaunted self-driving car, as imminent as it is illusory, will not transform the basic geometry of roads or significantly increase their capacity in cities like London that are medieval in their foundations. Perhaps such new technologies will squeeze out a few percent more efficiency from the legacy of the 1950s and 1960s, but it seems unlikely that they will catalyze the sort of urban transformation or social liberation of previous transport revolutions.

For a century, we lived off the legacy of rapid innovation. It allowed our cities to grow exponentially and, therefore, populations to urbanize. But we are now reaching the limits of what can tolerably be considered a city and there are not yet obvious technological revolutions on the horizon. We must make do mostly with building up and densifying the urban areas we already have. The challenge, therefore, is to make our increasingly populated cities not only tolerable to live in, but enjoyable, healthy, convivial and sustainable.

In this scenario, the role of good quality public space cannot be underestimated. It should be delivered in tandem with – and as part of – good infrastructure. Good public space does not exist in isolation without people travelling to it and through it. Without users it would be nothing more than a monument or a necropolis. Similarly, without integrating a human-centred approach to design – one predicated on social exchange – infrastructure risks continuing to function as separate from, rather than part of, the public realm. It is surely the successful

Figure 13.4: Broadgate Circle in the City of London

The city is where people choose to go – DSDHA's transformation of Broadgate Circle in the City of London from a corporate monoculture that was occupied predominantly during the working week to a vibrant and inclusive social space that attracts diverse audiences throughout the entire week.

272

combination of the two that ensures that *the city is where people choose to go.*

Notes

1   Marchetti developed a theory with Yacov Zahavi that the distribution of settlements is approximately one hour apart by foot, equating to 3–5 miles. The distribution of local amenity (food shops, bars, chemists, hairdressers, doctors, etc) in dense cities of approximately 400 metres is based on similar parameters for the maximum travel time of 10 minutes by foot that people will accept.

2   Urban theorist Kevin Lynch noted that people tend to follow links between landmarks and that those memorable places – churches, landscape features, etc – are the ones we recognize on walking and cycling journeys. Equally, while GPS and sat nav may have taken over the role of traditional map reading for some, it remains distinct from mental mapping.

References

Appleyard, D., Lynch, K. and Myer, J. (1964) *The View from the Road*, Cambridge MA: The MIT Press.

Brand, S. (1999) *The Clock of the Long Now: Time and Responsibility*, London: Weidenfeld & Nicholson.

Daley, P. (2016) 'Indigenous songlines: a beautiful way to think about the confluence of story and time', *The Guardian*, 4 July. www.theguardian.com/commentisfree/2016/jul/04/indigenous-songlines-a-beautiful-way-to-think-about-the-confluence-of-story-and-time

Duffy, E. (2009) *The Speed Handbook: Velocity, Pleasure, Modernism*, Durham, NC, Duke University Press.

English, J. (2019) 'The Commuting Principle that Shaped Urban History', *Citylab*, 29 August. www.citylab.com/transportation/2019/08/commute-time-city-size-transportation-urban-planning-history/597055/

Frampton, A., Solomon, J. D. and Wong, C. (2012) *Cities Without Ground: A Hong Kong Guidebook*, Singapore: ORO Editions.

Lynch, K. (1960) *The Image of the City*, Cambridge, MA: MIT Press.

Marchetti, C. (1994) 'Anthropological invariants in travel behavior', *Technological Forecasting and Social Change*, 47(1), September: pp 75–88.

Smithson, A. (1983) *AS in DS: An Eye on the Road*, Delft: Delft University Press.

Venturi, R., Scott Brown, D. and Izenour, S. (1977) *Learning from Las Vegas*, Cambridge, MA: The MIT Press.

14

Travel's Place in the Environment

Terry Hill

The environment is a tricky subject to deal with, with its almost mystic quality of unassailability. The environment is fragile and precious. Without our active care and protection, the sheer success and scale of the human species threatens to damage and destroy the environment. There are numerous examples to prove this.

And so this is truly the most important chapter in this important book. No environment, no travel. We have yet to find a truly sustainable solution to humanity's place in the environment and a balanced role for travel in it. This chapter will not conclude with a rational solution because our understanding and knowledge of a perfect relationship between travel on a scale we are currently experiencing, and a stable world ecology, is elusive. Having recognized the importance of the environment in our life on Earth, our expertise in knowing how to live a sustainable life is still in its infancy.

But this chapter will conclude with optimistic hope. The symptoms of the crisis have hit home, they have hit us hard in the last 50 years and most countries, most governments, most politicians and all international agencies are starting to say that they recognize the scale and urgency of the need to take action. But all of the people in these bodies are fearful of the consequences. Can politicians take the necessary actions (if we know what they are) and keep their communities in support? Do we know, and can we afford the costs of doing the right thing? (Can we afford the costs of not doing?) Beware the leader or sage who proclaims they know how to solve the triple challenge of human wellbeing, global

Figure 14.1a: Exhaust fumes from cars in a traffic jam

Figure 14.1b: Cyclists and pedestrians in Amsterdam, Netherlands

Human travel has a huge impact on our environment, contributing to air pollution, greenhouse gases and habitat destruction. But need the impact always be negative? Technological improvements – such as renewable-powered electric flights – and increased active travel might offer a brighter future.

healthy environment and universal economic prosperity. Often seen as competing aims (increasing one to the detriment of another), they are of course intricately interlinked.

Humans have always impacted and shaped our environment in some way, and often our ability and propensity to travel has spread the effects of our activities across wide areas. Sometimes these impacts have been very negative for other species – for example scientists attribute the extinction of many large mammals in pre-historic times to the activity of human hunting, finding that whenever humans (or our ancestors) migrated into a new area, the larger mammals tended to become extinct.[1] Other changes have been more complex: the great shift to sedentism and agriculture, moving away from a travelling, nomadic lifestyle (discussed in more detail in Chapter 3 'Travel and the Mind') had a large impact on our environment and many plant and animal species, both those we domesticated and those that came to fill the new ecological niches created. Despite this, we can say that throughout most of humanity's time on Earth we have tended to live in a more balanced relationship with our environment than we do now. One in which the impacts of human travel – powered in a pre-industrial age by renewable sources of wind and muscle – were on a smaller scale and slower to effect change than is the case today, and sometimes even beneficial to the environment, in tune with nature and the overall ecosystem.

For a brief time, say the past two centuries, we have become too confident, too arrogant, too colonial in our attitude to the environment. Seeing it as ours to colonize and exploit is a handy way of summarizing our relationship with the planet's mineral deposits, vital resources of water and sustenance, the rainforests to clear, the swamps to drain, rivers to train and so on; all to mobilize for our benefit. And while this attitude can be found in earlier times, I maintain that it is within those two centuries that our capabilities to colonize and exploit have increased so rapidly, growing hand-in-hand with our ambitions.

And now we know this just cannot go on. How on earth can we fix this broken system?

A balance sheet of humanity concludes that we are better off than ever; less poverty, increased life expectancy, better health, ever fewer conflicts. But this misses the point that we are enjoying better lives on the back of the environment, not intricately, intrinsically and intimately deep and dirty into it. If we do not make drastic changes soon, most of these positive trends look set to reverse.

And so, we get to the crux of the matter: how do we get back to the impact of a pre-industrial revolution 700 million global population living and travelling *in* the environment, from this current 7.7 billion people living *off* it? Well, it will not be by actually going *back* will it? This global perspective ignores the real impact of advocating limits to growth on local populations, communities and people. Limiting growth may be a strategy for the wealthy developed parts of the planet but a levelling off of global wellbeing indicators means denying the poorer parts of the world their surely rightful aspirations to benefit from the fruits of humanity's progress: food, health, shelter and, yes, travel. Our approach to travel will need to be transformed if we are to limit its harmful impacts on the environment and offer a more equitable future.

In the following sections we will look first at the interactions of travel and the environment throughout human history before moving on to examine prospects for the future of travel in a heating world.

The relationship between travel and the environment splits into three neat ages: that of muscle and wind, that after the realization of climate change and the 175 years between – the age without limits.

Muscle and wind: travel and the environment in balance

Before the 19th century, when travel was confined largely to human muscle and was enabled at most by animal assistance and the Earth's weather systems, travel was more in balance with nature, or was dominated by it. In fact the environment (wind and gravity) aided travel. Travel had many beneficial effects on human development as human ingenuity created footwear, the wheel, the barge and the ship all to aid migration, commerce and interchange of cultures.

Before the industrial revolution animals travelled more and further than humans. The vast herds migrating across the savannahs, prairies and steppes of the world and the annual north–south commute of birds and butterflies cover distances and numbers that are difficult to comprehend. The Arctic tern holds the record for distance – 90,000 kilometres per year and, for quantity, and excluding plankton, 1.3 million Sudanese white-eared kobs holds the record. Bruce Chatwin (1987) has an interesting observation on the relationship between travel and behaviour:

> As a general rule of biology, migratory species are less 'aggressive' than sedentary ones. There is one obvious reason why this should be so. The migration itself, like the pilgrimage, is the hard journey: a 'leveller' on which the 'fit' survive and stragglers fall by the wayside. The journey thus pre-empts the need for hierarchies and shows of dominance.

> The 'dictators' of the animal kingdom are those who live in an ambience of plenty. The anarchists, as always, are the gentlemen of the road.

Humans came to inhabit and populate and travel in all parts of the world. The larger human nomadic movement patterns were about survival, more economic and political than cultural: transhumance and migrations. Today, the biggest mass movements are social phenomena. Two million people take part in the 21st-century Hajj annually, and in the Chunyun spring festival (Chinese New Year) an estimated three billion trips were made in 2019 over the course of the festival; 2.46 billion trips by automobile, 413 million by rail − a rise of 8.3 per cent − and 73 million by air. And yet, even in pre-industrial times, a considerable number of people undertook long journeys with cultural and spiritual motivations (for more on this see Chapter 7 'Religious and Spiritual Travel'). By some estimates, as many as two million people per year may have made the pilgrimage to Santiago de Compestela in the 11th century, and this was just one of the popular devotional destinations in the medieval period (Stopford, 1994). This was a significant proportion of the European population of the time and such numbers must have had an impact on the routes and destinations through which pilgrims travelled. But in the pre-industrial age, with its power sources of wind and muscle, the environmental impact of such travel was not on the same scale as we see today.

Long-distance travel was a relative rarity and the numbers of journeys were dominated by commuting, the journey to work, from home to field and market. From the 16th century, mercantilism led to increasing volumes of international trade, but even this was small compared to locally sourced goods, and the average person's geographic range was limited. The relationship between human travel and human settlement has always been intimate and feasible journeys dictated town and village size and distribution, then as now (as discussed in Chapter 13 'Placemaking and Travel'). So it was that a market was a maximum of a day's walk from the limits of its catchment.

This era culminated in the 'Age of Enlightenment', which challenged tradition and faith through argument, reason and the evidence of the senses. From the end of the 17th century the enlightenment rapidly spread across Europe and to America and had travel as its foundation as ideas and knowledge migrated with the enlightened, and travel to ever-further parts of the globe quite literally expanded the bounds of human knowledge (for more on this see Chapter 11 'Travel as Exploration'). In parallel with the enlightened nobility's 'Grand Tour',[2] it was the enlightenment and its scientific quest that lead above all to major advances in science, engineering and to the industrial revolution and an age without any apparent limits to what could be achieved.

The age without limits: travel v the environment

Cornwall has a lot to answer for besides the pasty. While the origins of the first form of hydrocarbon power, the steam engine, are many, there is no doubt that in the 18th century Thomas Newcomen and Richard Trevithick's engines enabled work done to be at a huge multiple of individual human power. From this sped rapid and intense invention, innovation, population growth and travel volumes to an unprecedented extent. It might be said that the word 'exponential' was created to describe the hydrocarbon age. On this graph (Figure 14.2) the population kick at 1800 coincides precisely with the invention of Trevithick's steam locomotive demonstrated in Camborne, 90 years after Newcomen's steam mining pump on the Wheal Vor mine near Helston, both in Cornwall.

In the same way that the first agricultural revolution enabled society to move from a hunter-gatherer population to a settled farming economy, thus creating villages and then on to cities, so the industrial revolution's mechanized transport drove more people into towns and cities that supported a burgeoning population. There seemed to be no end to what could be achieved by powering industry and transport by

Figure 14.2: World population growth over the last 12,000 years

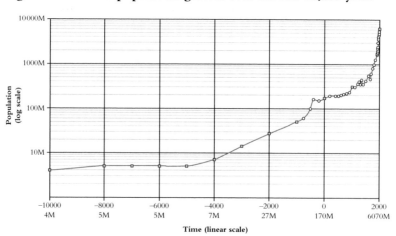

From 1800, the start of the 'hydrocarbon age', the world's population saw unprecedented exponential growth. With increasing wealth and population comes growing demand for travel – and increasing damage to our environment.

coal, and later gas and oil. This power transformed the former rural economies of agriculture and 'cottage' industries and so lead to rural depopulation, city urbanization and a population explosion.

This era, from 1800 to 1972, was perhaps the heyday of travel; benefits for the traveller with little or no realization of the increasing damage that mechanized transport does to the environment. But the allure of travel has changed and travel has been democratized. We live now in an era of mass travel. It is not only the aristocracy that can complete the Grand Tour as the glamour of air travel evolves to the ubiquity of low cost airlines and the utility of passenger sea liners is extinguished and is replaced by the massive cruise ship market. But perhaps the Grand Tour was not as sophisticated as it was reported to be. Maybe air travel was never glamorous, it merely had a gloss of luxury (and exclusivity) to make up for its discomfort of noise and cramped accommodation. My father-in-law, writing home from a trip to Australia on Imperial Airways in the late 1930s, spoke of the frequent stops en-route not only to refuel but for a bath and change of clothes because flying was dirty, dusty, noisy and sweaty. And the luxury liners carried most passengers in steerage.

So this nostalgia is tinged with heroism; the admiration of the intrepid explorer and the innate curiosity that we suspect is founded in our compulsion to travel and travel in quantities that far exceeds the utility of travel. Far more people travel than is attributable to their subsistence needs alone. Technology and operational efficiency has improved such that by car, train, air and sea we can all be explorers.

The democratization of travel is not merely mass tourism: going there, seeing it and coming back to tell the tale. The democratization of travel coupled with the population explosion has led to migration and a tremendous mixing, marbling and melding of people and of produce, across virtually all countries and cities. Of course, it causes tensions of immigration and racism and challenges of assimilation. And some bemoan the ubiquity of globalization, the continual assault of marketing to consume American fast food, quinoa, farmed ostrich or sushi.

But none of this is new:

> Our new, rapid, closed-in sort of travel has its sinister aspects, and here is one of them. When people moved slowly in their travel, there was time to establish proper communications with what was strange, to absorb, to adjust oneself. Now that we are whizzed about the world, there is no time for absorbing and adjusting. Perhaps it is for this

reason that the world that the traveller knows is beginning to show less and less variety. By the time we can travel at four hundred miles an hour we shall probably move over dead uniformity, so that the bit of reality we left at one end of the journey is twin to the bit of reality we step into at the other end. Indeed, by that time there will be movement, but, strictly speaking, no more travel. (J. B. Priestley *English Journey*, 1934)

However, we benefit enormously from the variety and richness of our cosmopolitan communities. We in the UK do not have to travel far to experience the different, the exotic.

It took a long time for the environment to be discovered. For many years the UK Institution of Civil Engineers had as its purpose 'the art of directing the great sources of power in nature for the use and convenience of man'. Nature and the environment were for our benefit and for us to exploit.[3]

How was it that during this era of seemingly limitless travel we came to consider that we were not a part of nature, were in some way superior to flora and fauna? Paradoxically it was probably because, while we thought we were masters of the world and all of its natural systems, we also thought it would always be there. Like many abusive relationships that rely upon a dysfunctional but mutual dependency; we probably thought that however much we over-exploit resources, species or habitats they would always be there for us. But they will not. Travel and the environment have got out of balance and in many situations the traveller and the environment are in conflict (as we will examine in more detail later in this chapter).

Within the policy world, there has been a steady and increasing understanding of the effects and impacts of transport investment and travel on the environment. In the UK the successive decades can be seen as being dominated by different frameworks of understanding:

- 1960s affordability: Ernest Marples' pledge to build 1,000 miles of motorway was a budgeted commitment, not a value for money justification.
- 1970s transport economics: COBA – cost/benefit appraisal – largely based on discounted cash flows of capital and operational cost savings and time-saving benefits based on a willingness to pay and the value of time.
- 1980s environmental impact appraisals: based on pseudo-rigorous and if possible quantified multivariate assessments.

- 1990s public engagement: consultation community sociology driven by a methodological assessment of transport problems.
- 2000s commerciality: PFI brought commerciality to the provision of transport facilities.
- 2010s sustainability: including limiting the effects of climate change.

Now this approach is web-based as the Department of Transport's Transport Analysis Guidance (WebTAG).[4] In addition to its economic procedures, its environmental and social headings are shown in the table below:

Environmental and social headings in WebTAG

Environmental	Social
Noise	Accidents★
Air quality★	Physical activity
Greenhouse Gases★	Security
Landscape/Townscape	Severance
Biodiversity/Ecology	Journey Quality★
Heritage	Option and non-use value★
Water Environment	Accessibility

While it may be thought that these topics are inherently qualitative in nature, in an attempt to square the circle of the economics v environment conflict, WebTAG tries to monetize several factors (marked ★) so that they can be set alongside the economic appraisal. While this goes some way to bringing environmental factors into consideration, we may find that, as a result, in the words of Oscar Wilde, we 'know the price of everything and the value of nothing'.

But are all of the environmental impacts necessarily negative? There is no doubt that the growth of travel, underpinned by transport infrastructure has been transformative, from the opening up of the US in the 19th century to the regeneration of London's East Thames Corridor and the development of China's high speed rail network in the 21st. Transport investment and travel have grown in parallel with wealth creation and the reduction in poverty. There is a rich body of literature demonstrating this link. However, I think we are going to have to conclude that, overall, the total effect of:

$$\frac{\text{population x trip rates x global heating x toxic emissions x resource depletion}}{\text{fragility of the world's ecosystem}}$$

means that on current trends, travel is unsustainable. We will have to change.

We have always travelled and will continue to do so in ever-increasing numbers, so long as population growth continues. Our appetite for motorized personal transport seems to be insatiable. In Figure 14.3, showing road traffic growth, the recessions of 1956, 73, 90 and 2008 can clearly be seen but recovery soon returns to the relentless 4% yearly growth rate. And there is no evidence that political policy swings between public or private transport investment make any difference.

Figure 14.3: Road traffic growth in Great Britain, 1949–2018

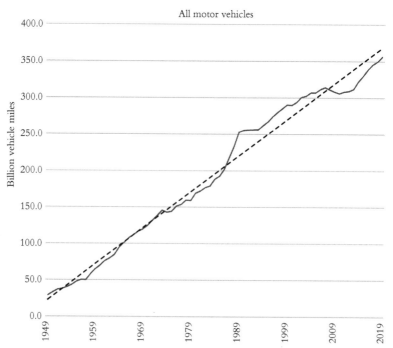

As this chart shows, car use has risen over the last 70 years (DfT statistics, table TRA0101). Separate ITC research has shown that per capita car usage (rather than aggregate total miles travelled) has stalled since 1990.

Encouragingly however there are signs that, on a per-capita basis, this has been stagnating in developed nations since 2000. This has been observed across countries from the US, to Germany, France, Australia and the UK. The Independent Transport Commission's own research has demonstrated that there has been a particular fall in demand for car travel by young men, and there is some debate over whether the millennial generation will travel less than its predecessors. However, Professor of Energy and Transport Andreas Schafer has shown that travel demand is often displaced by faster modes, and it could be that, as incomes increase, our appetite for car travel is being replaced by aviation and other forms of high-speed transport. The trend line for aviation is a resilient five per cent.

How much should be spent on satisfying this demand? And where should the balance be struck between economics and the environment? Traditionally policy makers have placed more emphasis on essential travel over discretionary, with higher monetary values put on the former. A possible ranking of the value of different journey purposes could be:

Essential

- migration; economic (seasonal and nomadic), refugees
- exploration
- journeys for and to work

Discretionary

- leisure – family, friends
- traveller/tourist[5]

Interestingly governments put high values of time on journeys *for* work, less on journeys *to* work and even less on non-work journeys. Conventional values of time coefficients assign higher values to those pursuits that potentially degrade the environment (work and commercial journeys), or are indifferent to its quality, than to those that need a high-quality environment to be appreciated (tourism and social journeys). Exploration and migratory journeys seem to be completely absent from the economic evaluation literature, yet migrants clearly pay large sums for undertaking arduous and often hazardous journeys. Conversely, in the aviation industries at least, discretionary journeys are seen as the future growth areas: 'Emerging markets throughout the world have shown that air travel is a discretionary expenditure, but it is one of the first discretionary items to be added as a consumer joins the middle class...In developed markets, demand for essential travel has been met, leaving growth to come from discretionary travel' (Boeing Current Market Outlook 2014–33). Andreas Schafer (2007) finds that while global average incomes and population more than doubled over the previous 50 years, and this translated into directly proportionate increases in passenger mobility, shares of budgets and personal time stayed roughly constant. At an aggregate level, five per cent of our daily time is spent travelling, a figure that holds true for residents of African villages, in Palestine, Peru, Japan, Western Europe and the US. And by switching to faster modes (low speed public transport to light vehicles to high speed rail and air) ever further distances are being travelled – average daily travel distances in North America have increased from 30 kilometres to 70 kilometres over the past 50 years.

What satisfaction do we get out of travel, and what is its relationship with the environment? First, it seems wrong to class travel and its impact as the optional and variable item, and the environment as fixed and immovable. What we now appreciate is that our world is in constant flux and little of what we know around us is as it always has been. And travel helps us understand this. Our environment changes, sometimes negatively through no fault of travel. And frequently through travellers' insights and revelations, it changes for the better. Travel brings former, different or 'better' environments to a wider audience and frequently induces vast improvements in degraded environments. And in the same way as zoos publicize endangered species and help protect them, so travel can help draw attention to endangered environments and so protect them.

Here are a couple of examples:

- Travel broadening the mind and bringing the destruction of habitats and heritage to our attention via wildlife and eco-tourism (which can reduce negative impacts, channel resources into conservation practices and create 'an emotional bond, where individuals learn and want to help' (Lemelin et al, 2012)), travel reporting and TV programmes (the so-called 'Attenborough effect').
- Transport investments for new travellers bringing huge investments to degraded environments, derelict and/or deprived areas such as Malmö in Sweden or the East Thames Corridor in London, both of which experienced a renaissance following major transport investments.

And so to the contention that travel is a derived demand. The UK Department for Transport's WebTAG under the heading 'Journey Quality' states:

> Travellers don't normally travel for its own sake. Travel is a derived demand that arises from people's desire to engage in activities. Therefore, a high-quality journey, when experienced, is often taken for granted. However, a poor journey quality, when experienced, can be easily recognised. Journey quality can be affected both by travellers and by network providers and operators.

Surely this must be challenged. Maybe it is correct that poor quality travel is commented upon more than good quality, but it is manifestly apparent that the days of travel as merely a means to other things, a means to an end, is over. What is the end? Are there other means? Peoples' 'discretionary' travel is increasing at a rate of over four per cent per year, among the highest of all sectors, whether for tourism, social or education purposes, and therefore we can deduce that there is a clear 'willingness to pay' – the usual litmus test of transport economic appraisal – for travel for its own sake.

If future travel increases are going to be generated in large part by 'discretionary' travel, and if, as we shall see, current methods of travel are increasingly damaging to the environment, what is to be done? If it is truly discretionary (eg visiting relatives) then economic logic leads us to conclude that it can be managed downwards with little or no overall economic disbenefit. And this management could mean reducing the amount of discretionary travel by pricing (eg Air Passenger Duty (APD)) or by rationing, as is happening at many over-visited tourist sites such as Machu Picchu, Similan Islands off Thailand, and Venice. Or the increasing numbers could be accommodated more sustainably using more park-and-ride, or investing in high speed rail for all short-haul air routes.

Climate change changes everything: regaining balance

Now we know that the world is finite. When did this revelation occur? In our lifetime. I learnt this when, at school, I read Peter Fleming's[6] *Brazilian Adventure* (1933) and he burst my inquisitive explorer's bubble: 'After all, nobody had been here before .... even if these and many other circumstances branded our adventure as the sheerest anti-climax – Roger and I would have done a thing which is becoming increasingly difficult to do – would have broken new ground on this *overcrowded* planet' (emphasis added). That was in 1933! So while, yes, it was before my lifetime, the realization that, not only were there few places on Earth left to explore, but that there were also limits to what we could extract from the Earth, came soon after.

When did we discover the environment? In the same fashion that Philip Larkin insisted that sex was discovered in 1963, so the environment was discovered in 1972. While there are many learned articles proving that humans first had an effect on the environment as far back as 11,500 years and more ago, it entered our recent common consciousness through the groundbreaking work of the Club of Rome and *The Limits to Growth* report. *The Limits to Growth* was published in 1972 and it floated the notion of resource depletion. There is only so much stuff left to fuel the travel we love, and the fuelling of it has damaged the Earth.

It is not the aim here to demonstrate the certainty of climate change, or humanity's causal role or the role of our CO_2 emissions. This is assumed. However, Figure 14.4 does demonstrate the seriousness and urgency of acting now.

Figure 14.4: Atmospheric carbon dioxide concentrations over the past 800,000 years

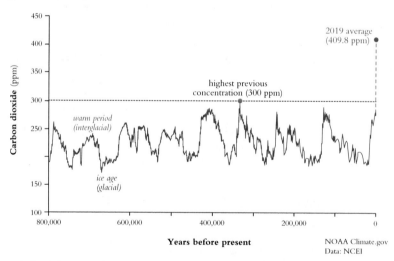

CO_2 levels have varied over the past 800,000 years but current levels are without precedent in that period.

The glacial and inter-glacial periods over the last 800,000 years are illustrated by the CO_2 levels deduced from arctic ice cores. And also illustrated is the current level of CO_2 concentration at 35 per cent higher levels than they have been over that timeframe. As noted earlier, the point of dramatic inflection is the start of the hydro-carbon fuelled industrial revolution – 1800.

Therefore, we know with certainty that it is now too late to avoid climate change and that, while we should do everything we can to reverse this trend, the time lag means that temperatures will rise, the weather will become more extreme and sea levels will rise – the latter estimated at one metre over the coming centuries, even if we are able to stick to commitments made in the 2015 Paris Agreement. In order to avoid even more destructive impacts we need to act quickly to reduce carbon emissions; scientists warn that every five years of delay now could lock in another 20 centimetres of sea-level rise in future (Mengel et al, 2018).

The damage we are doing to the environment and its ecology by travel is far greater than the single mechanism of CO_2 and the greenhouse effect leading to global warming. But the science of climate change has advanced so rapidly that it has now become the catalyst for change. The actions of environmental NGOs and campaigners, active since the 1970s, has taken a sharp increase prompted by new information and more severe and frequent examples of global heating. Extinction Rebellion wants, demands, governments to declare national emergencies, and the respected IPCC (UN Intergovernmental Panel on Climate Change) says we only have until 2030 to halt global warming in its tracks or else it will spiral out of control. Previous forecasts of the level and rate of increase of temperatures and its effects are found to be underestimates. Instances of extreme weather events, forest fires, glacier retreat and polar ice-cap melting are reported regularly.

The role of human travel within all this is substantial. According to the IPCC:

> Transport accounted for 28% of global final energy demand and 23% of global energy-related CO_2 emissions in 2014. Emissions increased by 2.5% annually between 2010 and 2015, and over the past half century the sector has witnessed faster emissions growth than any other. The transport sector is the least diversified energy end-use sector; the sector consumed 65% of global oil final energy demand, with 92% of transport final energy demand consisting of

oil products (IEA, 2017a), suggesting major challenges for
deep decarbonization. (Rogelj et al, 2018)

Different modes of transport are responsible for different levels of
emissions within this total, with road transport making up the bulk
(around 18 per cent of all emissions). Air travel, although responsible
for much less in total, is a fast-growing sector and particularly carbon
intensive.[7] It is now possible to calculate (approximately) the amount
of Arctic sea ice that is lost for each mile flown: for example a round-
trip from London to New York results in the loss of 6.6 m^2.

When we are counting up the climate impacts of human travel we
need to consider not only transport, but other activities that are entailed
in travel. Tourism is one of the world's largest industries, with well
over a billion international tourist arrivals every year (see Chapter 10
'Tourist Travel'). As might be expected for such a large industry, the
carbon footprint of the global tourism industry accounts for around
eight per cent of global carbon emissions. A large part of this is transport
of course, particularly air travel, but food and shopping also contribute
significantly (Lenzen et al, 2018).

Dramatic and fundamental though the current global warming
impacts and future threats are, there are also other immediate impacts
caused by travel and transport. Road and other vehicle emissions
are damaging health: according to the World Health Organization,
outdoor air pollution was responsible for 4.2 million premature deaths
globally in 2016, and transport is one of the biggest contributors to
that pollution.[8] Plastics, including many single-use items, are used
heavily within the tourist industry: the United Nations Environment
Programme estimates that 14 per cent of all solid waste each year
is produced by tourists (Muñoz and Navia, 2015). Often the waste
management systems of the destinations cannot deal with this waste
appropriately, or it is not responsibly disposed of (for example, cruise
ships have been found dumping rubbish in the ocean). This waste is
turning up in food chains and threatening the most remote and precious
environments, including those destinations that tourists want to visit
for their natural beauty.

High visitor numbers, and the construction of large resorts, golf
courses and other developments, have myriad impacts on destinations,
including soil erosion, degradation or pollution, natural habitat loss, and
damage to cultural heritage sites. Problems of water stress in popular
tourist and pilgrim destinations like Dubai and Mecca have been much
talked about in recent years, but even areas that might seem naturally
lush can suffer water stress due to intensive use. In Bali, around 60 per

cent of water is used by the tourist industry, and in the last ten years water tables have dropped by 50 metres.[9]

There is also the problem of human travel accidentally or intentionally introducing invasive species to new habitats, often with devastating effects. Examples abound: from the tiny, plant pathogen-carrying, one-millimetre long cotton whitefly, which has spread to every continent except Antarctica; to the 30,000 Burmese pythons (which can grow to 20 feet) that now live in the Florida Everglades eating endangered birds and alligators.[10] Impacts can be severe: European rabbits introduced to Australia are thought to have been a major cause of loss of native species and degradation of many habitats in Australia since the 19th century; and the introduction of zebra mussels (via ballast water from the Black Sea) is disrupting ecological systems across the eastern US and causing billions of dollars of damage to infrastructure.[11]

We are, therefore, heading towards a dramatically different future but one that needs us to return to being at one with nature. This next age, after those of muscle and wind, and of no limits, could have been called the ecological age. That could be the dream, but it is by no means certain. There seems to me to be two options: to achieve this by doing without, or else by doing with the levels of travel we have been used to. Increasing standards of living in poorer countries means that travel will continue to increase. And, of course, the answer will be both.

The 'do without' scenario asks if we can reduce our travel. Could it be that travel will become unappealing? Can we persuade the 80 per cent of the world's population who have never flown, as their incomes grow, to avoid the intensive international tourism habits of the other 20 per cent? Other unsocial pursuits have been tackled through nudging and persuasion, or concerted internationally agreed action. While travel is not in the same category, could we learn from other 'nudge' and global programmes, ozone-damaging chlorofluorocarbons eradication, anti-smoking, anti-drinking and no-litter/plastic campaigns? If, as is alleged, travel damages attractions, the issue could become self-correcting; less attractive destinations, less demand. And, perish the thought, many destinations lie below the rising sea levels. Venice's Piazza San Marco has recently suffered its second highest tide of all time. Much needed sea defences are under construction but are mired in corruption allegations and political obstacles – an example where good engineering and technological solutions to mitigate and adapt are available but the will gets frustrated.

The 'do with' scenario asks how we can travel comfortably, efficiently, safely and with much less environmental damage. Not a weak balance scorecard assessment of positive environmental impacts balancing negative environmental impacts or, worse, economic benefits offsetting environmental damage. There is much to be optimistic about. The efficiency of transport is increasing at an astonishing rate with cars reducing fuel consumption by about one per cent a year over the recent past, and aeroplanes achieving over twice that. The traction power used by the different modes of transport has become significantly more efficient and is emitting fewer noxious (SO_x, NO_x and CO_x) and greenhouse gases. Electric vehicles are becoming ever more attractive and, assuming the increase of renewable and zero carbon sources of energy (solar, wind and nuclear), this will help make travel environmentally benign, especially with improvements being made to batteries so that they use materials that are less harmful and not so rare. Electric flight is already here, being prototyped now. And there are no shortages of serious endeavours being made towards zero carbon travel, including the use of renewable energy to produce hydrogen fuel. But net emissions are still on the rise as the increases in total travelling volume far outweigh the unit reductions. Increases in efficiency and moves to renewable electrification will play a vital role but they will not be enough. We must also change our behaviour. And not by becoming sedentary and unadventurous, but by living, working and playing locally. Staycationing, rediscovering local attractions, pursuing different activities in our own communities. Walking and cycling instead of driving and flying. And, for work, living nearer our employment so that we can walk, cycle or take a short bus ride. Cities will have higher densities to achieve this, and the transport infrastructure will probably have to improve.

I am certain that we will not solve the climate change dilemma by the imposition of authoritarian controls, but regulations have an essential part to play and we are already seeing some regulations pointing in the right direction. While they are not coming quickly enough, and are too little too late for many economies, they are bringing results. Whether at trans-national, national or city level, regulations for vehicle emissions and electric cars are driving manufacturers to research and develop ever more ambitious performance of their products. And as they show such progress, authorities up their targets. The UK government recently brought forward its requirement to end production of petrol and diesel vehicles by five years to 2035.

But surely we can be more imaginative in living attractive lives more responsibly. So far we have barely scratched the surface of the new digital opportunities and their potential. While the last generation may struggle to keep up with developments, the next generation takes eLearning, eCommuncations and eExperiences for granted. Virtual travel is next. Combining Google Glass or other reality headsets, 3D binaural headphones (both exist) with smell, feel and vibration technologies (still in development), total immersive experience is in the pipeline. While Christian Wolf of the University of Texas says that this technology 'will probably never take away from the actual experience of travel' he is working on trying to deliver just that.[12] And for those who do not yearn for the effort and discomfort of hazardous adventurous travel, it could be just the ticket.

Conclusion

It is surprising that we have got this far through a chapter on the environment without ever asking, for the purposes of 'why travel?', just what we mean by the environment. I have been lax about using ecology, sustainability, nature and indeed climate change interchangeably because, while we know they each have clear definitions, they are all part of the stunningly immediate project to fix the planet by making travel fit for purpose. The standard neutral definition that the environment is 'everything around us' just does not do it for me. It does not capture the visceral distress that its loss arouses in people. 'You don't know what you've got 'till it's gone' is a powerful feeling that describes the emotions of experiencing intense air pollution brought about by vehicle emissions, plastics turning up in the Pacific Ocean garbage patch, or the realization that floods, forest fires and habitat/species extinctions are due to us, among other things, travelling. 'Everything around us' does not capture the concept of the vital, holistic, good support system we need to maintain and enhance our lives and the joy of living.

We cannot really know the environment without travel, whether to the end of our road to buy a loaf and post a letter, or to the ends of the Earth to experience other environments and reflect on our own. So how can this pleasure and utility be made harmless? Never has there been such a speed of transformation of mores, values and acceptability of the need for change. Examples of these improvements can be seen in:

- Increasing of cycling in cities that formerly spurned such a mode.
- Ride-hailing and car-pooling services increasingly accepted and challenging traditional models of taxis, car rental or owner-driving.
- Notions of 'Mobility as a Service' being tested, although with some way to go (see discussion in Chapter 12 'Technology and Travel').
- The diesel emissions scandal accelerating performance transparency and hence leading to public demand for improvements.

- Electric vehicles are here now with total market acceptance, with 'range anxiety' still an issue, but reducing fast. This, coupled with other possible benign fuels for freight (eg hydrogen) and with renewable, carbonless electricity generation could result, in time, in total elimination of CO_2 emissions in road transport.
- 'Flight shame' gaining credence among some sections of the community, meaning fewer flights and more local ground transportation, social media communications and investment in electric aviation (a survey in 2019 found 21 per cent of respondents had reduced their flying for environmental reasons).[13]
- Better designed infrastructure (tunnels, landscaping, urban integration) and greater investment in more sustainable transport modes.
- Gains in transport power and fuel efficiency across all modes.
- Autonomous vehicles being rolled out progressively; lane assist, auto emergency braking, speed-limiting, and engine stop/start technology all trending towards total driverless autonomy within the next ten years.
- Quieter road and air transport.
- An outpouring of academic and general readership literature all pointing to a large and rising interest in finding sustainable solutions (in one week during the writing of this chapter half a dozen books were published on the subject of climate change).

Will all this make travel both thrilling, pleasurable and environmentally acceptable, and will it be achieved in time? Different forecasts and targets aim to achieve this by 2050 (30 years from publication), or even 2030. By any measure this is indeed racing towards a cliff-edge, just in time to avert the forecasted environmental disaster. It is a race between increasing total travel demands, reducing unit damaging impacts and societal attitudes to new technologies and paradigms of travel. It is going to be a hell of a ride!

Notes

[1] www.theatlantic.com/science/archive/2018/04/in-a-few-centuries-cows-could-be-the-largest-land-animals-left/558323/
[2] Beginning in the late 16th century, it became fashionable for young aristocrats to visit Paris, Venice, Florence and, above all, Rome, as the culmination of their classical education. For more see Chapter 10 'Tourist Travel'.
[3] It has now modified this aim to include 'to create and maintain a sustainable natural and built environment'.
[4] https://assets.publishing. service.gov.uk/government/uploads/system/uploads/attachment_data/file/254128/webtag-tag-unit-a3-environmental-impact-appraisal.pdf

5 Traveller: forever off the beaten track, seeking the authentic, engage with locals. Tourist: 'Of all noxious animals... the most noxious is a tourist', wrote the clergyman-diarist Francis Kilvert (1840–79).
6 Author Ian Fleming's brother.
7 https://www.iea.org/topics/transport
8 www.who.int/en/news-room/fact-sheets/detail/ambient-(outdoor)-air-quality-and-health
9 www.smh.com.au/world/beneath-the-surface-of-tourism-in-bali-a-water-crisis-looms-20160908-grc1or.html
10 https://io9.gizmodo.com/10-of-the-worlds-worst-invasive-species-5833022
11 https://2001-2009.state.gov/g/oes/ocns/inv/cs/2304.htm
12 www.theguardian.com/vital-signs/2014/oct/06/environment-travel-tourism-virtual-3d-oculus-rift-voluntourism-volunteers
13 A survey by Swiss Bank UBS of 6,000 people in the US, Germany, France and the UK, found that 21 per cent had reduced their flying in 2019 due to environmental concerns and UBS predicts this could greatly reduce rates of growth in air travel: www.bbc.co.uk/news/business-49890057

References

Chatwin, B. (1987) *The Songlines*, London: Jonathan Cape.

Fleming, P. (1933) *Brazilian Adventure,* Oxford: Alden Press.

Lemelin, H., Dawson, J. and Stewart, E. J. (eds) (2012) *Last Chance Tourism,* London: Routledge.

Lenzen, M., Sun, Y., Faturay, F., Ting, Y.-P., Geschke, A. and Malik, A. (2018) 'The carbon footprint of global tourism', *Nature Climate Change*, 8, 522–8. doi:10.1038/s41558-018-0141-x.

Meadows, D. H. and Club of Rome (1972) *The Limits to Growth : A Report for the Club of Rome's Project on the Predicament of Mankind*, New York: Universe Books.

Mengel, M., Nauels, A., Rogelj, J., Schleussner, C.-F. (2018) 'Committed sea-level rise under the Paris Agreement and the legacy of delayed mitigation action', *Nature Communications*, 9(601). doi.org/10.1038/s41467-018-02985-8.

Muñoz, R. and Navia, E. (2015) 'Waste management in touristic regions', *Waste Management & Research*, 33(7): 593–4. doi: 10.1177/0734242X15594982.

Rogelj, J., Shindell, D., Jiang, K., Fifita, S., Forster, P., Ginzburg, V., Handa, C., Kheshgi, H., Kobayashi, S., Kriegler, E., Mundaca, L., Séférian, R. and Vilariño, M. V. (2018) 'Mitigation Pathways Compatible with 1.5°C in the Context of Sustainable Development', in V. Masson-Delmotte, P. Zhai, H.-O. Pörtner, D. Roberts, J. Skea, P. R. Shukla, A. Pirani, W. Moufouma-Okia, C. Péan, R. Pidcock, S. Connors, J. B. R. Matthews, Y. Chen, X. Zhou, M. I. Gomis, E. Lonnoy, T. Maycock, M. Tignor and T. Waterfield (eds) *Global Warming of 1.5°C. An IPCC Special Report on the impacts of global warming of 1.5°C above pre-industrial levels and related global greenhouse gas emission pathways, in the context of strengthening the global response to the threat of climate change, sustainable development, and efforts to eradicate poverty*, https://www.ipcc.ch/sr15/chapter/chapter-2/ (in press).

Schafer, A. (2007) 'Long-Term Trends in Global Passenger Mobility', in *Frontiers of Engineering: Reports on Leading-Edge Engineering from the 2006 Symposium*, Washington DC: The National Academies Press.

Stopford, J. (1994) 'Archaeology of Pilgrimage', *World Archaeology*, 26(1): 57–72.

15

Conclusion: What Have We Learnt?

Kris Beuret and Matthew Niblett

There is a bitter irony that when this book was first commissioned we were addressing the debate about the need to reduce travel on environmental grounds set against the contrasting view that human beings' demand for travel was irrepressible. Who would have thought that at the time of writing this concluding chapter, the whole world would be locked down due to a pandemic with advice to travel 'only when absolutely necessary'? Furthermore, silent airports, empty trains, buses and deserted city centres are a testament to the human ability to heed this advice and stay put. But for how long? Already there is evidence of growing mental illness, domestic abuse and non-compliance. Cabin fever is no longer an historical phenomenon.

So, the question 'why travel?' is now even more important as the world struggles to reinstate economic systems that were previously based on the implicit assumption of ever-growing demand for travel. Even Extinction Rebellion envisage a new deeply green transport strategy rather than pure localism, while others such as the CEO of Heathrow Airport predict that when the pandemic recedes travel demand will be of 'epic proportions'.

Thus, the role of travel demand and its associated motivation is even more relevant to our purpose in producing this book, and the wide range of perspectives chosen to discuss the overarching theme of 'why travel?' has been more than justified. The resulting 13 chapters from the different perspectives of the natural sciences, arts and social sciences is indicative of the value of cross-disciplinary study – something still too rare in intellectual discourse. Yet in spite of such different content

Figure 15.1: Older woman looks out of the window

Cabin fever and loneliness have become an important issue in ageing western societies, and increasingly familiar worldwide during the pandemic travel restrictions.

and theoretical perspectives, there is one conclusion shared by all our authors: the reasons for why we travel are more than practical responses for getting to and from a particular place. The common verdict is that there is a fundamental need for travel, in the absence of which humanity would not have survived in the past nor can prosper in the future. As Robert Louis Stevenson noted in a reflection of an old Taoist proverb: 'to travel hopefully is a better thing than to arrive' (1881: iv.190). Likewise, as stated recently by *The Independent's* Simon Calder: 'travel is an immense force for good. Tourism spreads wealth from richer countries to poorer destinations, creating jobs by the hundreds of millions, and providing life-enriching experiences' (Suleman, 2016).

If this view is accepted there are important implications for society, ranging from discussions about how to incorporate the need to travel without major damage to our world, right through to whether we have a right to travel. Taking Maslow's model of the hierarchy of needs, the question is whether travel is a physiological need along with food and shelter, or a higher level need, perhaps even self-actualization. The verdict has crucial and wide policy implications including whether there is an unfettered right to travel irrespective of climate change and other adverse impacts.

Figure 15.2: Maslow's hierarchy of needs

If human needs can be represented as a pyramid, as Maslow suggested, where does travel fall within such a hierarchy?

We shall return to this question. But first it is useful to refer to the view from the individual disciplinary contributions in the preceding chapters.

The fundamental motivations of travel

The chapters on Biology, the Mind, and Philosophy all describe how there are instinctive motivations that lie behind human travel beyond merely getting from point to point. This view is also the theme of the Economics chapter, which uses these insights to challenge conventional economic theories.

As Charles Pasternak explains in Chapter 2, from a biological perspective travel is tied intimately with the evolutionary development of humanity itself. He identifies the origins of our bipedal mode of travel with brain development and our social nature. There are also health issues related to travel and movement, which can be both positive, such as neurogenesis and endorphin release when we exercise, or of a more problematic nature, such as the effects of jet lag and exposure to new viruses when we travel far. Above all, he demonstrates that our inquisitive nature has resulted in our desire for travel stemming from a need to find quests and explore.

The evolutionary aspects of travel and movement also lodge themselves within our psychological needs and reactions to travel, which, as Tony Hiss explores in Chapter 3 on the Mind, have fundamental impacts on our cognitive and emotional wellbeing. He explains that there is strong evidence that the novelty and experience of travel are important for our cognitive abilities and derived from our ancestors scanning the horizon on the savannah. The links between movement and our emotional health are also strong, which is why confinement can have such negative impacts on wellbeing.

The question of what drives our travel has also occupied philosophers down the centuries, as explained by Matthew Niblett in the fourth chapter. He shows how, in the ancient world, movement was often viewed as an aid to thinking, and many philosophers built this into their teaching. More recently, the importance of travel for broadening the mind and as a formative part of learning has been emphasized by leading philosophers. At the same time, he recognizes that some philosophers have observed that travel can leave us disappointed and explores some of the reasons thinkers have given for this problem. The chapter also examines how travel and movement have begun to be considered a fundamental human right.

These insights, which show that there are instinctive drivers that lie behind human travel beyond merely getting from one location to another, call into question conventional economic theories. These are examined by Matthew Dillon and Alexander Jan in Chapter 5 on economics and travel, where they address head-on a fundamental theme of this book – namely to challenge the traditional approach whereby travel is calculated merely as a derived demand. They show the need to calculate the intrinsic value of the experience of travel itself, especially in the light of the ability to do other things during travel, ranging from working on trains to the sheer enjoyment of watching the scenery go by. After providing an overview of the economic explanations of travel behaviour, they look at how more recent understandings of our instinctive need to travel are being considered in economic valuations, as well as how to account for the economic costs of travel, such as its contribution to climate change. The latter approach clearly challenges the conventional emphasis on the value of reductions in travel time as the prime focus when calculating the benefits of projects and making investment decisions. We might ask why this traditional view remained fixed for so long and whether a new scepticism about modelling will help to accelerate the move away from the traditional approach. This seems likely since methods of quantifying the intrinsic value of travel have now been enabled by behavioural economics and new opportunities have arisen from technologies such as electronic connectivity and autonomous vehicles. In other words, these insights on the value of travel point policy makers in a direction away from 'predict and provide' and towards a more political and strategic approach of 'vision and validate'.

The fundamental overarching conclusion from these authors is that our motivations for travel are far wider than merely getting from A to B. We are human because we travel – our evolution depended on our being the best at a combination of speed and distance. Furthermore, there is much evidence of links between travel and mental and physical health with the view that challenge and novelty are beneficial to our cognitive abilities, including creativity, and that we would never have flourished to the same extent as a species without widespread travel. Even if the derived demand for travel could be met by some form of virtual communication, the consequences of preventing travel could be severe for individuals and humanity.

Travel for exploration and knowing ourselves

If biology and neuroscience see travel as fundamental to human life, the implications are also vast for our culture and civilisation, and the next set of chapters have taken this as a common theme from different perspectives across the humanities and social sciences.

As our authors show, travel can be about self-expression as well as mass identities. In Chapter 6 Kris Beuret and Roger Hall explore sociological perspectives, demonstrating how travelling impacts social structures as well as mobility through class and social status. Their examples of the search for freedom and social mobility show how mass movements have occurred due to the desire to move from the place and position in which people were born to different positions in the social structure. Moving from one socioeconomic group to another is strongly related with the ability to move jobs, housing, and social groups, all of which are enabled by travel. But unlike those who took the £10 offer to emigrate to Australia and had little opportunity to travel back for visits, the expansion of mass travel has enabled family structures to survive even though the traditional three-generational family residing and working near to each other has largely disappeared. Of course, such ability to travel freely is not available to all equally and the chapter also flags up the disadvantages caused by limited travel based on income, gender and disability. The chapter concludes with reflections about the way in which travel can reinforce political beliefs, or sharpen the difference between the world views of 'nativists' and 'globalists'.

Travel is at the core of many religious identities, and travel for spiritual reasons even today remains a strong motivation. In the chapter by Alison Kuznets, she explains the ways in which pilgrimage and spiritual travel have come to be so strongly engrained in world religions, enabling the pilgrim to be spiritually transformed and to become closer to their god/gods, both at the destination and also through the process of the journey. Missionary travel is also core to some religions, enabling the missionary to serve their god, 'save souls' and achieve salvation. Religious war can, for some, serve similar spiritual purposes to missionary travel, although of course creates great suffering. On an associated theme, religious persecution has existed throughout history and is still a driver of travel. Conversely, one of the benefits of migration can be the encouragement of toleration that sometimes accompanies exposure to other religions and beliefs.

At a more personal level, travel clearly has a major impact on human creativity and self-expression. These aspects are explored in the chapter on art and literature, which explains how travel has come to dominate our language through metaphor and idioms. How and why travel is such a central motif within our stories, art and literature is a core topic. It is important to be clear that a short chapter cannot cover all aspects of human creativity and, as such, there are inevitable omissions – such as the impact of travel on music. Nonetheless, it is hard to imagine many creative works that do not stem from some context of travel. Just imagine how much less rich human culture would be had van Gogh not travelled to the south of France or Christopher Wren to Italy, Wole Soyinka not escaped persecution in Nigeria, or had Freya Stark not trekked into the desert. The chapter also identifies the role of metaphors relating to travel as an integral part of artistic expression and the very essence of culture.

The chapters on anthropology, tourism and exploration each uncover the importance of exchange and discovery as motivators of human travel. Whether it be for new perspectives and knowledge, or for the trade and exploitation of physical commodities, the desire to know and possess new ideas and things has long driven humans to journey far and wide. These authors also highlight how, as worldwide travel has increased, this has generated an ever-strengthening paradox for a globalizing world – travel may open people's horizons and give them a bigger worldview and understanding of other peoples and places, but in so doing our travel impacts on those people and places we visit and can potentially take a heavy toll on those local cultures themselves.

As anthropologist Tom Selwyn shows in his chapter, human travel and hospitality involve cultural rituals whose differences and continuities offer interesting insights into why we travel in the way we do. Travel features as a core part of many myths of identity and stories of origin, which provide meaning to cultures and societies. Professor Selwyn demonstrates how important travel is for people to understand their place in the world, and discover their own identities, whether individual, group or national.

Today, most long-distance leisure travel is taken as a form of tourism. Hazel Andrews explains how, as people become richer, they choose to travel more, so much so that tourism represented ten per cent of the global economy before the COVID-19 pandemic. In her wide-ranging examination, she shows that the impulses behind tourist travel vary widely, including a search for authenticity, for knowledge, status, self-transformation/understanding, escape from constraints and routines of home, and in pursuit of social conformity. It is interesting that as people become richer their demand for travel increases. Wars and pandemics threaten this growth, but if these recede it is not unreasonable to expect a revival in tourism demand encouraged by a massive marketing industry. However, the kinds of tourism we do could change, with less focus on far-flung destinations, a greater emphasis upon sustainable tourism, and more interest in eco-friendly and slower travel methods.

Some of the most famous travels in history have been undertaken for the purpose of exploration: a phenomenon that continues in the human desire to explore outer space. Emily Thomas in her chapter on travel and exploration notes that exploratory travel goes back to the dawn of recorded history and is perhaps linked to the idea of humans as questing creatures (as outlined in Charles Pasternak's chapter). This search for new knowledge, she explains, was given added impetus in the early modern period through thinkers such as Francis Bacon, who developed the case for travel for scientific discovery. Exploration extends our understanding of the world by uncovering the past (archaeology) and expanding future horizons (space travel) with much else in between, including the relatively uncharted deeps of the ocean. She also identifies the more private aspects of exploration as an endeavour of discovery we can all achieve through travel.

The future of travel: limits and new horizons

Having identified the fundamental motivations that lie behind human travel, and how travel shapes society, our final part focuses on the need to understand how we can travel better. If travel is a human need, it also brings with it problems in terms of its potential impacts. The book's final section focuses on contemporary issues in the light of our overarching question 'why travel?' and implications for how we can travel better.

This last point is taken up by the chapter on technology in which Glenn Lyons raises the crucial link between the development of technology and our ability to travel more cheaply, more comfortably, faster and for longer distances – hence the massive growth of travel with all the attendant and varied impacts described in the chapters of this book. This then leads to a further question, which goes back to the debate about derived and intrinsic demand raised in the economics chapter, but here in the context of the enabling role of technology. In particular, the impact of substitutionary technology (eg telecommunications) or non-transport technology (eg better storage of food) is raised. However, there are reservations – we know people are not totally rational and the ways in which technology is used and developed are difficult to predict, as demonstrated by current debates about whether people will continue to work from home or whether city centre residents will continue to buy large polluting cars. Another problem is that there is frequently a lack of long-term planning and investment especially in the light of global targets for carbon reduction. The overall conclusion is that we need to develop resilient technologies to allow for uncertainty while tackling the need for sustainability in future travel.

The placemaking chapter, written by Deborah Saunt and Tom Greenall, starts from the view that why we travel is directly related to how we build and plan our settlements. Travel has shaped our towns and cities – but often not in a positive way, so we need to build better places that can take into account a fuller picture of our travel behaviours. This is necessary because, sadly, past urban design has led to many cities being dominated by cars and pollution, to the detriment of the quality of life of many residents, especially children and others with restricted mobility. In support of this view, the authors show how travel, place and human connectivity are intimately connected with physical, cultural and psychological perspectives. Therefore, if the public realm is to work well it should incorporate function, beauty, safety, a sense of belonging and also encourage sustainable travel. The authors provide case studies of examples that emphasize the methods, skills and challenges involved in achieving this outcome. Optimistically, they suggest that in the wake of the COVID-19 pandemic, this might yet be an impetus to bring more of the natural world and open space into our urban areas.

It is fitting that the final chapter in the book by Terry Hill focuses on the environment, with a timely reminder that travel is not a panacea, and the negative impacts of human travel are nowhere more evident than in the damage that is done to our environment and to the climate as a result of transport-related emissions. We are only at the start of the quest to see how we can live and travel sustainably in the context of the role played by travel in harming the environment – how can we change that? Do we need to restrict travel or are there solutions through which we can travel better? One view is that travel growth must be curtailed but the author suggests that this is only an option for wealthier countries. Rather we must find ways of making travel environmentally sustainable as well as offering a more equitable future for humankind. This is best done, Terry Hill suggests, not through authoritarian restrictions but through the use of behavioural 'nudging' techniques such as pricing and rationing to encourage more responsible travel and the development of sustainable travel technologies. At a time when the need to address climate change is a global priority, the chapter provides insights on the role that travel can play in leading to a more sustainable future.

Final thoughts

Returning to our initial question 'why travel?' – if the evidence in this book is correct, then there is also a strong case to be made for encouraging travel (in a sustainable way) or even for treating travel as a human right. Such a view is increasingly shaping international laws – as for example in Article 13 of the Universal Declaration of Human Rights, or in the European Union's Treaty of Maastricht, which guarantees free movement between member states. In today's world, there are few completely closed societies (even North Korea issues visas) (Lloyd, 2008), and the restrictions on travel caused by the COVID-19 pandemic have been an unpleasant shock to most people, even if the reduction in long-distance flying has helped to lower carbon emissions. At the same time, the importance of travel to our physical and mental health has become all too apparent during the pandemic as a result of lockdowns. We know now all too clearly why confinement has traditionally been used as a punishment. Looking ahead, perhaps a long-lasting result of the pandemic is the increasing recognition that even local travel, such as a daily walk in nature or bike ride round the neighbourhood, has a crucial innate value that can support our wellbeing. And it is possible that in future more attention will be given to the quality of our travel, rather than its speed or frequency.

To conclude: we travel because it is integral to what defines humanity and because it enables human progress and wellbeing, individually and socially. The challenge policy makers must now face is how to retain, encourage and extend travel without adverse effects. Exactly how this can be achieved is not the subject of this book. Encouragingly, however, it is a topic which others are beginning to address (Docherty and Shaw,

Figure 15.3: Signpost: which way now?

2019), and the insights in this book should help to provide a deeper context on the nature and value of travel, through which practical discussions and decisions about policy can be made. Our overriding hope is that, as the world struggles with a variety of medical, social and ecological challenges, the fundamental need for humans to travel will underpin a positive framework for navigating the road ahead.

For further insights and perspectives, please visit the project website, where the debate continues: www.whytravel.org.

References

Docherty I. and Shaw, J. (eds) (2019) *Transport Matters*, Bristol: Policy Press.

Lloyd, M. (2008) *The Passport: The History of Man's Most Travelled Document*, Canterbury: Queen Anne's Fan.

Stevenson, R. L. (1881) *Virginibus Puerisque*, London: Kegan Paul.

Suleman, K. (2016) 'Interview' in *PR Week*, 30 March 2016, London: Haymarket Media Group.

Index

Note: Page locators in *italic* refer to figures or tables.